SPIRITUAL DIRECTION
CONTEMPORARY READINGS

Edited with Introductions
by
KEVIN G. CULLIGAN, O.C.D.

LIVING FLAME PRESS
BOX 74 LOCUST VALLEY, N.Y. 11560

253.53
Cu 5

Cover: Robert Manning

Imprimi Potest: Benedict J. Bishop, O.C.D.
                   Provincial, Washington Province
                   Discalced Carmelites

Copyright © 1983 by Kevin Culligan, O.C.D.

ISBN: 0-914544-43-8

Published by: Living Flame Press, Box 74, Locust Valley, New York 11560

Printed in the United States of America

253.5
CUs

*To my students
with affection and esteem*

Preface

Twenty years ago, I thought spiritual direction was obsolete. It seemed out of touch with modern life and an obstacle to growth in personal responsibility and freedom. There was little doubt in my mind that psychological counselors and therapists would eventually replace spiritual directors as those best qualified to help persons with their inner struggles and longings. As a ministry in the Church, spiritual direction appeared to have no future.

Then came Vatican II. Through the power of the Holy Spirit released by that Council, an increasing number of Christians now seek their true identity and fulfillment through a deeper union with God. Their desire for reliable guides in this spiritual quest has also infused new life into the ministry of spiritual direction. Today many competent spiritual directors respond to the demand for guidance, new training programs prepare directors for the future, and the literature on spiritual direction grows steadily.

My purpose in this book is to introduce you to this revitalized ministry. By presenting readings from reliable authors and practitioners in the field, I hope to acquaint you with current thinking, practices, and issues in spiritual direction. Whether you are guiding others on their journey to God or simply making the journey yourself, I believe you will find these readings helpful.

The idea for this book came from my students in an introductory course in spiritual direction in the Pastoral Counseling Program at Loyola College in Maryland. When the course began in 1977, there were few books available to introduce students to contemporary spiritual direction; instead, we relied on selected journal articles and material from other sources. As suitable textbooks began to appear, my students continued to find the supplementary readings valuable for obtaining a view of the actual practice of spiritual direction in the United States. They convinced me that others would also value them; hence this book.

Space does not permit reprinting here all the articles used in that course. I have, however, selected those which would appeal to a wide range of readers so that this book might be useful both for courses, workshops and seminars and for private independent reading. I have arranged the readings into a logical sequence so that those questions most often asked by persons entering spiritual direction could be addressed: What is spiritual direction? What makes a good director? What happens in the direction process? Who can be a spiritual director? The articles do not answer all of these questions definitively; nor do I necessarily agree with all the authors on every point. Nevertheless, they will tell you what contemporary writers are saying about spiritual direction, its nature, its demands, its practice, its models.

The selections, of course, reflect my personal preferences. Since another editor might include different readings, I have added at the end of the collection listings of related material under each major heading. Should the articles in this book stimulate you to investigate these other sources, my efforts will be rewarded.

In presenting these readings, I wish to thank the following persons: Father Barry Estadt, OFM. Cap., Director of the Loyola Pastoral Counseling Program and my colleagues on the Loyola faculty for their support in developing the spiritual direction course in which these readings were first used; my students who encouraged me to publish these selections for a wider readership; Katherine Quevedo, Fr. Chris Aridas and Jacqueline Seitz of Living Flame Press for their help in the final selection and preparation of articles for publication; the authors and publishers who permitted the republication of these articles, all of which originally appeared elsewhere; my Carmelite brothers Kenneth Huppman, Steven Payne, and Bryan Paquette and Mr. Robert Slater for their assistance along the way. I also thank those who gave me such gracious hospitality and assistance during my 1981-82 sabbatical when I prepared these pages — the Discalced Carmelites of the Anglo-

Irish Province, the Irish Dominicans, the Jesuits at Milltown Park, Dublin, and the Atonement Friars at the Catholic Library, London. All these people have helped me bring these readings to you and, I trust, join me in the hope that this book will introduce you to a most exciting ministry in today's Church.

Contents

PART ONE

The Nature
of Spiritual Direction

I define spiritual direction as a counseling ministry in the Church which helps Christians draw closer to God, especially through prayer. This definition accurately states the nature of spiritual direction, although it fails to convey its special richness. To appreciate both the scope and uniqueness of this ministry, you must also know something of its history, its place in different Christian traditions and its relationship to other modern forms of counseling.

The articles that follow in this section provide an opportunity to explore these areas. Kevin Wall gives an overview of spiritual direction's development through twenty centuries of Christianity. Kallistos Ware and Sandra Schneiders discuss contemporary Orthodox and Roman views of this ministry. Eugene Geromel compares the ministry of spiritual direction with modern psychotherapy.

Taken as a whole, these articles reveal that spiritual direction cannot be limited to one point of view or strategy; rather, it can be understood and practiced in a variety of ways. The rich diversity of this ministry merely reflects the mystery it serves — God's infinite workings in human life. Yet, it is precisely this focus upon helping persons grow in their relationship with God through prayer that makes spiritual direction a distinctive form of modern counseling.

In practice, each spiritual director eventually arrives at his or her own approach to this ministry. The common bond among most of them, however, is their effort to guide persons to a deeper union with God by helping them listen to the Spirit who is the Chief Director of us all.

Spiritual Direction

Kevin A. Wall, O.P.

Spiritual direction is the guiding of a Christian soul in the path of perfection. On the part of the guide, or spiritual director, it demands knowledge of the general and more specific principles of Christian action as well as insight into the state of soul of the one directed. This requires that the director have considerable theological science and at least some degree of experience in spiritual matters to give him an understanding of the spiritual condition of the person whom he directs. Without such experience he could hardly have the penetrating perception classically known as discernment of spirits. Since he must have this, the spiritual director is ordinarily a man not only of theological learning, but also possessed of a degree of holiness. Direction itself supposes some lack of these qualities in the soul under direction, a deficiency that justifies the counseling in the sense that it makes counseling necessary or at least useful. This judicious counseling is the essence of spiritual direction.

In Catholic theology, especially during the last two centuries, the term has usually been taken to mean the counseling of individuals within the framework of sacramental confession. Historically the Christian tradition concerning it seems to have arisen from the same context, that is to say, as an extension of sacramental confession and revelation of conscience for absolution from sins. But since sacramental confession is connected with the total sacramental and hierarchical action of

This article originally appeared in the *New Catholic Encyclopedia,* IV, pp. 887-90. Copyright 1967 by The Catholic University of America. Reprinted by permission.

the Church, the extrasacramental counseling of individuals or groups, or hierarchical action, or other activities aimed at promoting the advance of souls in perfection can be included under the term. However the more restricted meaning of the counseling of individual souls has become common and is the accepted meaning today.

Understood in this way it is a peculiarly Christian phenomenon because of the special goal to which Christian counseling is directed. However, something generically similar to it has existed from time immemorial, even outside of the Christian tradition. The pagans of Western antiquity practiced a sort of moral guidance. Men put themselves under learned masters to develop in virtue. Socrates was a famous example of such a master and was thought to have genius in the area of moral decision. In the Buddhist tradition, a sort of psychological counseling has been used as a fundamental technique for the advancement of its disciples. In recent years this has become better known to the West through its growing acquaintance with Zen Buddhism. In brief, these and other examples make it clear that some generic form of spiritual direction seems to be a nearly universal phenomenon.

Early Eastern Christianity. In early Oriental Christianity spiritual direction seems to have developed chiefly because of its utility in the formation of monks, although it had broader roots. Indirect evidence suggests that bishops must have exercised it with respect to groups of Christians in their communities who sought a more perfect way of life in the practice of continence and prayer. At all events, it was a much-honored practice and Oriental Christianity gave tribute to it in the names it applied to spiritual directors, e.g., the honorable name of father. The spiritual director was conceived of as the progenitor of the one directed in the life of perfection. This was a peculiarly Christian conception that apparently arose from the community awareness that Our Lord had never codified His doctrine and made explicit all of its principles. Neither had the disciples and apostles done this. The major portion of these principles was therefore implicit, and it was the work of the spiritual father to make them explicit.

Early Western Christianity. Evidence of such spiritual direction in early times in the West is obscure and indirect. It seems reasonable to believe that the ascetics among the community in the early Church, particularly the holy virgins, were the object of special instruction by the bishops and that this instruction had of necessity to take something of the form of spiritual direction. Many early works hint at this. Tertullian and St. Cyprian wrote at considerable length about the guidance of virgins. However, unambiguous evidence is meager, and when it first appears it is chiefly in the form of letters and of legislative texts for monasteries, in which sources it is difficult to distinguish individual counseling from group direction.

St. Ambrose. This is not the case in the writings coming down from St. Ambrose. They contain a clearly identifiable example of the practice of spiritual direction aimed at the perfecting of particular souls. It was not the advanced sort of guidance associated with the higher stages of the spiritual life and with mysticism. St. Ambrose restricted himself to the stage of the beginner and encouraged those whom he directed to practice the fundamental Christian virtues, particularly those connected with the state of virginity. His accentuation of virginity gained for him the reputation of being a determined opponent of marriage, and his basic attitude toward the moral life has often been pointed to as indicative of his debt to the Stoics. Although his spiritual treatises, compiled from his sermons, concentrated on virginity, his letters manifested a much wider range of interest. Some of them show him to have been a true master of the art of spiritual direction.

St. Jerome. St. Jerome too was a talented counselor of souls as the term is now commonly understood. While in the East, he studied the ascetical practices of the monasteries. When he returned to Rome in 382, he was therefore well equipped to teach and to counsel the pious souls, particularly women, who sought him out. He was an excellent teacher, but an even more adept director of souls. From his writings it is clear that the moment he began to practice this art he became more at ease, more open, and more confident of himself. He did not hesitate to give orders and expected them to be obeyed. He was particularly at home in counseling concerning the life of virginity and of monastic perfection.

St. Augustine. The busy life of St. Augustine made it impossible for him to dedicate much time to the direction of particular souls. Nevertheless, he is important in the history of spiritual direction because of his efforts to set up and sustain monastic communities. This was the milieu in which he lived his own personal life from the time of his conversion, and it was particularly dear to him. His counseling therefore tended to concentrate on it, but he replied also to particular requests for help from individuals in every station of life. These replies gained him his reputation as an authority in spiritual direction.

5th and 6th Centuries. During the 5th and 6th centuries the major portion of spiritual counseling was devoted to the formation of novices to the monastic life. Cassian enjoyed a widespread reputation for this. His counseling was based on his youthful experience in the Near East, particularly in Egypt, where he received his own spiritual formation. He applied the fruits of this experience to the formation of novices in the monastic life of southern France. He put every novice under the guidance of an older member of the community, and the young monk was encouraged to reveal his conscience and the movements of his heart to the older monk assigned to direct him. Without his advice no spiritual enterprise was to be undertaken. Cassian warned that great care should be taken in choosing responsible directors. Any imprudence on the part of the director would cause the novice to lose confidence in the value of revealing his conscience. This work of Cassian was furthered and stabilized by the Rule of St. Benedict (c. 580). This stressed the importance of the spiritual director for the monastery, because the maintenance and conservation of community life depended on the formation of the new generation of its members.

7th to 11th Centuries. This tradition of spiritual direction, once firmly established by Cassian and St. Benedict, continued in effect during the period from the 7th to the 12th centuries. But its vigor varied with the decline and the revitalization of society at large. During the period of cultural decay preceding the Carolingian renaissance and following it, spiritual direction fell into decline. No doubt there were souls during this time who attempted a high level of spirituality and who sought out directors to aid them, but they could not have been very numerous, for the evidence of their existence is scanty. What direction remained took place, for the most part, within the monasteries. There is scarcely any evidence from the 10th and 11th centuries of spiritual direction as it is now understood.

12th to 15th Centuries. With the 12th century, however, it began to rise to a high level with St. Anselm of Canterbury. Anselm's efforts were directed primarily to the formation of the monks who were under his charge, but he also provided counsel for others in every walk of life. In his instruction he was gentle and kind, but at the same time forceful. He insisted on unceasing effort and continuing progress. He taught that the primary goal was not the negative one of avoiding sins, small and great, but the positive one of union with God. The high level of spiritual counseling as practiced by Anselm continued in vigor during the period from the 12th to the 15th centuries. For the most part it maintained its traditional purpose of forming novices to the monastic life, a direction given it by St. Benedict and generally followed in the newly emerging orders. An exception must be made for the Dominicans. Because of the specific purpose of their foundation, spiritual direction became one of their primary activities; and because the souls toward whom their apostolate was directed were primarily the laymen of the emerging medieval cities, their spiritual direction became oriented toward them. Even so, it still maintained some connection with the past in that it attempted to impart to laymen the maximum of the benefits of monastic experience that were compatible with their lives. The Third Order was the favorite vehicle for this, but the type of monasticism that could be adapted to this purpose was more primitive in form than that which derived from St. Benedict. This explains, in part, the spiritual direction given by St. Catherine of Siena, which was outside the hierarchical structure and fundamentally charismatic.

Other noted directors, such as St. Bernard of Clairvaux, in the 12th century, had exercised a strictly ecclesiastical direction. They were concerned with the diminishing authority of the Church, and therefore made submission to it a prime object of their counseling. St. Bernard preached, above everything else, the necessity of obedience. Since this was to be given to a spiritual director acting in the name of the Church, it placed enormous responsibility on him. St. Bernard, recognizing this, attempted to achieve the necessary balance by stressing the importance of choosing for this function only a person of recognized ability in the discernment of spirits.

In the Franciscan school the work of St. Bonaventure merits special attention. His spirituality was totally oriented toward the mystical, but his attitude toward the necessity of spiritual direction for this end was not rigid. He thought that those who had themselves the gift of discernment of spirits did not need it. However, he was convinced that there were few such souls and that most individuals needed spiritual guidance at least in the initial stages of their advance to perfection.

During the last centuries of the Middle Ages, the Dominicans exercised a great influence through their spiritual direction. This was a natural consequence of their specific mission in the Church. Teaching and preaching Christian doctrine naturally led them to the counseling of individual souls. St. Dominic had given the example of it by his own apostolic activity. He had also made it part of the legal structure of the order in abbreviating the Office, exempting the friars from manual labor, and granting dispensations liberally for the needs of study. All of this inevitably gave rise to increased activity in the area of spiritual direction. The *cura animarum* thus became primarily counseling of souls in the way of perfection. A striking case of this occurred when the Dominican friars took over the spiritual direction of the convents of Dominican sisters in the Rhineland. This particular apostolate gave rise to the remarkable school of Rhineland mysticism in which both directors and directed reached a high level of mystical perfection. In England Richard Rolle, an independent spirit living an eremitical life, hardly insisted on spiritual direction at all. But the author of the celebrated *Cloud of Unknowing* thought it necessary. Humble submission to a spiritual director is needed for spiritual progress. Among the Lowland writers, Ruysbroeck, who depended on the Rhineland mystics for many of his teachings, stressed the possession of the discernment of spirits on the part of the soul seeking perfection, as more necessary for progress than submission to a director. For this reason, although he consented to advise many souls on particular problems, he refused to do it in the continuous way ordinarily understood as spiritual direction. Gerard Groote followed Ruysbroeck's principles and stressed obedience to superiors as fundamental for the monk. However, the deplorable condition of many convents in his time led him to put limits to this. Thomas à Kempis, author or definitive editor of the *Imitation of Christ,* placed great importance on spiritual direction as one of the four ways to obtain deep peace of soul.

Modern Period. With the 16th century, the character of spiritual direction changed. It became institutionalized and empirical. In large part this was the result of the great success of the *Exercises* of St. Ignatius, which encouraged the practice of individual and group retreats. It was due also to a heightened appreciation of the necessity for the interior life to counter the forces that culminated in the Reformation. With respect to this, spiritual direction of a more institutionalized form had an obviously important role to play. The Dominicans of Florence, whose attention was drawn to it by the example of Savonarola, were among the initiators of the new movement. At Rome, the Oratory in the Church of S. Girolamo gave it great impetus through the work of St. Philip Neri. In his apostolate, spiritual direction was essential. He gave it with profound perception, being at the same time paternal and firm. The primitive form of the Oratory, with its considerable liberty of action, aided him in this work.

St. Philip Neri was only one of many who began at this time to practice spiritual direction intensely. Others too saw it as a necessary correction for the neglect of this sort of apostolate in the preceding period. To this neglect they attributed a large part of the spiritual decline of the Church. The absence of an intense sacramental life was felt to be a contributing cause. Spiritual directors therefore began to counsel an intense life of sacramental activity and of prayer. Through the influence of Savonarola and others of his brethren, the prayer took the special form of meditation on the Passion of Christ. Louis of Granada, in Spain, was one of the leading advocates of this form of meditation.

In Spain also the great works of Teresa of Avila and John of the Cross inculcated the necessity of spiritual direction for the renewal of the Church. St. Teresa took care to provide her convents with good confessors. Because many of the difficulties she encountered came from her failure to find them, she developed a great respect for theological learning and regarded it as a fundamental qualification in a spiritual director no less necessary than a personal experience of spiritual things. In his writings, St. John of the Cross aimed at illuminating not only souls seeking perfection, but also spiritual directors. He was severe against ignorant and timid guides. The role of the director as he saw it was that of an instrument of the Church who provided a vital sense of the Church's presence at each step in the advancement toward perfection. The director was not a master imperiously intervening in the affairs of the soul and limiting its progress by the standard of his own spiritual gifts, but an instrument to maintain contact with the Church in the soul as it developed through the operations of the Holy Spirit.

Another classical source for spiritual direction was provided by the *Exercises* of St. Ignatius. Although these were not properly a manual of direction, they constituted a standard framework of reference. This was particularly true for the doctrine of discernment of spirits. The *Exercises* taught that by this knowledge a prudent director can safely lead the soul into the first steps of the spiritual life. But he should do this, according to St. Ignatius, as a witness of God and should carefully avoid involving himself in any way except as one who mediates a divine action. The detailed revelations of the soul of the one whom he guides permit him to accomplish this, as long as he can truly perceive the spirits involved.

17th Century. The 17th century has been called the golden age of spiritual direction. During this period a rich literature arose on the subject. The general tendency was to regard it as continuous with sacramental confession. In the beginning this led to the mixing of matters of internal and external forum in the government of convents. Consequently there were many works of that time bearing on the external forum, but containing much excellent advice on the direction of souls. The leading director of the period was St. Francis de Sales. His passage in the *Introduction to the Devout Life* on the necessity of spiritual direction became classic. The ancient religious orders also occupied themselves extensively with spiritual direction during this period as did the secular clergy. Bishops Bossuet and Fénelon, Marie de l'Incarnation, and several lay men and women gained fame by their achievement in the apostolate of spiritual direction.

18th Century. The 17th century condemnation of the errors of Molinos and of Fénelon's *Maximes des Saints* tempered enthusiasm for the publication of spiritual writings and for the apostolate of spiritual direction. In some circles this gave rise to a spirit of obstinate resistance, as among the Jansenists. The result was an impoverishment of doctrine and a paucity of spiritual directors. Some outstanding examples of men skilled in the art of direction did emerge, however, such as the Jesuit Jean Pierre de Caussade, whose name is commonly associated with the doctrine of abandonment to divine providence. But even Caussade's estimation of the need of a director was much tempered by his experience. He once characterized a director of conscience as more an embarrassment than an aid. In this censure, however, he criticized certain faults in the relationship of director and directed, rather than the essence of the practice itself.

19th Century. With the end of the French Revolution and the termination of the Napoleonic Wars, Europe experienced a renewed interest in religion and therefore in spiritual direction. The basis for this was less theological than had previously been the case, but the charity animating it was undoubtedly genuine. Some founders of religious congregations made important contributions. G.J. Chaminade, founder of the Marianists; John Bosco, founder of the Salesians; and Charles de Foucauld, founder of the Little Brothers and Sisters of the Sacred Heart are only a few. The Dominican Lacordaire, and J.N. Grou, SJ, also made important contributions to the reviving spirituality. The Redemptorists, preachers by vocation and therefore naturally inclined to carry this forward into direct counseling of individual souls, made comparable contributions, as did various bishops and secular priests who distinguished themselves in this apostolate.

20th Century. All of this activity in the 19th century, but particularly the work of editing spiritual texts and the publication of studies in numerous spiritual periodicals, as well as the promulgation of a number of important papal documents, led to a flourishing of direction in the 20th century. The discouraging effects of the condemnation of quietism have been removed and directors have been freed to resume this important ministry now on a solid and authoritative basis, for the Holy See has given the movement considerable encouragement, although it has insisted on certain qualities in those who occupy themselves in giving direction.

The advancing knowledge of depth psychology has both aided and hindered spiritual direction. Although it is popularly surmised that a crisis is imminent in the apostolate of the director as a result of depth psychology, the demand for direction is greater than ever before. Depth psychology and guidance in

18

the life of grace are different things. Neither need be a hindrance to the other, but both may gain by mutual confrontation if the possibilities and the limitations on both sides are properly understood.

Bibliography: Francis de Sales, *Introduction to the Devout Life,* tr. M. Day (Westminster, Md. 1959); *Spiritual Directory for People Living in the World,* ed. J.E. Woods (Westminster, Md. 1959). John of the Cross, *The Dark Night of the Soul,* in *Collected Works,* tr. K. Kavanaugh and O. Rodriguez (Garden City, N.Y. 1964) bk. 1, ch. 2, 3, 6. Teresa of Avila, *The Way of Perfection* in v. 2 of *Complete Works,* ed. Silverio de Santa Teresa and E.A. Peers, 3 v. (New York 1964) ch. 5; *Interior Castle, ibid.* 6th Mansions, ch. 8; *Life,* tr. D. Lewis (Westminster, Md. 1962) ch. 5. Ignatius of Loyola, *Spiritual Exercises,* tr. L.J. Puhl (Westminster, Md. 1951). L. Scupoli, *The Spiritual Combat* (London 1935), tr. from It. F.W. Faber, *Growth in Holiness* (Westminster, Md. 1960) ch. 18. L. Lallemant, *The Spiritual Doctrine,* ed. A.G. McDougall (Westminster, Md. 1946), tr. from Fr. A. Tanquerey, *The Spiritual Life,* tr. H. Branderis (2d ed. Tournai 1930; repr. Westminster, Md. 1945) ch. 5.2. C. Marmion, *The English Letters of Abbot Marmion 1858-1923* (Baltimore 1962). R. Garrigou-Lagrange, *The Three Ways of the Spiritual Life* (London 1938; repr. Westminster, Md. 1950) v. 1, ch. 17. Leo XIII, "Testem benevolentiae" (letter to Cardinal James Gibbons, Jan. 22, 1899) ActSSed 31 (1898-99) 470-479, Eng. J.T. Ellis, ed., *Documents of American Catholic History* (Milwaukee 1956) 553-562. Pius XII, "Menti nostrae" (Apostolic exhortation, Sept. 23, 1950) ActApS 42 (1950) 657-702, Eng. *Catholic Mind* 49 (1951) 37-64. P.P. Parente, *Spiritual Direction* (rev. ed. New York 1961). *Workshop on Spiritual Formation and Guidance-Counseling in The CCD Program, 1961,* Cath. U. of Amer. (Washington 1962). E. des Places et al., DictSpirAscMyst 3:1002-1214. F. Wulf, LexThk² 574-575. P. Pourrat and M. Gaucheron, *Catholicisme,* 3:864-873. U. Bonzi da Genova, EncCatt 4:1687-96.

The Spiritual Father in Orthodox Christianity

The Right Reverend Kallistos Ware

He who climbs a mountain for the first time needs to follow a known route; and he needs to have with him, as companion and guide, someone who has been up before and is familiar with the way. To serve as such a companion and guide is precisely the role of the "abba" or spiritual father — of the one whom the Greeks call *geron* and the Russians *starets,* a title which in both languages means "old man" or "elder."[1]

The importance of obedience to a *geron* is underlined from the first emergence of monasticism in the Christian East. St. Antony of Egypt said: "I know of monks who fell after much toil and lapsed into madness, because they trusted in their own work. . . .So far as possible, for every step that a monk takes, for every drop of water that he drinks in his cell, he should entrust the decision to the old men, to avoid making some mistake in what he does."[2]

This is a theme constantly emphasized in the *Apophthegmata* or *Sayings of the Desert Fathers:* "The old men used to say: 'If you see a young monk climbing up to heaven by his own will, grasp him by the feet and throw him down, for this is to his profit. . . . If a man has faith in another and renders himself up to him in full submission, he has no need to attend to the commandments of God, but he needs only to entrust his entire will into the hands of his father. Then he will be blameless before God, for God requires nothing from beginners so much as self-stripping through obedience.' "[3]

This article originally appeared in *Cross Currents,* Summer-Fall 1974, pp. 296-313. Reprinted by permission.

This figure of the *starets,* so prominent in the first generations of Egyptian monasticism, has retained its full significance up to the present day in Orthodox Christendom. "There is one thing more important than all possible books and ideas," states a Russian layman of the 19th century, the Slavophil Kireyevsky, "and that is the example of an Orthodox *starets,* before whom you can lay each of your thoughts and from whom you can hear, not a more or less valuable private opinion, but the judgment of the Holy Fathers. God be praised, such *startsi* have not yet disappeared from our Russia." And a priest of the Russian emigration in our own century, Fr. Alexander Elchaninov (†1934), writes: "Their field of action is unlimited . . . they are undoubtedly saints, recognized as such by the people. I feel that in our tragic days it is precisely through this means that faith will survive and be strengthened in our country."[4]

The Spiritual Father as a "Charismatic" Figure

What entitles a man to act as a *starets?* How and by whom is he appointed?

To this there is a simple answer. The spiritual father or *starets* is essentially a "charismatic" and prophetic figure, accredited for his task by the direct action of the Holy Spirit. He is ordained, not by the hand of man, but by the hand of God. He is an expression of the Church as "event" or "happening," rather than of the Church as institution.

There is, however, no sharp line of demarcation between the prophetic and the institutional in the life of the Church; each grows out of the other and is intertwined with it. Thus the ministry of the *starets,* itself charismatic, is related to a clearly-defined function within the institutional framework of the Church, the office of priest-confessor. In the Eastern Orthodox tradition, the right to hear confessions is not granted automatically at ordination. Before acting as confessor, a priest requires authorization from his bishop; in the Greek Church, only a minority of the clergy are so authorized.

Yet, although the sacrament of confession is certainly an appropriate occasion for spiritual direction, the ministry of the *starets* is not identical with that of the confessor. The *starets* gives advice, not only at confession, but on many other occasions; indeed, while the confessor must always be a priest, the *starets* may be a simple monk, not in holy orders, or a nun, a layman or laywoman; for there are in the Orthodox tradition spiritual mothers as well as spiritual fathers. The ministry of the *starets* is deeper, because only a very few confessor priests would claim to speak with the former's insight and authority.

But if the *starets* is not ordained or appointed by an act of the official hierarchy, how does he come to embark on his ministry? Sometimes an existing *starets* will designate his own successor. In this way, at certain monastic centers such as Optina in 19th-century Russia, there was established an "apostolic succession" of spiritual masters. In other cases, the *starets* simply emerges spontaneously, without any act of external authorization. As Fr. Alexander Elchaninov says, they are "recognized as such by the people." Within the continuing life of the Christian community, it becomes plain to the believing people of God — which is the true guardian of Holy Tradition — that this or that person has the gift of spiritual fatherhood or motherhood. Then, in a free and informal fashion, others begin to come to him or her for advice and direction.

It will be noted that the initiative comes, as a rule, not from the master but from the disciples. It would be perilously presumptuous for someone to say in his own heart or to others, "Come and submit yourselves to me; I am a *starets,* I have the grace of the Spirit." What happens, rather, is that — without any claims being made by the *starets* himself — others approach him, seeking his advice or asking to live permanently under his care. At first, he will probably send them away, telling them to consult someone else. Eventually the moment comes when he no longer sends them away but accepts their coming to him as a disclosure of the will of God. Thus it is his spiritual children who reveal the *starets* to himself.

The figure of the *starets* illustrates the two interpenetrating levels on which the earthly Church exists and functions. On the one hand, there is the external, official and hierarchical level, with its geographical organization into dioceses and parishes, its great centers (Rome, Constantinople, Moscow, Canterbury), and its "apostolic succession" of bishops. On the other hand, there is the inward, spiritual and "charismatic" level, to which the *startsi* primarily belong. Here the chief centers are, for the most part, not the major primatial and metropolitan sees, but certain remote hermitages, in which there shine forth a few personalities richly endowed with spiritual gifts. Most *startsi* have possessed no exalted status in the formal hierarchy of the Church; yet the influence of a simple priest-monk such as St. Seraphim of Sarov has exceeded that of any patriarch or bishop in 19th-century Orthodoxy. In this fashion, alongside the apostolic succession of the episcopate, there exists that of the saints and spiritual men. Both types of succession are essential for the true functioning of the Body of Christ, and it is through their interaction that the life of the Church on earth is accomplished.

Flight and Return: the Preparation of the *Starets*

Although the *starets* is not ordained or appointed for his task, it is certainly necessary that he should be *prepared*. The classic pattern for this preparation, which consists in a movement of flight and return, may be clearly discerned in the lives of St. Antony of Egypt (†356) and St. Seraphim of Sarov (†1833).

St. Antony's life falls sharply into two halves, with his fifty-fifth year as the watershed. The years from early manhood to the age of fifty-five were his time of preparation, spent in an ever-increasing seclusion from the world as he withdrew further and further into the desert. He eventually passed twenty years in an abandoned fort, meeting no one whatsoever. When he had reached the age of fifty-five, his friends could contain their curiosity no longer, and broke down the entrance. St. Antony came out and, for the remaining half century of his long life, without abandoning the life of a hermit, he made himself freely available to others, acting as "a physician given to Egypt by God." "He was beloved by all," adds his biographer, St. Athanasius, "and all asked to have him as their father."[5] Observe that the transition from enclosed anchorite to spiritual father came about, not through any initiative on St. Antony's part, but through the action of others. Antony was a lay monk, never ordained to the priesthood.

St. Seraphim followed a comparable path. After sixteen years spent in the ordinary life of the monastic community, as novice, professed monk, deacon, and priest, he withdrew for twenty-one years of solitude and almost total silence. During the first part of this period he lived in a forest hut; at one point he passed a thousand days on the stump of a tree and a thousand nights of those days on a rock, devoting himself to

23

unceasing prayer. Recalled by his abbot to the monastery, during the latter part of his time of solitude he lived rigidly enclosed in his cell, which he did not leave even to attend services in church; on Sundays the priest brought communion to him at the door of his room. Though he was a priest he did not celebrate the liturgy. Finally, in the last eighteen years of his life, he ended his enclosure, opening the door of his cell and receiving all who came. He did nothing to advertise himself or to summon people; it was the others who took the initiative in approaching him, but when they came — sometimes dozens or even hundreds in a single day — he did not send them empty away.

Without this intense ascetic preparation, without this radical flight into solitude, could St. Antony or St. Seraphim have acted in the same degree as guide to those of their generation? Not that they withdrew *in order* to become masters and guides of others. They fled, not in order to prepare themselves for some other task, but out of a consuming desire to be alone with God. God accepted their love, but then sent them back as instruments of healing in the world from which they had withdrawn. Even had He never sent them back, their flight would still have been supremely creative and valuable to society; for the monk helps the world not primarily by anything that he does and says but by what he *is,* by the state of unceasing prayer which has become identical with his innermost being. Had St. Antony and St. Seraphim done nothing but pray in solitude they would still have been serving their fellow men to the highest degree. As things turned out, however, God ordained that they should also serve others in a more direct fashion. But this direct and visible service was essentially a consequence of the invisible service which they rendered through their prayer.

"Acquire inward peace," said St. Seraphim, "and a multitude of men around you will find their salvation." Such is the role of spiritual fatherhood. Establish yourself in God; then you can bring others to His presence. A man must learn to be alone, he must listen in the stillness of his own heart to the wordless speech of the Spirit, and so discover the truth about himself and God. Then his word to others will be a word of power, because it is a word out of silence.

Shaped by the encounter with God in solitude, the *starets* is able to heal by his very presence. He guides and forms others, not primarily by words of advice, but by his companionship, by the living and specific example which he sets. He teaches as much by his silence as by his speech. "Abba Theophilus the Archbishop once visited Scetis, and when the brethren had assembled they said to Abba Pambo, 'Say something to the Archbishop, so that he may be edified.' The old man said to them, 'If he is not edified by my silence, he will not be edified by my speech.' "[6] A story with the same moral is told of St. Antony. "It was the custom of three Fathers to visit the Blessed Antony once each year, and two of them used to ask him questions about their thoughts and the salvation of their soul; but the third remained completely silent, without putting any questions. After a long while, Abba Antony said to him, 'See, you have been in the habit of coming to me all this time, and yet you do not ask me any questions.' And the other replied, 'Father, it is enough for me just to look at you.' "[7]

But the real journey of the *starets* is spiritually into the heart, not spatially into the desert. External solitude, although helpful, is not indispensable, and a man may learn to stand alone before God while yet continuing to pursue a life of active service in the midst of society. St. Antony of Egypt was told that a doctor in Alexandria was his equal in spiritual achievement: "In the city there is someone like you, a doctor by profession, who gives all his money to the needy, and the whole day long he sings the Thrice-Holy Hymn with the angels."[8] We are not told how this revelation came to Antony, nor what was the name of the doctor, but one thing is clear. Unceasing prayer of the heart is no monopoly of the solitaries; the mystical and "angelic" life is possible in the city as well as the desert. The Alexandrian doctor accomplished the inward journey without severing his outward links with the community.

There are also many instances in which flight and return are not sharply distinguished in temporal sequence. Take, for example, the case of St. Seraphim's younger contemporary, Bishop Ignaty Brianchaninov (†1867). Trained originally as an army officer, he was appointed at the early age of twenty-six to take charge of a busy and influential monastery close to St. Petersburg. His own monastic training had lasted little more than four years before he was placed in a position of authority. After twenty-four years as abbot, he was consecrated bishop. Four years later he resigned, to spend the remaining six years of his life as a hermit. Here a period of active pastoral work preceded the period of anachoretic seclusion. When he was made abbot, he must surely have felt gravely ill-prepared. His secret withdrawal into the heart was undertaken continuously during the many years in which he administered a monastery and a diocese; but it did not receive an exterior expression until the very end of his life.[9]

Bishop Ignaty's career may serve as a paradigm to many of us at the present time, even though we fall far short of his level of spiritual achievement. Under the pressure of outward circumstances and probably without clearly realizing what is happening to us, we become launched on a career of teaching, preaching and pastoral counselling, while lacking any deep knowledge of the desert and its creative silence. But through teaching others we ourselves may begin to learn. Slowly we recognize our powerlessness to heal the wounds of humanity solely through philanthropic programs, common sense and psychiatry. Our self-dependence is broken down, we appreciate our own inadequacy, and start to understand what Christ meant by the "one thing that is necessary" (Luke 10:42). That is the moment when a man may perhaps begin to enter upon the path of the *starets*. Through his pastoral experience, through his anguish over the pain of others, he is brought to undertake the journey inwards, to ascend the secret ladder of the Kingdom, where alone a genuine solution to the world's problems can be found. No doubt few if any among us would dare to think of ourselves as a *starets* in the full sense, but provided we seek with humble sincerity to enter into the "secret chamber" of our heart, many of us can share to some small degree in the grace of the spiritual fatherhood. Perhaps we shall never outwardly lead the life of a monastic recluse or a hermit — that rests with God — but what is supremely important is that each should see the need to be a hermit of the heart.

The Three Gifts of the Spiritual Father

Three gifts in particular distinguish the spiritual father. The first is *insight and discernment (diakrisis),* the ability to perceive intuitively the secrets of another's heart, to understand the hidden depths of which the other is unaware. The spiritual father penetrates beneath the conventional gestures and attitudes whereby we conceal our true personality from others and from ourselves; and, beyond all these trivialities, he comes to grips with the unique person made in the image and likeness of God. This power is spiritual rather than psychic; it is not simply a kind of extra-sensory perception or a sanctified clairvoyance but the fruit of grace, presupposing concentrated prayer and an unremitting ascetic struggle.

With this gift of insight there goes the ability to use words with power. As each person comes before him, the *starets* knows — immediately and specifically — what it is that the individual needs to hear. Today we are inundated with words, but for the most part these are conspicuously *not* words uttered with power. The *starets* uses few words, and sometimes none at all; but by these few words or by his silence he is able to alter the whole direction of a man's life. At Bethany Christ used three words only, "Lazarus, come out" (John 11:43); and yet these three words, spoken with power, were sufficient to bring the dead back to life. In an age when language has been shamefully debased, it is vital to rediscover the power of the word; and this means rediscovering the nature of silence, not just as a pause between words, but as one of the primary realities of existence. Most teachers and preachers talk far too much; the true *starets* is distinguished by an austere economy of language.

But for a word to possess power, it is necessary that there should be not only one who speaks with the genuine authority of personal experience, but also one who listens with attention and eagerness. If someone questions a *starets* out of idle curiosity, it is likely that he will receive little benefit; but if he approaches the *starets* with ardent faith and deep hunger, the word that he hears may transfigure his being. The words of the *startsi* are for the most part simple in verbal expression and devoid of literary artifice; to those who read them in a superficial way, they will often seem jejune and banal.

The spiritual father's gift of insight is exercised primarily through the practice known as "disclosure of thoughts" *(logismoi)*. In early Eastern monasticism the young monk used to go daily to his father and lay before him all the thoughts which had come to him during the day. This disclosure of thoughts includes far more than a confession of sins, since the novice also speaks of those ideas and impulses which may seem innocent to him, but in which the spiritual father may discern secret dangers or significant signs. Confession is retrospective, dealing with sins that have already occurred; the disclosure of thoughts, on the other hand, is prophylactic, for it lays bare our *logismoi* before they have led to sin and so deprives them of their power to harm.[10] The purpose of the disclosure is not juridical, to secure absolution from guilt, but its aim is self-knowledge, that each may see himself as he truly is.

Endowed with discernment, the spiritual father does not merely wait for a person to reveal himself, but shows to the other thoughts hidden from him. When people came to St. Seraphim of Sarov, he sometimes answered their difficulties before they had time to tell him why they had come. On many occasions the answer at first seemed quite irrelevant, and even absurd and irresponsible; for what St. Seraphim answered was often not the question his visitor had consciously in mind, but the one he ought to have been asking. In all this St. Seraphim relied on the inward light of the Holy Spirit. He found it important, he explained, not to work out in advance what he was going to say; in that case, his words would represent merely his own human judgment, which might well be in error, and not the judgment of God.

In St. Seraphim's eyes, the relationship between *starets* and spiritual child is stronger than death, and he therefore urged his children to continue their disclosure of thoughts to him even after his departure to the next life. Before his death, he told the nuns under his care: "When I am dead, come to me at my grave, and the more often, the better. Whatever is on your soul, whatever may have happened to you, come to me as when I was alive and, kneeling on the ground, cast all your bitterness upon my grave. Tell me everything and I shall listen to you, and all the bitterness will fly away from you. And as you spoke to me when I was alive, do so now. For I am living, and I shall be for ever."

The second gift of the spiritual father is *the ability to love others and to make others' sufferings his own*. Of one of the Egyptian *gerontes,* it is briefly and simply recorded: "He possessed love, and many came to him."[11] *He possessed love* — this is indispensable in all spiritual fatherhood. Unlimited insight into the secrets of men's hearts, if devoid of loving compassion, would not be creative but destructive. He who cannot love others will have little power to heal them.

Loving others involves suffering with and for them; such is the literal sense of compassion. "Bear one another's burdens, and so fulfill the law of Christ" (Galatians 6:2). The spiritual father is the one who *par excellence* bears the burdens of others. "A *starets*," writes Dostoevsky in *The Brothers Karamazov,* "is one who takes your soul, your will, into his soul and his will." It is not enough for him to offer advice. He is also required to take up the soul of his spiritual children into his own soul, their life into his life. It is his task to pray for them, and his constant intercession on their behalf is more important to them than any words of counsel.[12] It is his task likewise to assume their sorrows and their sins, to take their guilt upon himself, and to answer for them at the Last Judgment.

All this is manifest in a primary document of Eastern spiritual direction, the *Book of Varsanuphius and John,* embodying some 850 questions addressed to two elders of 6th-century Palestine, together with their written answers. "As God Himself knows," Varsanuphius insists to his spiritual children, "there is not a second or an hour when I do not have you in my mind and in my prayers. . . . I care for you more than you care for yourself. . . . I would gladly lay down my life for you." This is his prayer to God: "O Master, either bring my children with me into Your Kingdom, or else wipe me also out of Your book." Taking up the theme of bearing others' burdens, Varsanuphius affirms: "I am bearing your burdens and your offences. . . . You have become like a man sitting under a shady tree. . . . I take upon myself the sentence of condemnation against you, and by the grace of Christ I will not abandon you, either in this age or in the age to come."[13]

Readers of Charles Williams will be reminded of the principle of "substituted love", which plays a central part in his novel *Descent into Hell.* The same line of thought is expressed by Dostoevsky's *starets* Zosima: "There is only one way of salvation, and that is to make yourself responsible for all men's sins . . . to make yourself responsible in all sincerity for everything and for everyone." The ability of the *starets* to support and strengthen others is measured by his willingness to adopt this way of salvation.

Yet the relation between the spiritual father and his children is not one-sided. Though he takes the burden of their guilt upon himself and answers for them before God, he cannot do this effectively unless they themselves are struggling wholeheartedly for their own salvation. Once a brother came to St. Antony of Egypt and said: "Pray for me." But the old man replied: "Neither will I take pity on you nor will God, unless you make some effort of your own."[14]

When considering the love of a *starets* for those under his care, it is important to give full meaning to the word "father" in the title "spiritual father." As father and offspring in an ordinary family should be joined in mutual love, so it must also be within the "charismatic" family of the *starets*. Yet it is primarily a relationship in the Holy Spirit, and while the wellspring of human affection is not to be unfeelingly suppressed, it still needs to be purged of emotional excitement and transfigured. In this connection there is a significant story in the *Apophthegmata*. A young monk looked after his elder, who was gravely ill, for twelve years without interruption. Never once in that period did his elder thank him or so much as speak one word of kindness to him. Only on his death-bed did the old man remark to the assembled brethren, "He is an angel and not a man."[15] The story is valuable as an indication of the need for spiritual detachment, but such an uncompromising avoidance of all outward tokens of affection is not typical of the *Sayings of the Desert Fathers*, still less of Varsanuphius and John.

A third gift of the spiritual father is *the power to transform the human environment*, both the material and the nonmaterial. The gift of healing, possessed by so many of the *startsi*, is one aspect of this power. More generally, the *starets* helps his disciples to perceive the world as God created it and as God desires it once more to be. "Can you take too much joy in your Father's works?" asks Thomas Traherne. "He is Himself in everything." The true *starets* is one who discerns this universal presence of the Creator throughout creation, and assists others to discern it also. In the words of William Blake, "If the doors of perception were cleansed, everything will appear to man as it is, infinite." The *starets* is one in whom the doors of perception have been cleansed. For the man who dwells in God, there is nothing mean and trivial: he sees everything in the light of Mount Tabor, transfigured by the love of Christ. "What is a merciful heart?" inquires St. Isaac the Syrian. "It is a heart that burns with love for the whole of creation — for men, for the birds, for the beasts, for the demons, for every creature. When a man with such a heart as this thinks of the creatures or looks at them, his eyes are filled with tears. An overwhelming compassion makes his heart grow small and weak, and he cannot endure to hear or see any suffering, even the smallest pain, inflicted upon any creature. Therefore he never ceases to pray with tears even for the dumb animals, for the enemies of truth, and for those who do harm to it, asking that they may be guarded and receive God's mercy. And for the reptiles also he prays with a great compassion, which rises up endlessly in his heart after the example of God."[16]

An all-embracing love, like that of St. Isaac or of Dostoevsky's *starets* Zosima, transforms its object, making the human environment transparent, so that the uncreated energies of God shine through it. A momentary glimpse of what this transfiguration involves is provided by the celebrated "conversation" between St. Seraphim of Sarov and Nicolas Motovilov, one of his spiritual children. They were walking in the forest one winter's day and St. Seraphim spoke of the need to acquire the Holy Spirit. This led Motovilov to ask how a man can know with certainty that he is "in the Spirit of God":

> Then Fr. Seraphim took me very firmly by the shoulders and said: "My son, we are both at this moment in the Spirit of God. Why don't you look at me?"
>
> "I cannot look, Father," I replied, "because your eyes are flashing like lightning. Your face has become brighter than the sun, and it hurts my eyes to look at you."
>
> "Don't be afraid," he said. "At this very moment you have yourself become as bright as I am. You are yourself in the fullness of the Spirit of God at this moment; otherwise you would not be able to see me as you do. . . . But why, my son, do you not look me in the eyes? Just look, and don't be afraid; the Lord is with us."
>
> After these words I glanced at his face, and there came over me an even greater reverent awe. Imagine in the center of the sun, in the dazzling light of its mid-day rays, the face of a man talking to you. You see the movement of his lips and the changing expression of his eyes and you hear his voice, you feel someone holding your shoulders, yet you do not see his hands, you do not even see yourself or his body, but only a blinding light spreading around for several yards and lighting up with its brilliance the snow-blanket which covers the forest glade and the snowflakes which continue to fall unceasingly.[17]

Obedience and Freedom

Such are, by God's grace, the gifts of the *starets*. But what of the spiritual child? How does he contribute to the mutual relationship between father and son in God?

Briefly, what he offers is his full and unquestioning obedience. As a classic example, there is the story in the *Sayings of the Desert Fathers* about the monk who was told to plant a dry stick in the sand and to water it daily. So distant was the spring from his cell that he had to leave in the evening to fetch the water and he only returned in the following morning. For three years he patiently fulfilled his abba's command. At the end of this period, the stick suddenly put forth leaves and bore fruit. The abba picked the fruit, took it to the church, and invited the monks to eat, saying, "Come and taste the fruit of obedience."[18]

Another example of obedience is the monk Mark, who while copying a manuscript was summoned by his abba: so immediate was his response that he did not even complete the circle of the letter O that he was writing. On another occasion, as they walked together, his abba saw a small pig; testing Mark, he said, "Do you see that buffalo, my child?" "Yes, Father," replied Mark. "And you see how powerful its horns are?" "Yes, Father," he answered once more without demur.[19] Abba Joseph of Panepho, following a similar policy, tested the obedience of his disciples by assigning ridiculous tasks to them, and only if they complied would he then give them sensible commands.[20] Another *geron* instructed his disciple to steal things from the cells of the brethren;[21] yet another told his disciple (who had not been entirely truthful with him) to throw his son into the furnace.[22]

Such stories are likely to make a somewhat ambivalent impression on the modern reader. They seem to reduce the disciple to an infantile or sub-human level, depriving him of all power of judgment and moral choice. We are tempted to ask with indignation: Is this the "glorious liberty of the children of God" (Rom. 8:21)?

Three points must here be made. In the first place, the obedience offered by the spiritual son to his abba is not forced but willing and voluntary. It is the task of the *starets* to take up our will into his will, but he can only do this if by our own free choice we place it in his hands. He does not break our will, but accepts it from us as a gift. A submission that is forced and involuntary is obviously devoid of moral value; the *starets* asks of each one that he offer to God his heart, not his external actions.

32

The voluntary nature of obedience is vividly emphasized in the ceremony of the tonsure at the Orthodox rite of monastic profession. The scissors are placed upon the Book of the Gospels, and the novice must himself pick them up and give them to the abbot. The abbot immediately replaces them on the Book of the Gospels. Again the novice takes up the scissors, and again they are replaced. Only when the novice gives him the scissors for the third time does the abbot proceed to cut his hair. Never thereafter will the monk have the right to say to the abbot or the brethren: "My personality is constricted and suppressed here in the monastery; you have deprived me of my freedom." No one has taken away his freedom, for it was he himself who took up the scissors and placed them three times in the abbot's hand.

But this voluntary offering of our freedom is obviously something that cannot be made once and for all, by a single gesture. There must be a continual offering, extending over our whole life; our growth in Christ is measured precisely by the increasing degree of our self-giving. Our freedom must be offered anew each day and each hour, in constantly varying ways; and this means that the relation between *starets* and disciple is not static but dynamic, not unchanging but infinitely diverse. Each day and each hour, under the guidance of his abba, the disciple will face new situations, calling for a different response, a new kind of self-giving.

In the second place, the relation between *starets* and spiritual child is not one-sided but mutual. Just as the *starets* enables the disciples to see themselves as they truly are, so it is the disciples who reveal the *starets* to himself. In most instances, as we have already noted, a man does not realize that he is called to be a *starets* until others come to him and insist on placing themselves under his guidance. This reciprocity continues throughout the relationship between the two. The spiritual father does not possess an exhaustive program, neatly worked out in advance and imposed in the same manner upon everyone. On the contrary, if he is a true *starets,* he will have a different word for each; and since the word which he gives is, on the deepest level, not his own but the Holy Spirit's, he does not know in advance what that word will be. The *starets* proceeds on the basis not of abstract rules but of concrete human situations. He and his disciple enter each situation together, neither of them knowing beforehand exactly what the outcome will be, but each waiting for the enlightenment of the Spirit. Each of them, the spiritual father as well as the disciple, must learn as he goes.

The mutuality of their relationship is indicated by certain stories in the *Sayings of the Desert Fathers,* where an unworthy abba has a spiritual son far better than himself. The disciple, for example, detects his abba in the sin of fornication, but pretends to have noticed nothing and remains under his charge; and so, through the patient humility of his disciple, the spiritual father is brought eventually to repentance and a new life. In such a case, it is not the spiritual father who helps the disciple, but the reverse. Obviously such a situation is far from the norm, but it indicates that the disciple is sometimes called to give as well as to receive.

In reality, the relationship is not two-sided but triangular, for in addition to the *starets* and his disciple there is also a third partner, God. Our Lord insisted that we should call no man "father," for we have only one father, who is in Heaven (Matthew 23:9). The *starets* is not an infallible judge or a final court of appeal, but a fellow-servant of the living God; not a dictator, but a guide and companion on the way. The only true "spiritual director," in the fullest sense of the word, is the Holy Spirit.

This brings us to the third point. In the Eastern Orthodox tradition at its best, the spiritual father has always sought to avoid any kind of constraint and spiritual violence in his relations with his disciples. If, under the guidance of the Spirit, he speaks and acts with authority, it is with the authority of humble love. The words of *starets* Zosima in *The Brothers Karamazov* express an essential aspect of spiritual fatherhood: "At some ideas you stand perplexed, especially at the sight of men's sin, uncertain whether to combat it by force or by humble love. Always decide, 'I will combat it by humble love.' If you make up your mind about that once and for all, you can conquer the whole world. Loving humility is a terrible force; it is the strongest of all things and there is nothing like it."

Anxious to avoid all mechanical constraint, many spiritual fathers in the Christian East refuse to provide their disciples with a rule of life, a set of external commands to be applied automatically. In the words of a contemporary Romanian monk, the *starets* is "not a legislator but a mystagogue."[23] He guides others, not by imposing rules, but by sharing his life

34

with them. A monk told Abba Poemen, "Some brethren have come to live with me; do you want me to give them orders?" "No," said the old man. "But, Father," the monk persisted, "they themselves want me to give them orders." "No," repeated Poemen, "be an example to them but not a lawgiver."[24] The same moral emerges from the story of Isaac the Priest. As a young man, he remained first with Abba Kronios and then with Abba Theodore of Pherme; but neither of them told him what to do. Isaac complained to the other monks and they came and remonstrated with Theodore. "If he wishes," Theodore replied eventually, "let him do what he sees me doing."[25] When Varsanuphius was asked to supply a detailed rule of life, he declined, saying: "I do not want you to be under the law, but under grace." And in other letters he wrote: "You know that we have never imposed chains upon anyone. . . . Do not force men's free will, but sow in hope; for our Lord did not compel anyone, but He preached the good news, and those who wished hearkened to Him."[26]

Do not force men's free will. The task of the spiritual father is not to destroy a man's freedom, but to assist him to see the truth for himself; not to suppress a man's personality, but to enable him to discover himself, to grow to full maturity and to become what he really is. If on occasion the spiritual father requires an unquestioning and seemingly "blind" obedience from his disciple, this is never done as an end in itself, nor with a view to enslaving him. The purpose of this kind of "shock treatment" is simply to deliver the disciple from his false and illusory "self," so that he may enter into true freedom. The spiritual father does not impose his personal ideas and devotions, but he helps the disciple to find the vocation that is distinctively his own. In the words of a 17th-century Benedictine, Dom Augustine Baker: "The director is not to teach his own way, nor indeed any determinate way of prayer, but to instruct his disciples how they may themselves find out the way proper for them. . . . In a word, he is only God's usher, and must lead souls in God's way, and not his own."[27]

In the last resort, what the spiritual father gives to his disciple is not a code of written or oral regulations, not a set of techniques for meditation, but a personal relationship. Within this personal relationship the abba grows and changes as well as the disciple, for God is constantly guiding them both. He may on occasion provide his disciple with detailed verbal instructions, with precise answers to specific questions. On other occasions he may fail to give any answer at all, either because he does not think that the question needs an answer, or because he himself does not yet know what the answer should be. But these answers — or this failure to answer — are always given within the framework of a personal relationship. Many things cannot be said in words, but can be conveyed through a direct personal encounter.

In the Absence of a *Starets*

And what is one to do, if he cannot find a spiritual father?

He may turn, in the first place, to *books*. Writing in 15th-century Russia, St. Nil Sorsky laments the extreme scarcity of qualified spiritual directors; yet how much more frequent they must have been in his day than in ours! Search diligently, he urges, for a sure and trustworthy guide. "However, if such a teacher cannot be found, then the Holy Fathers order us to turn to the Scriptures and listen to our Lord Himself speaking."[28] Since the testimony of Scripture should not be isolated from the continuing witness of the Spirit in the life of the Church, the inquirer will also read the works of the Fathers, and above all the *Philokalia*. But there is an evident danger here. The *starets* adapts his guidance to the inward state of each; books offer the same advice to everyone. How is the beginner to discern whether or not a particular text is applicable to his own situation? Even if he cannot find a spiritual father in the full sense, he should at least try to find someone more experienced than himself, able to guide him in his reading.

It is possible to learn also from visiting *places* where divine grace has been exceptionally manifested and where prayer has been especially concentrated. Before taking a major decision, and in the absence of other guidance, many Orthodox Christians will go on pilgrimage to Jerusalem or Mount Athos, to some monastery or the tomb of a saint, where they will pray for enlightenment. This is the way in which I myself have reached the more difficult decisions in my life.

Thirdly, we can learn from *religious communities* with an established tradition of the spiritual life. In the absence of a personal teacher, the monastic environment can serve as *guru;* we can receive our formation from the ordered sequence of the daily program, with its periods of liturgical and silent prayer, with its balance of manual labor, study and recreation.[29] This seems to have been the chief way in which St. Seraphim of Sarov gained his spiritual training. A well-organized monastery embodies, in an accessible and living form, the inherited wisdom of many *startsi*. Not only monks, but those who come as visitors for a longer or shorter period, can be formed and guided by the experience of community life.

It is indeed no coincidence that in 4th-century Egypt the kind of spiritual fatherhood that we have been describing emerged initially, not within the fully organized communities under St. Pachomius, but among the hermits and in the semi-eremitic *milieu* of Nitria and Scetis. In the former, spiritual direction was provided by Pachomius himself, by the superiors of each monastery, and by the heads of individual "houses" within the monastery. The Rule of St. Benedict also envisages the abbot as spiritual father, and there is virtually no provision for further direction of a more "charismatic" type. In time, of course, the coenobitic communities incorporated many of the traditions of spiritual fatherhood as developed among the hermits, but the need for those traditions has always been less intensely felt in the *coenobia*, precisely because direction is provided by the corporate life pursued under the guidance of the Rule.

Finally, before we leave the subject of the absence of the *starets*, it is important to recognize the extreme flexibility in the relationship between *starets* and disciple. Some may see their spiritual father daily or even hourly, praying, eating, and working with him, perhaps sharing the same cell, as often happened in the Egyptian Desert. Others may see him only once a month or once a year; others, again, may visit a *starets* on but a single occasion in their entire life, yet this will be sufficient to set them on the right path. There are, furthermore, many different types of spiritual father; few will be wonder-workers like St. Seraphim of Sarov. There are numerous priests and laymen who, while lacking the more spectacular endowments of the *starets*, are certainly able to provide others with the guidance that they require. And, alongside spiritual fatherhood or motherhood, there are always opportunities also for spiritual brotherhood and sisterhood.

Many people imagine that they cannot find a spiritual father, because they expect him to be of a particular type: they want a St. Seraphim, and so they close their eyes to the guides whom God is actually sending to them. Often their supposed problems are not so very complicated, and in reality they already know in their own heart what the answer is. But they do not like the answer, because it involves patient and sustained effort on their part: and so they look for a *deus ex machina* who, by a single miraculous word, will suddenly make everything easy. Such people need to be helped to an understanding of the true nature of spiritual direction.

Contemporary Examples

In conclusion, I wish briefly to recall two *startsi* of our own day, whom I have had the happiness of knowing personally. The first is Father Amphilochios (†1970), for a time abbot of the Monastery of St. John on the Island of Patmos, and in later life spiritual father to a community of nuns which he had founded not far from the Monastery. What most distinguished his character was his gentleness, the warmth of his affection, and his sense of tranquil yet triumphant joy. Life in Christ, as he understood it, is not a heavy yoke, a burden to be carried with resignation, but a personal relationship to be pursued with eagerness of heart. He was firmly opposed to all spiritual violence and cruelty. It was typical that, as he lay dying and took leave of the nuns under his care, he should urge the abbess not to be too severe on them: "They have left everything to come here, they must not be unhappy."[30] When I was to return from Patmos to England as a newly-ordained priest, he insisted that there was no need to be afraid of anything.

My second example is Archbishop John (Maximovich), Russian bishop in Shanghai, in Western Europe, and finally in San Francisco (†1966). Little more than a dwarf in height, with tangled hair and beard, and with an impediment in his speech, he possessed more than a touch of the "Fool in Christ." From the time of his profession as a monk, he did not lie down on a bed to sleep at night; he went on working and praying, snatching his sleep at odd moments in the twenty-four hours. He wandered barefoot through the streets of Paris, and once he celebrated a memorial service among the tram lines close to the port of Marseilles. Punctuality had little meaning for him. Baffled by his unpredictable behavior, the more conventional among his flock sometimes judged him to be unsuited for the administrative work of a bishop. But with his total disregard of normal formalities he succeeded where others, relying on worldly influence and expertise, had failed entirely — as when, against all hope and in the teeth of the ''quota'' system, he secured the admission of thousands of homeless Russian refugees to the USA.

In private conversation he was very gentle, and he quickly won the confidence of small children. Particularly striking was the intensity of his intercessory prayer. When possible, he liked to celebrate the Divine Liturgy daily, and the service often took twice or three times the normal space of time, such was the multitude of those whom he commemorated individually by name. As he prayed for them, they were never mere names on a lengthy list, but always persons. One story that I was told is typical. It was his custom each year to visit Holy Trinity Monastery at Jordanville, NY. As he left at the close of one such visit, a monk gave him a slip of paper with four names of those who were gravely ill. Archbishop John received thousands upon thousands of such requests for prayer in the course of each year. On his return to the monastery some twelve months later, at once he beckoned to the monk and, much to the latter's surprise, from the depths of his cassock Archbishop John produced the identical slip of paper, now crumpled and tattered. ''I have been praying for your friends,'' he said, ''but two of them'' — he pointed to their names — ''are now dead and the other two have recovered.'' And so indeed it was.

Even at a distance he shared in the concerns of his spiritual children. One of them, Fr. (now Archbishop) Jacob, superior of a small Orthodox monastery in Holland, was sitting one evening in his room, unable to sleep from anxiety over the problems which faced him. In the middle of the night the telephone rang; it was Archbishop John, speaking from several hundred miles away. He had rung to say that it was time for the monk to go to bed: ''Go to sleep now, what you are asking of God will certainly be all right.''[31]

Such is the role of the spiritual father. As Varsanuphius expressed it, ''I care for you more than you care for yourself.''

[1]The fullest study on spiritual fatherhood in the Christian East is still I. Hausherr, SJ, *Direction spirituelle en Orient autrefois (Orientalia Christiana Analecta* 144: Rome 1955). An excellent portrait of a great *starets* in 19th-century Russia is provided by J.B. Dunlop, *Staretz Amvrosy: Model for Dostoevsky's Staretz Zossima* (Belmont, Mass. 1972); cf. I. de Beausobre, *Macarius, Starets of Optino: Russian Letters of Direction 1834-1860* (London

1944). For the life and writings of a Russian *starets* in the present century, see Archimandrite Sofrony, *The Monk of Mount Athos. Staretz Silouan: 1866-1938* (London 1973); *Wisdom from Mount Athos* (London 1974). ²*Apophthegmata Patrum,* alphabetical collection *(PG* 65), Antony the Great, 37 and 38; ET Benedicta Ward, SLG, *The Sayings of the Desert Fathers* (London 1981), pp. 8-9. ³*Apophthegmata Patrum,* anonymous series (Nau/Guy), 244 (112) and 290 (158): ET Benedicta Ward, SLG, *The Wisdom of the Desert Fathers* (Fairacres Publication 48: Oxford 1975), pp. 34, 45. ⁴A. Elchaninov, *The Diary of a Russian Priest* (London 1967), p. 54. ⁵*The Life of Antony,* chapters 87 and 81: ET R.C. Gregg *(The Classics of Western Spirituality:* New York 1980), pp. 94, 90. ⁶*Apophthegmata Patrum,* alphabetical collection, Theophilus the Archbishop, 2: ET, p. 81. ⁷*Ibid.,* Antony, 27: ET, p. 7. ⁸*Ibid.,* Antony, 24: ET, p. 6. ⁹Compare the lives of St. Tikhon of Zadonsk (†1753) and of Ignaty's contemporary, Bishop Theophan the Recluse (†1894). ¹⁰Evergetinos, *Synagoge* i, 20: ed. Victor Matthaiou, vol. i (Athens 1957), pp. 168-9. ¹¹*Apophthegmata Patrum,* alphabetical collection, Poemen 8: ET, p. 167. ¹²For the importance of a spiritual father's prayers, see for example *Apophthegmata Patrum,* anonymous series, 293 (160): ET, pp. 45-46. ¹³*The Book of Varsanuphius and John,* ed. Sotirios Schoinas (Volos 1960), *Letters* 208, 39, 353, 110 and 239. A critical edition of part of the Greek text, accompanied by an English translation, has been prepared by D.J. Chitty: *Varsanuphius and John, Questions and Answers (Patrologia Orientalis* xxxi, 3: Paris 1966). There is a French translation of the whole collection by L. Regnault: *Barsanuphe et Jean de Gaza, Correspondance* (Solesmes 1972). ¹⁴*Apophthegmata Patrum,* alphabetical collection, Antony, 16: ET, p. 4. ¹⁵*Ibid.,* John the Theban, 1: ET, p. 109. ¹⁶*Mystic Treatises of Isaac of Nineveh,* ET A.J. Wensinck (Amsterdam 1923), p. 341 (translation altered). ¹⁷"Conversation of St. Seraphim on the Aim of the Christian Life," in *A Wonderful Revelation to the World* (Jordanville, NY 1953), pp. 23-24. ¹⁸*Apophthegmata Patrum,* alphabetical collection, John the Dwarf, 1: ET, pp. 85-86. ¹⁹*Ibid.,* Mark the Disciple of Silvanus, 1 and 2: ET, pp. 145-146. ²⁰*Ibid.,* Joseph of Panepho, 5: ET, p. 103. ²¹*Ibid.,* Saio, 1: ET, p. 229. The *geron* subsequently returned the things to their rightful owners. ²²*Apophthegmata Patrum,* anonymous series, 295 (162): ET, p. 47. There is a parallel story in the alphabetical collection, Sisoes, 10: ET, p. 214. Compare Genesis 22 (Abraham and Isaac). ²³Fr. André Scrima, "La tradition du père spirituel dans l'Eglise d'Orient," *Hermès,* 1967, no. 4, p. 83. ²⁴*Apophthegmata Patrum,* alphabetical collection, Poemen, 174: ET, p. 191. ²⁵*Ibid.,* Isaac the Priest, 2: ET, pp. 99-100. ²⁶*The Book of Varsanuphius and John, Letters* 23, 51 and 35. ²⁷Quoted by Thomas Merton, *Spiritual Direction and Meditation* (Collegeville, Minn. 1960), p. 12. ²⁸"The Monastic Rule," in G.P. Fedotov, *A Treasury of Russian Spirituality* (London 1950), pp. 95-96. ²⁹But see Merton, *op. cit.,* pp. 14-16, on the dangers of rigid monastic discipline without proper spiritual direction. ³⁰I. Gorainoff, "Holy Men of Patmos," *Sobornost* (The Journal of the Fellowship of St. Alban and St. Sergius), series 6, no. 5 (1972), pp. 343-344. ³¹Bishop Savva of Edmonton, *Blessed John: The Chronicle of the Veneration of Archbishop John Maximovich* (St. Herman of Alaska Brotherhood: Platina, Calif. 1979), p. 104.

The Contemporary Ministry of Spiritual Direction

Sandra Schneiders, I.H.M.

One of the striking phenomena in the post-conciliar Church is the evident renewal of interest in "spiritual direction" on the part of priests, religious, and laity. In an age characterized by intense social consciousness, serious reserves about authority, and a deep distrust of anything which suggests alienation, this interest can appear regressive and anachronistic. Consequently, before discussing the subject of spiritual direction in itself it might be useful to situate the current interest within the contemporary socio-religious context.

The Context of the Spiritual Direction Question

The interest in spiritual direction (however the term is understood) is part of a larger cultural phenomenon of our times which might be called the quest for personal authenticity through interiority. Although this quest has given rise to a certain amount of bizarre behavior and unrealistic dabbling in the esoteric, it cannot be dismissed as basically misconceived or ephemeral. It is the result of many factors, the analysis of which is outside the scope of this article, but among which are a growing disaffection with runaway consumerism, disgust with the politics of power, fear of massive structural injustice, cosmic insecurity in a nuclear age, and a generalized rejection of the value-system which has made the person an expendable commodity in a throw-away economy. The pursuit of interiority is basically a search for personal meaning, a quest for

This article originally appeared in *Chicago Studies,* 15, Spring 1976, pp. 119-35. Reprinted by permission.

the "who" and the "why" in a world of "what" and "how."

The interest of many contemporary Christians in spiritual direction is part of the specifically religious manifestation of this quest, that is, it is part of the current interest in spirituality in general. Although spirituality is by no means exclusive to Christianity, our reflections in this article will deal only with Christian spirituality. For the Christian, the spiritual life is faith-life, the relationship of the person with God in Christ through the power of the Spirit within the believing community. This life has many aspects but the one we are concerned with here is that which has been traditionally called the "interior life," that is, the life of personal prayer and ongoing personal self-evaluation and re-formation.

Prior to Vatican II the ordinary Christian life was lived within a complex structure of obligations and practices that tended to obscure the personal character of the spiritual life and foster an illusion of religious adequacy in anyone who "practiced" faithfully. In such a religious context both the interior life and social responsibility tended to be underdeveloped aspects of Catholic spirituality. The dissolution of a good deal of the pre-conciliar structure has, fortunately but painfully, thrown the sincere Christian back upon his/her own resources and many people are spiritually disoriented by a freedom for which they were not prepared.

From time immemorial, and in every religious tradition which encourages personal spiritual evolution in its adherents, some form of spiritual direction (although seldom called by that name) has had an important place. Such direction has a particularly important place at the beginning of the spiritual life and in times of crisis and disorientation. Consequently, it is not at all surprising that many post-conciliar Catholics who are trying to develop a mature interior life in a context of decreasing religious structure and who are finding themselves both inexperienced in this domain and disoriented in a rapidly changing Church, are experiencing the need for spiritual direction. Their expressed desire for direction is not always met with enthusiasm by those within the ecclesial community to whom it is addressed.

The Ministerial Imperative

It is perhaps not inopportune to devote a moment's reflection to two of the major reasons, one speculative and one psychological-personal, for this reserve on the part of those within the community to whom Christians seeking spiritual direction often turn by preference. There is, of course, no essential relationship between any state of life and the ministry of spiritual direction. In the history of Christian spirituality laity, religious, and clergy have exercised this ministry and all three groups are represented among contemporary spiritual directors. Nevertheless, it is a fact that most requests for spiritual direction are addressed to priests and religious. This is no doubt due to the justifiable assumption that men and women who are full-time ministers within the ecclesial community *should* have both the interest in and the competence for assisting their brothers and sisters in spiritual growth and development. However justifiable this assumption, it is unfortunately not always well-founded in fact.

One reason that some otherwise zealous ministers of the Word are not receptive to a request for spiritual direction is the suspicion that such a request springs from an overly introspective concern with the interior life, a concern which needs to be redirected toward healthy apostolic involvement in the extension of Christ's reign in this world.

It is undoubtedly true that some people's interest in the interior life is a flight from reality, but it does not take much experience to recognize this pseudo-interiority. In the Christian whose spiritual life is fundamentally balanced (or at least potentially so) the concern for interiority is part of a healthy dialectic among several components of the spiritual life. The desire to grow in prayer and spiritual judgment, that is, in the interior life, is no more the enemy of apostolic involvement than is the liturgical life, the practice of virtue, or theological reflection and study. Any component of the spiritual life can be exaggerated; the solution is not to abandon the component but to integrate it. One of the aims of spiritual direction is precisely this integration. The minister who fears that any desire for the intensification of the interior life is a flight from apostolic involvement should perhaps confront the question of whether his/her own insistence on apostolic involvement might not be a flight from healthy interiority.

This suggests the second (and probably more widespread and fundamental) reason why some men and women involved in ministry shy away from a request for spiritual direction, namely, personal uncertainty in unfamiliar territory. However

43

well-founded in fact this sense of personal inadequacy may be, it does not justify simply closing the door on the topic.

Ministry is essentially a response to real needs and real needs must be determined by a prayerful reading of the signs of the times. One of the clearest signs of our times is the interest in spirituality in general and particularly in the two aspects of Catholic spirituality which have been seriously neglected until very recent times: genuine interiority and apostolic involvement in the quest for justice and peace. Spiritual direction is intimately related to both of these aspects.

This means that the contemporary minister is called, by the situation of and in the Church, to take the same kind of interest in spiritual direction that he/she has been called to take in liturgy, liberation and justice, group prayer, Scripture, and so on, in the years since Vatican II. The desire for spiritual direction is the expression of an authentic and widespread need in the contemporary Church. Consequently, it constitutes an imperative for contemporary ministry. The main purpose of this article is to discuss briefly four basic questions concerning the ministry of spiritual direction in an attempt to clear the ground for the reader who is trying to situate this topic within his/her ministerial perspective.

I. The Meaning of Spiritual Direction

A. The Problem of Terminology

Although most people involved in or writing about spiritual direction today would agree that the terminology is unsatisfactory, most also would recognize that there is little possibility of changing it, both because it is consecrated by a very long tradition, and because no one has come up with a really adequate alternative. Rather than attempting to change all of the terminology it seems preferable to learn to understand most of it differently and to gradually change, by usage, only what is really unsalvageable.

1. Spiritual Direction

The term "spiritual direction" is somewhat objectionable because it suggests (and historically it has often meant) that the "director" assumes an authoritarian role in relation to the "directee," who, by obedience, relinquishes some or all personal responsibility for the orientation of his/her interior life. Today, in the light of modern psychology and of an evolved Christian anthropology, such a relationship would be correctly judged to be alienating and irresponsible. Furthermore, our theological understanding of the dialectic between human and divine freedom makes largely unacceptable the conception of obedience upon which such a relationship rests.

Nevertheless, there is a way to understand the traditional term "spiritual direction" which would be both true to the essence of the experience in question and consonant with the evolution of our understanding of God, of the human person, and of the relationship between them. Spiritual direction can be understood as a process, carried out in a one-to-one interpersonal context, of establishing and maintaining a growth-orientation (that is, direction) in one's faith life. This process has two moments which are in a constant dialectical relationship with each other, namely, listening to and articulating God's call in one's life, and progressively elaborating an integrated and adequate response to that call. The term "direction," then, does not designate the activity of one person upon another (directing him/her) but the final object of the process (self-orientation toward growth in the life of faith).

2. Director

Although the one-to-one relationship which is both the context of the process and an integral part of it is not purely egalitarian, it is not an authority-obedience nor superior-subject relationship. For that reason the traditional terminology of "director-directee" is even more open to misinterpretation than is "spiritual direction" itself. In fact, "director" is so unsatisfactory that many alternates have been suggested and it seems likely that the term "director" will eventually be replaced by something like spiritual "guide" or "companion."

The role of this person is analogous to that of the guide in a mountain climb or a wild game hunt. The spiritual guide is a person who, at the request of the primary actor in the direction situation, puts his/her competence at the service of the other's spiritual project. The guide neither selects nor imposes the goal or even the means. Rather, the guide assists the person in various ways to discover and to achieve that which God is asking of him/her, for example, by helping the person to recognize avoidable pitfalls, to avoid the unprofitably dangerous, to see and capitalize on the helpful, to select efficacious means to the goals the person espouses, and especially to objectify the various aspects of his/her experience of God. And the guide is a companion in the inevitable loneliness and difficulties as well as in the joys of the spiritual life.

3. Directee

The term "directee" is foreign to American ears and can easily suggest alienation. But precisely because it is so unfamiliar it has the advantage of not evoking the difficulty-problematic of a word like "client." And, if "directee" is understood to mean someone seeking, establishing, and pursuing a direction rather than one being directed by someone else the term is perhaps salvageable.

In any case, what is important in the present terminological *impasse* is not to resolve the question of which words to use. It is to be very clear both about what we *are* talking about and what we *are not* talking about and especially to be certain that both persons in a given direction situation mean the same thing when they use the same words.

B. Definition of Spiritual Direction

Spiritual direction could be defined as a process carried out in the context of a one-to-one relationship in which a competent guide helps a fellow Christian to grow in the spiritual life by means of personal encounters that have the directee's spiritual growth as their explicit object. We will examine briefly each of the elements of this definition.

First, spiritual direction is a *process*. It is not a single or occasional consultation about some particular problem but an ongoing relationship characterized by a certain continuity and consistency. In practice, good spiritual direction usually involves regular (e.g., weekly, bi-weekly, monthly) meetings between the two persons. The rhythm may intensify in times of crisis but the process is essentially not crisis-dominated but growth-oriented. Consequently, a good spiritual direction situation maintains its continuity in times of spiritual well-being as well as in times of difficulty, the former being no less significant in the spiritual life than the latter. However, it is not so much the frequency but the regularity of the meetings and the continuity of their content which is most important.

Secondly, spiritual direction involves a *one-to-one relationship*. This distinguishes it from all types of group formation, however valuable these may be or whatever role such experiences may play in the overall spiritual project in which the directee is involved. Spiritual direction is a one-to-one relationship because its primary concern is with the recognition of God's unique and personal call to the individual and the personal and unique response of the individual to that call. Christian spiritual life is essentially communitarian, but no matter how intimately we are bound up with one another in Christ there is an ultimately unique dimension of our experience of God because the revelation of God in Jesus, offered to all, must eventually be internalized by the individual. This internalization of revelation, however analogous to the experience of others, has all the intimate and solitary uniqueness of growing up or of falling in love. Spiritual direction is concerned primarily with this personal experience and thus it involves a one-to-one relationship in which there is no generalization of experience but a concentration on the individual's experience in all its particularity.

Thirdly, the relationship involves two Christians, one of whom is *exercising a particular competence* in respect to the other who is profiting by this competence. This does not imply that the guide is necessarily a fully mature and perfect Christian. A person who may be a competent spiritual guide may (and often does) also consult someone who exercises that same role of guide for him or her. In the role of guide the person exercises the competence he or she possesses. In the role of directee he/she appeals to the same type of competence in another. This is, of course, not just a matter of changing hats and scripts. Levels of competence and stages of growth can be quite diverse. Someone well able to guide a high school student may not yet have the competence to guide a mature contemplative.

Although many people prefer, as spiritual guide, someone who is more experienced in the spiritual life than themselves, it is not necessarily true that the spiritual guide must be more advanced in the spiritual life than the directee. What is important is that the guide who is chosen be competent to assist the directee in the stage at which the latter is. Once a person is spiritually mature he/she is usually able to assist even those who might be actually more advanced in prayer. However, until a certain level of spiritual maturity is attained the question of relative competence remains crucial. We will discuss this question of competence in the section on the director or guide.

Fourthly, the objective of the spiritual direction process is the *growth of the directee*. This seemingly self-evident point is too easily forgotten, especially when the direction situation arises in an institutional context such as a seminary or a novitiate. Spiritual direction should not be "used" for disciplinary or evaluative purposes or even as a method of forming a candidate for a particular state of life. The only valid objective of spiritual direction is the growth of the directee. What growth consists in for the person in question is not to be determined by the guide, much less by a third party. It must be worked out by the directee in his/her relationship with God. The spiritual guide is at the service of the directee's own spiritual project, not of someone else's (or the director's own!) project for the person.

Fifthly, the primary means used in the spiritual direction process is *personal encounter* between the guide and the directee. Normally, this means face-to-face conversations although it sometimes includes shared experiences of another type, correspondence, etc. The nature and content of these encounters will be discussed below in the section on the direction process.

Sixthly, the encounters between guide and directee have the spiritual growth of the latter as their *explicit object*. Consequently, spiritual direction is not a by-product or unrecognized component of some other process such as group therapy, parish board work, academic counseling, youth group leadership, or the like. Any of these situations may be useful for someone's spiritual growth and all of them can be utilized for indirect spiritual counseling. But spiritual direction in the strict sense of the word is a process initiated by the directee for the explicit purpose of personal growth and development in the life of faith and into which the guide enters by invitation to facilitate that growth.

C. Types of Spiritual Direction

The foregoing paragraphs amount to saying that spiritual direction is a specific process which can be distinguished from other processes in the spiritual life. Nevertheless, there are several types of spiritual direction situations which differ in important respects and which can too easily be confused. We will distinguish here only three types whose confusion can have seriously detrimental consequences.

A first type, and one which is not the primary concern of this article, could be called *educative spiritual direction*. This type of direction process is characteristic of initial spiritual formation situations in which a significant part of the guide's role is the imparting of theological, moral, and spiritual information. This type of direction situation is temporary, usually has a fairly explicit beginning and end, and often involves a very inexperienced directee with a very experienced guide. The educative direction situation tends naturally to involve a certain "authority" pattern simply because of its educative character and of the clear disparity between guide and directee.

Unfortunately, this educative type of direction (and often enough a very unsatisfactory form thereof) is the only kind of spiritual direction many priests and religious have ever experienced. They therefore tend to think of spiritual direction as a return to the seminary or novitiate. Understandably, they have no desire to relive that experience, even if it was a relatively constructive one, and no desire to involve other adult Christians in anything similar. This is a valid reaction. Educative spiritual direction is usually not what the adult Christian needs or wants. But this means that the guide must develop some other model of spiritual direction.

A second type of spiritual direction, and one which is also not the primary concern of this article, is that which we have all read about in the lives of the saints, namely, *spiritual paternity or maternity*. This is an extraordinarily close, usually life-long relationship which is very rare and which is usually initiated in and by unusual circumstances. It is characterized by an intense and filial (though not childish) affectivity and the unreserved totality of the mutual sharing between the two persons. Like true spiritual friendship (to which it is closely akin) it is an extraordinary gift of God and not the product of human initiative.

Unfortunately, in houses of formation and in spiritual writing this relationship was often implicitly or explicitly presented as the ideal toward which every spiritual direction situation should tend. This is quite simply an error. The relationship of spiritual filiation is rare and not to be sought. It is not necessary for the majority of people, and, in any case, is not subject to our wishing. It is both futile and dangerous to try to establish such a relationship or to try to introduce its characteristics into the ordinary direction situation. If such a relationship occurs the people involved will know it and they will have both the joy and the difficulty of learning to deal with it. But it is not the subject of the present discussion.

A third type of spiritual direction, and the kind with which we are concerned here, is *fraternal spiritual direction*. This situation involves an adult relationship between two mature Christians, one of whom has a certain competence in regard to the spiritual life which he/she is placing at the service of a brother or sister's growth in the life of faith. The relationship involves a difference in competence but no superiority or authority. The real basis of the relationship is the fraternal friendship between two adult children of the same Father. Consequently, on the directee's part the relationship entails openness and responsiveness but no abandonment of critical judgment nor alienation of personal responsibility. A *fortiori* it must involve no infantilism or psychological regression. The guide is not a parent or superior surrogate but simply a friend and companion who possesses a certain competence in an area important to the directee. The latter may be, and probably is, more competent than the guide in many other areas, for example, in the apostolate, in his/her profession, etc., and this can be profitably borne in mind by both persons.

II. The Person Seeking Spiritual Direction

In one sense, namely the purely theoretical one, everyone should seek spiritual direction at least at certain stages of the spiritual life for the same reason that everyone should make a retreat from time to time. But in the far more important sense, namely the practical one, the only person who should enter into spiritual direction is the person who can profit from it. That means, in the concrete, the person who feels the need of direction and who wants it enough to ask for assistance and accept the demands of the relationship.

A person is likely to feel the need of spiritual direction at "growing points" in the spiritual life. Such points, whatever may precipitate them (e.g., simple human maturation, crises, changes in prayer, changes in life situation, etc.), involve a certain felt need to integrate, or re-integrate, one's spiritual life at a new level. If the person feels the need of assistance or companionship in undertaking this re-integration he/she may well seek the help of a spiritual companion or guide. This request for assistance in progressing in the spiritual life normally initiates the direction relationship.

Both the prospective guide and the directee must, during the first few encounters, make some kind of provisional judgment about the feasibility of the relationship and the chances that it will be productive. The guide is looking, first of all, for a basic openness in the directee and a predominant concern with the real objective of spiritual direction. It is not only possible but likely that these two essential characteristics will be mixed, at the outset, with other less desirable components. Part of the skill of the experienced spiritual guide is the ability to distinguish between a directee with problems and a problem personality who is seeking, in the spiritual direction situation, what should be sought through psychological counseling or some other form of assistance.

Secondly, it goes without saying that a minimum of human compatibility between the two persons is essential for an effective relationship.

III. The Spiritual Director or Guide

Spiritual direction is a ministry and, like other ministries, it arises at the juncture between divine vocation and human response. The vocation to this particular ministry, as to others, is heard both in the needs of persons asking for this service and in the natural aptitude and spiritual inclination which leads a person toward this ministry. If individuals are asking this service of a particular person, that very asking is a fairly good indication to the person that he/she has the qualities that others desire in a spiritual guide. Consequently, even if the person has never considered this ministry it is perhaps time to do so. Often enough the call to the ministry of spiritual direction comes through institutional circumstances such as appointment to a position which leads almost inevitably to requests for assistance in the spiritual life.

The person who feels called to the pastoral ministry of spiritual direction by a persuasive combination of factors may very well feel completely inadequate to exercise such a role. Such a reaction is basically very healthy for no one is really adequate to participate in the dialogue between God and the individual person. But this well-founded reaction should not induce apostolic paralysis. A serious response to this vocation, as to others, involves preparation for what is admittedly a difficult and delicate (although deeply rewarding) ministry. Once the initial preparation is assured, ongoing formation and growing experience will gradually produce a certain ministerial proficiency.

The requirements for effective ministry in the area of spiritual direction are determined by the final end of the process itself, namely, the spiritual maturity of the directee. Spiritual maturity is a fully-integrated life with God characterized by freedom, fidelity, and fruitfulness. Helping another grow toward such maturity requires a certain amount of knowledge, experience, and psychological-spiritual skill.

1. Knowledge

Christian spirituality is the experience of God that consists in participating in the revelation dynamic centered in Jesus of Nazareth. Throughout the twenty centuries since that dynamic was initiated, participation in it has assumed an amazing variety of forms without losing its fundamental identity as the work of the Spirit realizing the filiation of Jesus in the hearts of his disciples. The good spiritual guide needs a basic knowledge of the history of spirituality in order to be able to recognize both the fundamental type of spirituality that a given directee represents and also its originality. He/she should also have some knowledge of systematic spiritual theology, that is, of the structure and function of the spiritual life. Thirdly, the prospective guide needs a sound preparation in modern biblical (especially New Testament) study in order to be able to guide the directee in the intensified participation in revelation that the direction situation involves. Finally, a basic knowledge of human psychology is necessary for understanding and dealing with the people one will be called to accompany.

Ministerial preparation programs are still notably deficient in the first two areas and the person who feels called to work in the field of spiritual direction will undoubtedly have to do some self-education, at least by reading, and preferably also by formal course work. Once the basic spade work in overall history and systematics is done the practicing director can flesh out this skeleton by reading the great spiritual classics through which he/she will come in contact with the most profound instances of Christian religious experience that have been recorded. The works of and about Francis of Assisi, Catherine of Siena, Catherine of Genoa, Julian of Norwich, the author of the *Cloud of Unknowing,* Ignatius of Loyola, John of the Cross, Teresa of Avila, Francis of Sales, Vincent de Paul, and Therese of Lisieux, among others, will supply an increasing knowledge of Christian spirituality and a certain vicarious experience of the inner dynamics of the spiritual life.

2. Experience

Spiritual direction is a pastoral and, therefore, essentially practical ministry. Consequently, experience is at least as important as theoretical knowledge. Experience in this field begins not by giving spiritual guidance but by receiving it (although a limited entrance into the ministry of spiritual direction sometimes can begin fairly soon after the person has entered into the experience him or herself). Seeking a spiritual guide and entering seriously into the process of spiritual direction may well be the most difficult part of the preparation for the ministry of spiritual direction, especially for those priests and religious whose only experience in this area has been an ineffectual or even traumatic component of seminary or novitiate formation. The prospective guide's willingness to enter into the experience is a good test of his/her seriousness of purpose. If there is anything worse than a dearth of good spiritual guides it is surely the existence of dabblers in this area. Someone who has not had a relatively extended, productive experience of personal spiritual direction is normally not qualified to exercise this ministry for others. One learns what spiritual direction is all about by engaging in it, first as directee and eventually as guide.

Once a person has begun to serve others in the direction situation a dialectic is set up between theoretical knowledge obtained by reading and study, the experience of one's own growth in and through spiritual direction, and the ministerial experience. The three elements become mutually enlightening and encouraging. As this dialectic develops the person becomes gradually "experienced" in the sense in which that term is used to speak of a person who is sure and sensitive, strong and gentle in dealing with others.

3. Psychological-Spiritual Skill

Fundamentally, the skill of the good spiritual guide consists in the ability to create and maintain a growth situation. The primary inner qualification of the guide is spiritual freedom which enables him/her to be completely non-possessive and non-manipulative in the direction situation while ensuring a certain forward movement to the process as a whole. To try to move another according to one's own program of "shoulds" is the occupational temptation of anyone working in the area of interpersonal guidance. Teachers and priests are perhaps more beset by this temptation than others because of the over-developed conviction of intellectual and moral "rightness" and of the duty to militantly communicate to others the true and the good which is often deeply engrained by religious, priestly, and professional formation. The inner freedom necessary to let another find and follow his or her own path under the guidance of the Spirit is the result of personal growth in spiritual freedom. A certain maturity in this area is absolutely essential for an effective ministry in spiritual direction.

Given this primary inner qualification, the person working in spiritual direction will face the challenge of developing a certain skill in the one-to-one spiritual dialogue. The task is to create a growth atmosphere, that is, an interpersonal climate in which the directee becomes progressively free of fear, spiritually perceptive, generous, and able to assume responsibility and to take initiative in the spiritual life. To a large extent this skill is a psychological one and counseling techniques will be very helpful.

But it is also a spiritual skill which can only be acquired by reflective analysis of one's own experience of the interior life. The effective spiritual guide must be a person of prayer, that is, a person whose own interior life is rich and developing. The "feel" for the spiritual movement in another's life cannot be taught. It has to be developed "from the inside out" so to speak.

From what has been said about the requirements in the spiritual guide, namely, knowledge, experience, and skill, it should be evident that the organizing principle is experience. Theoretical knowledge helps to illuminate one's own and others' experience. And skill is the ability to relate creatively one's own experience to someone else's. Consequently, the most important component of preparation for the ministry of spiritual direction is to enter deeply into the experience of the interior life. It is precisely in the context of prayer and experienced spiritual direction that one becomes able to judge when and to what extent one is ready to exercise an active ministry in the field of spiritual direction.

IV. The Process of Spiritual Direction

The introductory nature of this article prohibits a lengthy discussion of the process of spiritual direction, that is, of what should go on in the direction dialogue, and how to make sure that it does. However, the recent bibliography on this topic is lengthening rapidly and can easily be consulted by the interested reader. Consequently, we will limit ourselves to a brief indication of the content and object of the direction process.

Basically, the direction dialogue consists in an open sharing between guide and directee on the fundamental activity of the interior life, namely, prayer, both as it is directly experienced by the directee and as it affects his/her daily life. The guide's primary effort is devoted to assisting the directee to objectify, appropriate, and then evaluate the experience by distinguishing between what is positive and to be encouraged and what is negative and to be discouraged. The director's contribution to this evaluation process (often called spiritual discernment) and to the formative effort includes listening, questioning, waiting, challenging, encouraging, and, in some cases, a certain amount of clarifying. In short, it includes whatever can facilitate the directee's effort to objectify, evaluate, integrate, and orient his/her life in the light of faith toward a more intense experience of and response to God in Jesus.

It is also the guide's task to read the signs in the situation in order to judge whether the process as a whole is proceeding positively, that is, whether or not the person is growing. If prayer is becoming more contemplative, if formal prayer and the rest of life are being progressively integrated, if the person is becoming interiorly more free, and if the person's faith commitment is deepening and finding expression in a more balanced, intense, and effective apostolic involvement, then the direction situation is achieving its objective.

It goes without saying that there is usually no straight-line development in the spiritual life. There will be setbacks, declines, eruptions, regressions, and any or all of the crises that characterize growth. The director's challenge is to continually evaluate the overall process and to distinguish between the negativities that are inherent to growth and a fundamentally negative situation. Again, only the experience of growing enables a person to recognize growth in another and to foster it.

Nevertheless, even the experienced guide can expect to make a certain number of more or less serious mistakes in dealing with others' spiritual experience. These mistakes will be less serious in proportion to the real freedom and self-determination that the guide has enabled the directee to achieve. Reading and consultation with experienced colleagues are important aids to ministerial growth in this area as they are in any other.

There are few types of ministry which involve the person more deeply and personally than that of spiritual direction, but this involvement, with all the real suffering it inevitably entails, is fruitful not only for the individual directee and for the Church whose health and fecundity are proportionate to the real holiness of her members, but also for the minister who will experience in and through this demanding service a particularly effective challenge to personal spiritual growth.

Depth Psychotherapy and Spiritual Direction

The Reverend Eugene Geromel

Feeling that I needed to know more about myself if I were to do counseling, I found myself entering psychotherapy while in seminary. Midway through this very rewarding experience I happened upon St. Francis De Sales' *Introduction to the Devout Life.* The more I read, the more convinced I became that if I had a spiritual director such as this I would learn as much about myself as I did in therapy. More importantly I would be deepening my relationship with Jesus Christ.

Spiritual direction is often defined as, "The help one person gives another to enable him to become himself in faith."[1] Merton describes it as "a continuous process of formation and guidance, in which a Christian is led and encouraged in his special vocation, so that by faithful correspondence to the graces of the Holy Spirit he may attain to the particular end of his vocation and to union with God."[2] In much more flowery rhetoric St. Gregory of Nazianzen writes, "The diagnosis and cure of our habits, passions, lives, wills and whatever else is within us, by banishing from our compound nature everything brutal and fierce and introducing and establishing in their stead what is gentle and dear to God, and arbitrating fairly between soul and body."[3] Spiritual direction can be simply defined as a formal relationship in which an individual is guided closer to God. The emphasis here is on the individual. This does not mean that the only guiding done by the Church is on an individual basis. Fr. Isabell in his monograph[4] on

This article first appeared in *Review for Religious*, 36, September 1977, pp. 753-63. Reprinted by permission.

direction, points out that direction occurs on various levels. There is the *general level* in which the Church as a whole guides through her teaching, morality and rituals. There is the *institutional or group level* in which religious communities or groups, i.e., marriage-encounter or cursillo, direct the faithful to God. There are the *hidden directors,* or those individuals who have influenced our lives. While these three levels will not be examined in this paper it must be recognized that direction does occur on various levels.

Individual direction seems to have begun with the earthly ministry of Jesus Christ. In the eleventh chapter of the Gospel of St. Luke our Lord deals with the question of prayer. Over and over again he deals with problems of individuals and their relationship to God. Later in the Church we find examples of men such as St. Anthony of the Desert who aided others in their quest for a deeper relationship with Christ. The early Bishops of the Church, Gregory I, Gregory of Nazianzen and St. Chrysostom, deal in their writing with the problems involved in direction. Spiritual direction as a formal process seems to have been expanded and nurtured within the monastic environment.

Having defined spiritual direction and given a very brief history I would like to explore and compare this relationship with that of counseling or psychotherapy. Since all light comes from the Giver of Light it behooves us to use whatever knowledge is available to help individuals deepen their relationship with Christ. Therefore we might ask ourselves, "What are the things we learn in psychotherapy which apply to spiritual direction?" One way in which this can be done is by describing those factors which aid healing in the counseling process and relate them to spiritual direction. The curative factors described here, with a few revisions, are those of Dr. Irvin Yalom. These are described in great length in his book, *The Theory and Practice of Group Psychotherapy.* [5] It should be noted that the experimental work done to develop and analyze these factors occurred in groups; they are the curative factors of group therapy. However on a concept level, I believe, the ones described here are also valid on an individual basis. Some of his factors will not be used in this paper. For instance, group cohesiveness is a very important factor in group therapy. It would obviously not occur on a one-to-one basis. However, it should be noted that in terms of the *general direction* of the Church, it has dramatic impact.

The eight factors which shall be discussed here are: the instillation of hope; universality; imparting of information; altruism; imitative behavior; interpersonal learning; catharsis; and existential factors. The three factors which shall be omitted are: group cohesiveness; development of socializing techniques; and the corrective recapitulation of the primary family group. It should be remembered that the purpose of relating these factors is for exploration, not to prove that direction is analogous to group therapy. The curative factors will be defined and then related to direction.

The Instillation of Hope

If therapy is to be effective, Yalom contends, the patient must believe that hope exists. Hope must be instilled and maintained if growth is to ensue. Unfortunately this very simple and "obvious" factor is often overlooked. Unless a patient believes he can "get well" why should he continue or even begin therapy?

In St. Athanasius' life of St. Anthony we see many examples of the instillation of hope. When speaking with those who wished to know Christ as he did, his encouragement was great. "To begin with, let us all have the same zeal, not to give up what we have begun, not to lose heart." Later we are told, "As Anthony discussed these matters with them, all rejoiced. In some the love of virtue increased, in some negligence was discarded and in others conceit was checked."[6]

One of the questions that must be asked is "Do we instill and maintain hope, so the goals of direction can be reached?" It is important that in the process of spiritual direction a sense of hope be present.

Universality

Many individuals who enter therapy have a sense that their problems are unique to them. They "alone" have these fears and anxieties. "The disconfirmation of their feelings of uniqueness is a powerful source of relief."[7]

How often do we encounter individuals who are so paralyzed by the feeling that they alone have this malady, that they are unable to work through the problem. Their despair over this "uniqueness" only adds to their alienation. In fact it can take on greater significance than the actual problem. Recently in an adult education class the subject of forgiving others arose. Nearly a third of the class was relieved to find that they were not the only ones who had difficulty in this area. Once they removed this burden they were able to deal with the actual problem of forgiveness.

This "negative" sense of uniqueness can often be a barrier to growth. It is often dealt with very simply. But not until one recognizes how very important and destructive a feeling it can actually be.

Imparting of Information

Explanation and clarification are often effective curative agents in therapy. "Under this general rubric I include the didactic instruction about mental health, mental illness and general psychodynamics given by the therapists, as well as advice, suggestions or direct guidance about life problems offered either by therapist or other patients."[8]

For many centuries spiritual direction had a very strong emphasis on instruction. It often appears to have taken autocratic forms. Merton states that in "the earliest days of Christian monasticism the spiritual fathers did much more than instruct and advise. The neophyte lived in the same cell with him, day and night, and did what he saw his father doing. He made known to the father 'all the thoughts that came into his heart' and was told on the spot, how to react."[9]

One has the impression that because of the abuses of the past, instructional aspects of spiritual direction are downplayed. Greater emphasis seems to be on "freedom" and the "relationship." Perhaps we need to re-examine the value of instruction in spiritual direction.

Altruism

"In therapy groups, too, patients receive through giving, not only as part of the reciprocal giving-receiving sequence but also from the intrinsic act of giving."[10] Individuals must transcend themselves and become absorbed in someone or thing outside themselves to grow.

Since the time of our Lord the goal of the Christian is to go beyond himself. "He who seeks to save his life will lose it, and he who loses it will be saved." "I live not for myself but for

Jesus Christ.'' Thomas Merton suggests that a "contemplative is not one who takes his prayer seriously, but one who takes God seriously, who is famished by truth, who seeks to live in generous simplicity, in the spirit.''[11] Our liturgy, our ethic, our total life in Christ seeks to lead us beyond ourselves. It might be of immense value to remember that altruism is not just a philosophical concept but that which brings man to wholeness.

Imitative Behavior

Social psychologists such as Bandura have suggested that modeling behavior after another person can be therapeutic. Yalom believes that imitative behavior, learning by imitating others, is one of the curative factors.

Undoubtedly, imitative behavior seems like an anathema to the modern mind, especially those involved in direction. We no longer wish to reproduce that system whereby, as quoted earlier, individuals are told what to think and do. Modern direction demands freedom. It stresses the uniqueness of the individual. Our clinically trained minds associate imitation with transference (which will be dealt with later) and respond with disgust. Yet perhaps we have overreacted.

If it is natural for a pipe-smoking therapist to have patients who try pipes, perhaps we should expect that the director will be imitated. His style of prayer or relating to others might be tried. Imitative behavior might allow the directee to try various styles of prayer or behavior. This would only be dangerous if they were locked into it or if we strongly encouraged it.

Interpersonal Learning

"Interpersonal learning, as I define it, is a broad and complex curative factor representing the group analogue of such individual curative factors as insight, working through transference, the corrective emotional experience.''[12] This is that aspect of therapy which is written about so often and thoroughly. It is exposing the patient, under better circumstances, to experiences which were difficult in the past. It is the interpretation of actions and dreams. It is the working through of transference. It is the gaining of insight.

Obviously this also occurs in direction. Insight into our nature, needs, and feelings as well as those areas of blockage, must be gained in order to grow in our relationship to Christ.

"But the whole of our treatment and exertion is concerned with the hidden man of the heart and our welfare is directed against that adversary and foe within us, who uses ourselves as weapons against ourselves."[13] An understanding of our relationships with others, past and present, reflects our ability to relate to Christ.

Fr. McCall[14] has suggested that there are various types of remarks in the spiritual dialogue. There are *continuation remarks* which encourage expression. There are *strengthening remarks* which support the directees in their progress. There are *explanatory remarks* which impart information. Lastly, there are *interpretative remarks* which seek to improve insight.

Throughout the ages much has been written on the process of spiritual direction. While they may not be couched in terms such as the "corrective emotional experience," these issues have been dealt with.

Catharsis

This is the open expression of affect or emotions. The spilling out, if you will, of feelings. Since 1895 when Freud and Breuer published their work on hysteria, the "talking cure" has been in evidence. Few theorists, however, believe that catharsis is enough. It does not automatically bring about change. Yet there must be a freedom of speech; a freedom to express one's needs and feelings, before growth is experienced.

"But those who are over others should show themselves to be such that their subjects may not blush to disclose even their secrets to them."[15]

While many of the spiritual directors have emphasized directing, there seems to have been, and still is, an emphasis on the directee's freedom to express himself. However, this has been seen more as a way for the director to come to know the other. Perhaps we could recognize that besides improving the relationship, catharsis allows the directee to bring feelings, fears, and needs out into the open.

Existential Factors

Much to his amazement one of the foremost curative factors discovered by Yalom was this one. His first instrument for exploring what brought about a cure excluded existential factors. Yet, man's ability to find meaning in life came to be considered an important curative factor. "Several issues are represented in this cluster: responsibility, basic isolation, contingency, the recognition of our own mortality, and the ensuing consequences for the conduct of our life, the thrownness or capriciousness of existence."[16]

One of the interesting phenomena of our time is that the secular world has begun to deal with the questions of existence, life and death, meaning and commitment, because the church has down-played these issues. While this may be a simplistic view, listening to sermons on Sunday morning would show that it contains truth.

Viktor Frankl has emphasized the healing power of meaning. In his book *Christotherapy,* Bernard Tyrrell affirms this need and reminds us that the gospel strongly proclaims it. "Christotherapy is fraternally related to Frankl's logotherapy in its basic emphasis on the healing power of meaning. But it differs in insisting that meaning itself has been made flesh in Christ and that the light of Christ is able to heal all those who are open to its beneficent presence."[17]

The Relationship

Nothing is more written of in the field of psychotherapy than the relationship between patient and therapist. Studies indicate that there are common characteristics in the "successful" relationships regardless of the therapist's orientation. For Yalom, group cohesiveness is the key to success in group work. In individual therapy the key remains the relationship between patient and therapist. The relationship is to be one with an atmosphere of acceptance in which there are high levels of empathy, warmth which is non-possessive and with a sense of genuineness. In this atmosphere of acceptance openness is encouraged and maintained. It is one in which self-knowledge and self-realization materialize.[18] It is an atmosphere in which the patient is treated with "unconditional positive regard," to use a Rogerian term. He is treated as a unique human being, not categorized and classified. Lastly, it is a professional relationship. Confidences are kept and trust is high. A relationship nurtured in this environment is a very important curative factor.

Just as much has been written on the relationship in therapy, so also has much been written on the relationship in spiritual direction. Modern writers emphasize strongly the freedom and acceptance of the directee. "We see, then, that the dialogue of direction, whether it is envisaged in its early stages or at a later point in the spiritual life, cannot develop unless it respects the freedom of the other. Direction is not an arbitrary matter; it must pay attention to the personal development and possibilities of an individual."[19] "The director is not to teach his own way, nor indeed any determinate way of prayer, but to instruct his disciples how they may themselves find out the proper way. . . . In a word, he is only God's usher and must lead souls in God's way, and not his own." "What we need to do is to bring the director into contact with our own real self, as best we can, and not fear to let him see what is false in our false self. Now this right away implies a relaxed, humble attitude in which we *let go* of ourselves and renounce our unconscious efforts to maintain a facade."[20] These writers contend that the relationship must contain openness, trust, and acceptance.

The stress is also upon unconditional positive regard and the uniqueness of the individual. "A true director can never get over the awe he feels in the presence of a person."[21]

The early church fathers laid heavy emphasis upon the fact that all individuals were different and must be treated as such. The great works on the priesthood and the episcopate by Gregory the Great, St. Chrysostom, and St. Gregory of Nazianzen stress that all persons are aided and treated in varying ways. "So also are souls treated with various instructions and guidance. To this treatment witness is borne by those who have experience of it."[22] All three of these church fathers have long lists of the different types of people that might be encountered, lists which go on for pages, pointing out the uniqueness of every individual.

Spiritual direction is also a professional relationship. The word "professional" raises many eyebrows and frowns. It is looked upon with disfavor. Perhaps we are overreacting against a pompous image, rather than recognizing that it is a role in which demands are placed upon the director. It is a relationship in which whatever is said must be kept in confidence. It is also professional in that it is not a "peer" relationship.[23] No matter how much transparency (to be described shortly) the relationship has, the director is in a professional role. He is there to share the gifts God has given him with another. This is done with a sense of responsibility, it is a relationship in which it is the director's responsibility to evaluate the progress being made.

Transference and Countertransference

Transference is a term which has been developed in psychoanalytic thought and practice. In its strictest sense it refers to the tendency of the patient to displace onto the therapist feelings, ideas, and so forth which originate with previous figures, often parental, in the patient's life. In the less strict sense, it is the tendency to displace onto another feelings, ideas, and so forth of other relationships. Harry Stack Sullivan refers to this as parataxic distortion. In essence, when a person is transferring to us, he is placing another's face upon us. To my knowledge, this phenomenon is not discussed by early Christian writers. (Which means, undoubtedly, that after the final draft of this paper is typed, someone will offer such a reference.)

In therapy, transference is dealt with in various ways, depending upon the school of thought to which the therapist subscribes. Some, such as the Freudian psychoanalytic, encourage transference, believing that the working-through is an important curative factor. Others, such as the Rogerian, have developed ways to seek to eliminate it. Some believe that Rogerian therapy was developed to avoid transference. Others such as Gestalt therapy, also seek to eliminate it, by living in the here and now.

It appears that the more aloof and neutral a figure the therapist is, the greater the tendency to transfer. The more transparent a therapist is, the less transference will occur. Transparency refers to the tendency of a therapist to show his true self and feelings. In short, the more a therapist is himself, the more difficult it is to put a face on him. It should be recognized, however, that even when transparency is present, transference still occurs, but to a lesser degree.

In spiritual direction it seems unlikely that transference would be sought or encouraged. It would be more of a barrier. It would therefore be of value if the director were able to make himself more transparent. However, there is a caution. Sandor Ferenczi, an early student of Freud's who experimented with this issue, suggests that disclosure (transparency) not take place too soon in the process.[24] It might well be that disclosure of weakness and limitations too early negates the instillation of hope and undermines trust.

Countertransference occurs when the therapist relates to the patient as though he were some other individual, or when the therapist's needs or emotions become involved in the relationship. This can obviously be destructive. Therapists have sought to control countertransference in three ways. The first is through self-exploration and self-knowledge. Freudian analysts are required to undergo a didactic analysis of their own. Other schools stress that the therapist should know himself. They suggest, rather than require, personal therapy. The second way is through the use of supervision and consultants, in which the therapists can share the work they are doing and explore personal needs and motives. The third is by trying to have enough patients that one's life does not become overly involved in one patient. Frieda Fromm-Reichmann suggests that a new therapist always have more than one patient.

There is little doubt that countertransference occurs in direction. Andre Godin's book *The Priest as Counselor*[25] provides a list of warning signs which might indicate when countertransference is occurring. Certainly such examination should take place in all our pastoral work, especially counseling and direction. We might also learn from those involved in psychotherapy. It might be of value to find some method of self-exploration. It certainly would be of value to find a mentor; someone with whom we could reflect upon the work we are doing. And it certainly would be important to have more than one individual for whom we are director.

Counseling vs. Direction

It is important to have a clear distinction of the difference between counseling, or psychotherapy, and spiritual direction.

"The approach of spiritual direction accents, more than counseling or psychotherapy, advice and exercises to help a person experience God and people in depth."[26] This definition is based on what happens, the methodology or technique used, to explain the difference. Its only limitation is that the methodology of some schools of therapy is based on advice, instruction and exercises.

"A person needs counseling when he or she is absorbed in some partial aspect of life. I say 'absorbed' to indicate that the individual is preoccupied with this to such an extent that other values or aspects of life are neglected.[27] This is a very practical guide to determine whether an individual needs therapy rather than direction. It is a good rule of thumb, but we're still left with an incomplete definition.

"The focus in counseling is more on problem solving, of effecting better personal integration and adjustment in the process of human maturation. The focus in spiritual direction, on the other hand, is more on growth in prayer and charity."[28] This brings us closer to the difference.

It is doubtful that any behavioral therapist, who used instruction, advice and exercise, would see as the end goal "to help a person experience God and people in depth." However, it is possible. A definition based on intent or focus will transcend methodology. Both therapy and direction, if they are good, deal with the whole person; both may use varied techniques and methodologies, but the *stated* intent of spiritual direction is growth in "prayer and charity" to the fulfillment of one's discipleship.

Qualities of a Director

The qualifications of a therapist vary from school to school. All seem, however, to have two general requirements. The individual must have an awareness of self as defined by that school. He must also have an understanding of man as perceived by that school of thought. For example, a Freudian analyst would undergo psychoanalysis and have an understanding of the theories of psychodynamics, pathology, and methodology.

Writers on the subject of direction seem to emphasize that the director be a man of prayer and a theologian. He must be a whole person; his theology and life of prayer are integrated so that he lives his faith.

"His first duty, if he wants to be an effective director, is to see to his own interior life and take time for prayer and meditation, since he will never be able to give to others what he does not possess himself."[29]

St. Teresa stresses over and over again that a director must be a theologian. She seems to have been upset often because she could not find directors who had a good theological background.

Morton Kelsey emphasizes that a pastor must possess four things in order to teach the faith. These are: 1) knowledge of the limitations and possibilities of the church; 2) must know

67

and understand the world view of the people with whom he deals; 3) must have experience — a prayer life and knowledge of mystical tradition; 4) a knowledge of depth psychology.[30] (These I believe also apply to direction.) In essence, a director must know where his people are, must know both God and his church, and have insight into the workings of the individual.

The emphasis on knowing the individual is a valuable one. It also has implications for our theological ability. Often when referring to a person as a theologian, we conjure up images of an academician, primarily because the theology we are taught tends to be philosophical theology. Martin Thornton suggests that there are five types or functions of theology:

> First, theology has a prior revelational function; the disclosure and proclamation of revealed knowledge.
>
> Second is practical or straight theology, the implications of which are obvious and which necessitate a spontaneous reaction.
>
> Third is pastoral theology, or that which is employed by Christian pastors in ministering to their flocks. Pastoral theology, as a subject of study, means the drawing out of the practical implications of theological statement and formulae.
>
> Fourth is applied theology, sometimes called ascetic theology, which guides, or is used to guide, individual Christians in their uniquely personal interpretation of discipleship, according to temperament and circumstances.
>
> Fifth is what I should call the negative or testing function of theology which guards people and communities from error in prayer, and therefore in practical life.[31]

We are told if we are to be with our people then we must have an understanding of where they are. This implies that we are able to speak to where they are. It indicates that the type of theological expertise necessary is not (1) or (2), above, but rather pastoral and applied (3 and 4). The director must have the ability to instruct in the faith so that it can be both understood and applied to life.

We also, I believe, need to learn from the dynamic therapies. We need some form of continual direction for ourselves or at least a mentor with whom we can share our work.

As I began the work for this paper, I felt that the insights of psychotherapy would provide "new" material for spiritual direction. This is obviously not the case. Much of our "new" insights have been known for centuries. They may have been

68

couched in different terms, disguised in flowery rhetoric, but nevertheless present in the works of the Fathers. It is, I believe, one of the "heresies" of our time to believe that we are the discoverers of new information and that what went before does not relate to the present.

This does not exempt us, however, from being aware of the insights of depth psychology. They provide us with methodology which can bring what we do into focus. We are provided with information on the workings of a dynamic relationship. We are given an understanding of conscious and unconscious motivation. They show us ways of monitoring our own work. In investigating Yalom's work, we are allowed to examine what we do in light of research. This work shows us the value of the various aspects of direction which promote growth. It is growth which is sought; growth which leads to wholesomeness in and through Christ.

¹J. LaPlace, *Preparing for Spiritual Direction* (Chicago: Franciscan Herald Press, 1975).   ²T. Merton, *Spiritual Direction and Meditation* (Collegeville, MN: The Liturgical Press, 1960).   ³St. Gregory Nazianzen, *Nicene and Post-Nicene Fathers,* v. 7 (New York: The Christian Literature Co., 1894).   ⁴D. Isabell, *The Spiritual Director* (Chicago: Franciscan Herald Press, 1976).   ⁵New York: Basic Books, 1975.   ⁶St. Athanasius, *The Life of St. Anthony* (Westminster, MD: The Newman Press, 1950), pp. 34, 57.   ⁷Yalom, *op. cit.,* p. 7.   ⁸*Ibid.,* p. 9.   ⁹Merton, *op. cit.,* p. 9.   ¹⁰Yalom, *op. cit.,* p. 13.   ¹¹Merton, *op. cit.,* p. 33.   ¹²Yalom, *op. cit.,* p. 19.   ¹³St. Gregory Nazianzen, *op. cit.,* p. 209.   ¹⁴In Isabell, *op. cit.*   ¹⁵St. Gregory the Great, *Nicene and Post-Nicene Fathers,* v. 10 (Grand Rapids, MI: Wm. B. Eerdmans, 1968).   ¹⁶Yalom, *op. cit.,* p. 85.   ¹⁷B. Tyrrell, *Christotherapy* (New York: Seabury, 1975), p. 28.   ¹⁸K. Horney, *Neurosis and Human Growth* (New York: W.W. Norton, 1950).   ¹⁹Laplace, *op. cit.,* p. 28.   ²⁰Merton, *op. cit.,* pp. 12, 24.   ²¹*Ibid.,* pp. 25-26.   ²²St. Gregory Nazianzen, *op. cit.,* p. 211.   ²³S. McCarty, "On Entering Spiritual Direction," *Review for Religious* 35, 6, pp. 854-867.   ²⁴Yalom, *op. cit.*   ²⁵Techny, IL: Divine Word Publications, 1968.   ²⁶W. Kraft, "Psychology and the Religious Life," *Review for Religious,* 35, 6, pp. 889-896.   ²⁷Isabell, *op. cit.,* p. 32.   ²⁸McCarty, *op. cit.,* p. 858.   ²⁹Merton, *op. cit.,* pp. 19-20.   ³⁰M. Kelsey, "Interview: Morton Kelsey," *Your Church,* 23, 2, pp. 11-14; 67-71.   ³¹M. Thornton, *The Function of Theology* (London: Hodder and Stoughton, 1968), p. 26.

PART TWO

Preparing
for Spiritual Direction

The principal Guide of every Christian is the Holy Spirit; a spiritual director is but a human instrument of this indwelling Paraclete. This is a fundamental principle in the ministry of spiritual direction; but one entering spiritual direction or preparing for this ministry may still ask: What makes a spiritual director an effective instrument of the Spirit? Spiritual writers over the centuries have noted many qualities that make a good director; of these, I like to emphasize experience, learning, and skill in helping relationships.

Experience means that a director knows God's ways of leading persons to Himself through observing closely this divine action in his or her own life and in the lives of others. Learning means that a director has a solid grasp of the knowledge which can be gained through a serious study of Sacred Scripture, theology, spirituality, hagiography, modern human sciences, literature — any field, in fact, which illuminates God's workings in the human heart. Skill in helping relationships means that the director understands the dynamics of interpersonal relationships and uses these to help persons respond more readily to God's guidance.

A spiritual director is thus likely to be an effective instrument of the Spirit in the lives of others to the degree that he or she possesses experience, learning, and helping skills. The chapters in this section address each of these areas: William Barry describes the experience of prayer; Matthias Neuman indicates several essential areas of learning; and James Gau demonstrates the importance of interpersonal relationships in spiritual direction.

In presenting these articles, I assume that spiritual direction is not limited to a charismatic activity practiced by a gifted few; I see it, rather, as a ministry of the Church for which persons open to God's action in their own lives and willing to undertake the discipline of study and training can prepare. Since there is no limit to our experience of God, to learning His ways, to improving interpersonal skills, I am also convinced that spiritual directors who are continually growing in each of these areas make the most effective instruments of the Holy Spirit.

Prayer in Pastoral Care: A Contribution from the Tradition of Spiritual Direction

William Barry, S.J.

Recent issues of *The Journal of Pastoral Care* have brought the issue of prayer and other religious resources to the forefront of our consciousness. Paul Pruyser in 1972 exhorted us to make more use of the traditional religious resources in our pastoral care and counseling.[1] In 1974, Gerald May wrote a thought-provoking article exploring the reasons why "my pastoral colleagues and I have not been able truly to integrate spirituality or spiritual experience into our counseling with clients."[2] Don Browning in 1975 pointed to the neglect of method in religious living and to the need for such a method and he singled out the method of practical moral reasoning associated with Pharisaism.[3] Finally, John Morgan made us aware of the possibilities for pastoral care contained in the Quaker tradition of silence.[4] In this essay I want to contribute to the dialogue the method of contemplative prayer associated with at least one strand of the tradition of spiritual direction, that strand which sees spiritual direction as a form of pastoral care whose purpose is to help another to relate consciously to the living God and to let God relate to him, to grow in that relationship, and to live its truth.[5]

At the Center for Religious Development in Cambridge we decided to take an empirical approach to the development of a spirituality for our time. We had a tradition behind us, a tradition that at its best helped people to be free before the living God. But we wondered how people in this time and place were

This article first appeared in *The Journal of Pastoral Care*, 31, June 1977, pp. 91-6. Copyright 1977 by the Association for Clinical Pastoral Education. Reprinted by permission.

experiencing the Lord in prayer. We took it as our primary task not to tell people what they ought to experience, nor to put them through a program of prayer experiences whose end we foresaw, but to help them to pay attention to what happened to them when they prayed. Then we invited them to discuss with a director what they experienced in order to "discern the spirits," i.e., to make religious sense out of what they experienced. Our task, then, was to help people to be real before a free God and to take seriously what happened to them when they did this. In our model of spiritual direction experiences in prayer are the main matter to be looked at when a person comes to a spiritual director for a session. What we discovered from this empirical approach should be of interest to pastoral counselors even if they do not use prayer as the principal tool in their work. At the end I will indicate some possibilities for the use of contemplative prayer in pastoral counseling.

One of our earliest discoveries was that some ways of praying were helpful, some not. Prayer that proceeded solely from a sense of obligation or duty rarely led to wholeness and life. Resolutions to pray more regularly whose basic source was the feeling that God demanded it most often were smothered in the tedium and boredom that ensued. Obligation and duty without hope of enjoyment are not the best bedrock upon which to build a love relationship. We also found that many people saw prayer as a time for petitions, for thinking, for making resolutions, and again that an exclusive use of these ways of prayer did not lead to the enthusiasm associated with any close relationship of love. Biblical prayer is first and foremost a response to a God who has acted and is acting, and we noticed that people began to enjoy prayer when they spent time looking at and listening to what God had done. Thus, we rediscovered for ourselves the fruitfulness of contemplative prayer, a prayer in which one looks at and/or listens to the works and words of the Lord and lets one's response be elicited by what is seen or heard. We began to stress contemplation in its etymological sense as a royal road to the enjoyment of prayer.

The contemplative attitude[6] is an attitude of wonder and openness before the other, whatever or whoever the other is. It shows itself when we listen to music, look at a painting, watch the sun set or rise, and let what we see or hear evoke in us a response. It is evident when we listen to a friend's grief and are moved to sorrow by what we hear. Children seem to be natural contemplatives as they look around themselves in wonder. Lovers are contemplatives insofar as they find their love elicited by the beauty and goodness of the beloved.

What hinders contemplation is self-preoccupation. It is difficult to be captivated by the beauty of the sunset if one has an empty stomach and feels hopeless about where the next meal will come from. Children are not wonderers when they have a bad toothache. People find it difficult to listen to the joy of a friend if they are overwhelmed by their own sorrows. Thus, we found that the kind of prayer that many people were engaging in made contemplation difficult, made it hard, in other words, to see and hear the wonders of the Lord and His good news. The reason was that the prayer was often concentrated on the self and one's own problems. For instance, a person may be praying for forgiveness for some fault or sin in such a self-preoccupied way that he or she cannot experience the forgiving look or word of the Lord. Recently, a woman said that she could not read the Bible because it made her feel bad. It turned out that she was so troubled by guilt feelings that when she read passages such as those in Hosea she saw only her own ''badness'' being depicted and failed to hear the words of love addressed by Yahweh to sinful Israel. In other words, self-preoccupation hindered her from hearing the word of the Lord.

We have found that it often takes time and patience and even creativity to help people to assume a contemplative attitude in prayer. They have been so schooled to see prayer as duty, as thinking, as petitioning that they find it difficult to believe that prayer can be as natural as looking at stars or the smile on another's face and responding to what one sees. Yet, the Psalms are full of prayers of praise, responses elicited by seeing the stars, the sea, a rainbow, or by feeling the cool of water on parched and dry throats, or by hearing the thunder and the wind. When people begin to listen and to look, they begin to notice that they feel grateful or happy or filled with awe, or anger, or whatever. Then we are able to point out that these responses are responses to the world God has made, and we can show them how the psalmists tried to put such responses into words. In other words, their responses are prayers if they are somehow aware that they are in the presence of God as they look and listen.

Besides looking at and listening to nature and natural beauty, we can also listen to Scripture itself as a privileged place to "find" God. But again we need to listen to Scripture and not to our own preoccupations. As people begin to do this, they begin to hear the passionate love of Yahweh for His people more than to catalogue their own sins and compare them favorably or unfavorably to biblical characters. For example, a woman who identifies with the woman with a flow of blood in Mark 5 will have difficulty listening to the whole passage if she is overcome with feelings of helplessness and hopelessness at the length of her own sufferings; she will be listening more fully if she, too, senses the power of the Lord to heal that led the woman to say, "If I touch even his garments, I shall be made well." Many people with whom we have worked at the Center for Religious Development have felt such faith and hope and have found themselves made spiritually and psychically whole when they reached out to the Lord.

Another thing that we discovered was that people's desires became clearer to them as they prayed in this manner. We try to help people to be aware of what they want of the Lord in prayer and to ask for it as they begin a period of prayer. Thus, a man may just want some peace of mind for a half hour and ask the Lord to help him to attain it. Then he might walk along the beach looking at the waves rolling in. Later as he reflects, he may realize that while he was intent on the waves, and the sun reflecting off them, he felt deeply peaceful and in the presence of someone who cares; but whenever he began to try to figure out his problem, he became agitated. So the next time he prays, he may desire to experience that presence of God again and may ask to know God more intimately, to be more aware of His presence, to be less self-preoccupied. If this desire is answered, he may begin to realize that such a God is not only attractive, but also fearsome — and he may thus become aware of the ambivalence of his desires for intimacy with God. Then he may have only the desire to get help with his ambivalence — to be so assured of the goodness and kindness of God that he will be able to tolerate the closeness to Him that lays bare his dark areas. In other words, real people before the real God find themselves full of conflicting desires and feelings and need help to sort out what they really want. The process of prayer itself — like the process involved in any close relationship — reveals the ambivalence of desires and hopes, and careful spiritual direction can help a person to resolve the ambivalence by staying with the relationship to the Lord.

It should be obvious that this kind of spiritual direction makes a radical assumption in faith; namely, that the Lord is actually and actively engaged now with His people as individuals, that He desires their intimacy, and that His people can experience that intimacy. Moreover, it assumes that such a desire for intimacy is for the benefit of His people and hence that this kind of prayer leads to the fruits of the Spirit, "love, joy, peace, patience, kindness, goodness, faithfulness, gentleness, self-control" (Gal. 5:22-23).

The next question is whether these fruits of the Spirit are experienced as a result of contemplative prayer. In order to answer adequately I will have to go into some detail about the process that seems to occur in most cases. These fruits are not experienced if a person cannot get beyond self-preoccupation in order to look at the Lord and His works. With some people it may take time and patience and quality pastoral care and/or pastoral counseling or psychotherapy to help them to this point. No one has ever achieved the fruits mentioned by self-absorption or by trying harder.

When people begin to look and listen, their initial responses are usually very positive; they feel more alive, more hopeful, more grateful, and their prayers are prayers of praise and thanksgiving. In other words, they experience God as creator and provider, as caretaker, as father and mother. There also are usually feelings of fear or anxiety, feelings that seem to be a response to the awesome in the God-experience. The experience seems to be what T.S. Eliot tried to describe in *The Cocktail Party:*

> *But let me tell you, that to approach the stranger*
> *Is to invite the unexpected, release a new force,*
> *Or let the genie out of the bottle.*
> *It is to start a train of events*
> *Beyond your control. . . .*

But these feelings of fear do not usually keep the person from continuing to enjoy prayer. It is more and more my belief that such positive experiences of being in the presence of a good and kind God are necessary before people will allow themselves to open up their dark sides to the Lord. I believe that preachers make a serious mistake when they inveigh against sin before people have a deep and prolonged experience of being loved by God.

When people have such experiences and are enjoying prayers, the next step most often is the experience of some form of resistance to growing in the relationship. Some people begin to feel unworthy and revert to preoccupation with their "sins" and with resolutions to be better. Some begin to doubt the validity of the earlier positive experiences. One woman said that the experience was too highfalutin for the likes of her. Prayer, it seems, becomes heavy and burdensome again. When we examine what is going on, we find self-preoccupation, busyness, and brooding have once again become the order of the day in prayer. Usually these are symptoms of a turn away from letting the Lord see them as they really are. At some level they have sensed that the Lord's look is penetrating areas of themselves and their lives they had rather not investigate. They are, in other words, resisting conversion to a full realness before God. Now they need help to be able to look Him in the face, to ask for healing, forgiveness, atonement. The Lord is revealing sinfulness now — and they are resisting while yet wanting to be able to stand the revelation.

In our practice we try to help persons experiencing such a crisis to turn to the Lord for help. We suggest the imaginative use of the healing passages in the Gospels. For instance, in the passage about Bartimaeus (Mark 10:46-52) a man might be able to identify with the blind man and shout out to Jesus and then feel the negativity of the crowd rebuking him; the man might sense the temptation he has to give up, to forget the quest for sight, to keep his life style unchanged. I have heard people say that they could not continue to cry out, that they felt Jesus might do it for someone else but not for them. Then they knew that they needed to pray for faith, perhaps as the father did in Mark 9: "I believe; help my unbelief."

But if they stay with the process and continue to be as real and honest as they can be, eventually they feel the power of the Lord as a stronger attraction than their own resistance, and they can, like Bartimaeus, shout all the more, "Son of David, have mercy on me." Then they, too, may hear the words: "What do you want me to do for you?" If they can then say that they want to see, they can experience the freeing power of God and look on Jesus and see Him looking with love and forgiveness. Jesus is real to them and they are real to Jesus —

and they come to know deeply that they are loved sinners. Both words are needed to describe this experience. People do experience themselves as alienated, as wounded, as unintegrated, and as in some way responsible for their own condition, i.e., as sinners. But they also experience themselves as accepted, as understood, as healed, as loved by this Stranger to whom they are attracted and whom they had feared. Tolkien has a scene that hits off something of this experience. Dwarves and elves traditionally mistrust one another. Gimli, the dwarf, has been treated with such mistrust in Lothlorien, the forest of the elves ruled by Celebron and Galadriel. At one point Galadriel "looked upon Gimli, who sat glowering and sad, and she smiled. And the dwarf . . . looked up and met her eyes; and it seemed to him that he looked suddenly into the heart of an enemy and saw there love and understanding. Wonder came into his face, and then he smiled in answer."[7]

In this process the spiritual director's task is to keep helping the person to look at the Lord and not to let himself get locked into self-absorption — even when the self-absorption seems virtuous. Many a confession of sinfulness is little more than self-absorption. The Lord alone can reveal sinfulness to us and when He does it, we experience the revelation as painful, yes, but also, and more deeply, as healing and enabling change. The self-absorbed never seem to change.

People who have experienced the gaze of Jesus in this healing, forgiving way feel freed, renewed, saved and very grateful. They also feel more tolerant of others' flaws and foibles and generally more optimistic about life. For many the next step becomes the desire to know Jesus better in order to live their lives more in accordance with His Spirit. Thus, the next step becomes what is traditionally called the following of Jesus. That process is less a healing process and much more a growing process, a process of putting on the mind of Christ Jesus. For present purposes we need not dwell on this process.

Are there any possibilities for using contemplative prayer as I have described it in pastoral counseling? I believe so. In a recent conversation Charles Kemp mentioned his use of "homework" in pastoral counseling. Pastoral counselors may well find that time spent in helping people to engage in contemplative prayer as homework is well worth it. For one thing, clients will be encouraged to use the religious resources of the tradition, resources which rely on their faith and the power and desire of the Lord to heal. Thus, clients will be encouraged to work on their own time as well as in the counseling sessions and in a way that is consonant with the counseling process itself. It may even be that clients will want to talk about experiences in such prayer and that the experiences will themselves be grist for the counseling mill. For pastoral counselors, then, contemplative prayer, like Quaker silence or Kemp's free writing, may become another rich religious source for our work.

[1] Paul W. Pruyser, "The Use and Neglect of Pastoral Resources," *Journal of Pastoral Care,* 1972, 23, pp. 5-17.   [2] Gerald G. May, "The Psychodynamics of Spirituality," *Journal of Pastoral Care,* 1974, 28, p. 84.   [3] Don S. Browning, "Method in Religious Living and Clinical Education," *Journal of Pastoral Care,* 1975, 29, pp. 157-167.   [4] John H. Morgan, "Silence as Creative Therapy: A Contemplative Approach to Pastoral Care," *Journal of Pastoral Care,* 1975, 29, pp. 248-253.   [5] An excellent introduction to this kind of spiritual direction is: William J. Connolly, "Contemporary Spiritual Direction: Scope and Principles. An Introductory Essay," *Studies in the Spirituality of Jesuits,* 1975, p. 7, Monograph no. 3. St. Louis: The American Assistancy Seminar.   [6] Further descriptions of the contemplative attitude may be found in Connolly, W.J., *op. cit.* and in William A. Barry, "The Contemplative Attitude in Spiritual Direction," *Review for Religious,* 1976, 35, pp. 820-828.   [7] J.R.R. Tolkien, *The Fellowship of the Ring* (New York: Ballantine Books, 1965), p. 461.

Letter to a Beginning Spiritual Director

Matthias Neuman, O.S.B.

Dear Sister Susan:

Last week brought a real joy when I received your letter
and read the exciting account of your first months as a
spiritual director. Even though you have entered upon the task
by pressure of personal requests, I sense that the role fits you
very well. I can also appreciate your hesitations and fears upon
entering this new ministry; but be assured that no Christian
service is without its anxieties. In this particular ministry the
challenge seems staggering; it is an immense responsibility to
take on the guidance of human lives, especially the sifting,
discerning and supporting of the innermost secrets of hearts.
You would do well to reflect on St. Benedict's advice to the
abbot of a monastery: "He should recognize the difficulty of
his position — to care for and guide the spiritual development
of many difficult characters. One must be led by friendliness,
another by sharp rebuke, another by persuasion. The abbot
must always remember his task is the guidance of souls (for
which he will be held accountable)." There can be no doubt
that this practice of spiritual direction produces an awe, a
humility, and a proper fear in the heart of anyone who
assumes its yoke of service.

Those feelings of inadequacy you worry about arise quite
naturally, then. This initial period of eight months has accurately indicated that special abilities are required to do the
work well. This is so true and your intuitions are right on tar-

This article first appeared in *Review for Religious,* 37, November 1978, pp.
882-88. Reprinted by permission.

get. The talent of being a spiritual guide goes far beyond a simple facility at helping people to "clarify their prayer life" or "to discern with them God's will in the Scriptures." Spiritual direction has unfortunately assumed a somewhat faddish image in our day and too many people approach the title without a clear awareness of these demands. At the same time, I don't wish to make this ministry seem overly professional; the gift of assisting a life to God demands a personal living of faith that no learned technique will ever provide. But we do well to remember that while this work of service moves beyond professionalism it still includes professional capabilities in its wake. Let me briefly list some of these for you.

The constant study and assimilation of the modern psychological sciences remain paramount. The in-depth exploration of the human psyche stands as one of the great achievements of the twentieth century. In particular you should attend to the study of growth processes, normal maturational patterns, and the functioning of human needs and motivations. All these elements recur again and again in spiritual direction for individuals of all ages. As your first encounters have made clear, human motivation is incredibly complex. How often self-love mingles with love of God, and vice versa! How often people cannot separate the parts! One of your major tasks as a spiritual director and the place where you will begin many probings with individuals will be the purification of motives. Hours upon hours will be spent in this task, for people — even in their lives of faith — are desperately searching for *why* they do what they do. As you assist them to find answers, the path of freedom open to God's Mystery will slowly show through the mist. To accomplish that purifying effort in the critical moments of a direction session requires that the advance homework has been done; the books have been read and pondered; the possibilities of growth, need, and motivation internalized in your own understanding. That all means study on a serious level. I have found the works of Erik Erikson, Abraham Maslow and other developmental psychologists to be helpful. Even a semi-popular work like Gail Sheehy's *Passages* will provide many insights into the common human maturational steps. Applications to the spiritual context will emerge easily. Don't neglect this fundamental area in your ongoing preparation.

Besides the study of psychology you should know well our

contemporary American culture, that encompassing environment in which both small and momentous decisions are shaped. We live in an age when cultural pressures influence behavior as never before. I believe it was a Carnegie Foundation Report of last year which concluded that, by the senior year of high school, peer pressure has become the single dominant factor in the behavior of young adults. Similar thrusts toward social conformity extend up and down the age scale in the United States. These cultural factors deeply affect the awareness and living of Christian faith, even when people vocally denounce such influences. Know well the values spread through our mass media system; unless a man's or a woman's decision for faith includes a direct confronting of these pressures, the house is being built on sand. A primary task of the spiritual director looks to this examining of the decision for faith in a person's life. You must help them sort out the demands of a Christian life-style in a twentieth-century, pluralistic, consumer society; that's where faith is struggling to live in our United States. Your study of this culture should not be confined to religious analyses of pop culture, though that's a good place to begin. Modern fiction traces many typical personal struggles analogous to real ones. The novels and short stories of Joyce Carol Oates forcefully penetrate the mystery of human emotions in our modern society; *The Wheel of Love* has as much material for meditation as many religious books. A recent novel by Mary Gordon, *Final Payments,* surveys cultural confrontations that you should be familiar with. And of course there are television and films. Too frequently we ignore these by reason of "poor content" in favor of spiritual reading. But those visual media are far more of a factor in shaping people's contemporary perception of reality than all the armloads of books that can be shoved at them. Regularly schedule some movies and some television into your agenda. The time won't be wasted, but will contribute a necessary learning of the ethos which underlies the common struggle for faith today. A spiritual director must be sharply in touch with that cultural base.

Lastly, and the most important among the learned abilities of a director, you must develop in your own mind and heart a firm grasp of the theology of God *within* human life and experience. What I mean by this is that you must be able to see consistently how a fundamental human issue or action possesses definite links to one's openness or closedness to true faith. Achieving a good self-image, holding correct attitudes on sexuality, power, work, valuing the honesty of good personal relationships — all these will powerfully affect a person's view of faith and the ways in which he or she will accept the Christian mystery. It is frequently said in today's anthropological theology that every statement about God is a statement about human life. As a spiritual director you should accept that completely, and *also* affirm that every statement about human life is a statement about God. In this realm you assume a mediator's role in the truest sense, because you bridge the gap between people's seemingly enclosed, secular experiences and their emerging life of faith. While going through emotional traumas it is usually hard, and sometimes practically impossible, for people to relate to God in any other way than as "immediate helper." Sometimes God is forgotten or the object of intense anger. In a real sense the mediating link between that person's painful experience and a learning of faith will be maintained *in your heart;* your prayer and memory will keep the lines open, until the individual can begin to pick up the pieces again. That's an awesome responsibility for a spiritual director, but it's your ministry because you have been given the talents to do it. A continual study of God in human experience will aid your ability to hold and continue those lines of connection. There are many good works in theology that explore this mystery of God within human life; Rosemary Haughton's works, *The Theology of Experience* and *The Transformation of Man,* provide good starting points.

Let me now turn to some consideration of the specific and difficult case you had to confront last semester. The young woman approached you with a problem in her prayer life (a quite common beginning), but soon it became apparent that other troubling issues were stirring deep within her. In your judgment, her affectivity was blocked and unable to be released ("she couldn't emotionally relate to anyone"). Then suddenly it came gushing out towards you. That's a common occurrence in direction relationships; it was precisely your care and concern for her that unlocked the welled-up torrents of emotion. Don't be afraid of such changes in people's lives; you will see them often. The vastly more important concern centers around how you follow up and respond to this affective burst.

This first time you found yourself full of relief when the semester ended and she went home. You sensed in yourself a backing-off, an inability to relate directly to her dependency. Well, don't feel too bad about that. A great deal was learned — as your later reflections indicated — and next time you will have a bit more courage and straightforward resolve to keep going. In a dependency situation, a very delicate middle ground must be attained between allowing her to feel your support and acceptance, while slowly correcting and setting boundaries for the sharing of affections. The ability to make that practical judgment will come only with the wisdom learned through trial and error. So, take courage! The experience will prove beneficial in the long run. A director, too, must be tried by fire. That means both you and your directees will be singed occasionally.

We might do well at this point to reflect a bit more about the religious life-style of a spiritual director. I'm sharing reflections here that have come from a brief nine years of experience, although with a fairly wide variety of individuals. Lord knows, there's still so much to learn. We never attain full mastery of the skill of directing lives.

First of all, through the instances of direction you will acquire a sense of the immense pain within human lives. Through the inner sharing of thoughts and feelings you will meet people who have harbored incredible suffering in their hearts for years, suffering you haven't believed possible. After a while you may even find yourself nodding to Thoreau's observation that most people "lead lives of quiet desperation." You will cry often! I have. Especially when a gentle soul is encountered who has never really had a chance to be kind or to be loved. Believe me, this human agony will constitute a real temptation for you — the desire to simply close off sensitivity and forbid any more stories of human despair. Please keep your tenderness and gentleness finely honed; they are the gifts which brought you to the ministry of direction in the first place. Sensitivity will be the necessary means for your ongoing growth and deepening as a wise director. Take care to check yourself regularly on this.

A second aspect of a spiritual director's life-style focuses on the courage to recognize and live with personal failure. This is already happening in your hesitating response to the young student. It won't be the last failure. Each year will find your efforts with some people ending up with unsatisfactory resolutions; the failures will be both partial and total. Sometimes people will move away from your area just as progress is beginning. A feeling of unfinished business will frequently be your lot. As human beings we hate a lack of closure. As Christians living with a religious ideal we easily tend to internalize that lack into our own guilt. This is a common temptation in all kinds of pastoral ministry. To live life happily you must learn to accept an incompleteness about your efforts. This resembles the unfinished quality of Christ's ministry. Even with the great efforts of His teaching and mission, the full richness of the Spirit came only after His death and in His physical absence. Remember that, like St. Paul, you are planting seeds. God alone gives the growth and that may flourish long after the person has left your immediate presence.

One of the director's essential functions is to serve as a reality principle for people, and that causes change in one's life-style. The result shows up in the virtue of radical honesty, a virtue which constitutes a signal characteristic of the spiritual-direction ministry. You will need to be bluntly honest, first of all, about your own feelings and attitudes, honest to yourself and to your own spiritual director. We know how easy it is to play games. Only if you acknowledge emotions, both destructive and tender, within yourself will there be courage enough to give straight and honest answers to advisees. A spiritual director at least ought to be able to "tell it like it is" without beating around the bush. No double-talk here; people get more than enough, even from their friends. This personal honesty may involve "telling it like it is" all the way from uncouth personal habits to a life that is totally messed up. If you won't tell them, probably no one will. Pray often for that gift of radical honesty.

The daily work of spiritual direction will revamp your prayer life. Expect this to happen and the conflict that arises will not be so great when the transition begins. The emotions raised in your heart from struggling with other people in their grasping for faith, love, truth, self-acceptance, the courage to risk, will not be easily contained. They will tend to overflow into your times of personal prayer; the hopes and needs of others will surge in and overturn the private agenda you had fixed. Don't fight this intrusion; adjust your mood and integrate these feelings into the style and content of your prayer.

One of the finest spiritual gains of this ministry will occur through the deep prayer you offer *for* those and *in the name of* those you are serving as director. At times when they cannot pray in the Body of Christ you will be their *alter ego*. Appreciate this change in the style of your prayer as a great treasure.

Another element of your spirituality will be an increased sense of the pressure of conversion in daily life. Conversion becomes more and more that slight, step-by-step, painstaking work of attaining a redirection or a better direction in one's life lived towards God. So many of the people who will come to you are seeking some kind of clarity in faith and the means to effectively internalize it. When this day-by-day striving to slowly purify intentions, lessen weaknesses and form new ways of acting has become a constant part of your personal awareness and action, you will discover ever greater treasures to place at the disposal of your directees. Most conversions in people's lives are not dramatic, instantaneous flashes; instead there is a patient living with and working out of the faith possibilities inherent in their life-situations and in the very talents they have been given. Most evidently you will soon learn this truth.

There are other significant changes which will be forced on your life-style because you have taken on this ministry, but these few points will suffice to indicate some of the adjustments a director is called on to make. This brings to mind another dimension which bears examination: the self-image of a spiritual director. How should or does this ministry change your view of yourself as a Christian?

A spiritual director must have the conviction of being a shaper of God's mystery in people's lives. Through you, their image of God as good or punishing, gentle or demanding will be affected. In many ways they will see God dealing with them as you deal with them. Therefore you must carry that honor conscientiously, for it counts as an awesome burden. You will need a gentleness of spirit to live with such a responsibility. So in your heart see yourself as a tender person no matter how hard and demanding your external conduct must be. Be happy, and nourish this kindly interior. Along with this sensitivity you need also the surety that your own personal spiritual life possesses unique and worthwhile qualities. It is important to have a positive appreciation of one's own spirituality. Know deeply and honestly that you have something eminently good to share: the gift of faith given by God to you. Always have a high estimation of that gift.

Your self-image ought to possess the sense of being a humble person. Humility is always necessary when confronting the mysteries of God, the human person, and God entering into human life. Recognize the style you practice in leading people into a deeper awareness of God's reality. That recognition should lead to the judgment you have to make about who will profit from your assistance and who won't. It takes humility to say, "I can't really help you; someone else is needed." Perhaps that admission will be a catalyst for much growth in the advisee's life. And be sure to help the individual find another director who has the abilities or style necessary.

In some way you will have to incorporate the aspect of being a challenger or confronter. This will be hard because it's the exact opposite to being an interiorly gentle person. One of the toughest tasks a director faces is having to confront individuals and tell them directly where they are deceiving themselves, failing in promises, or just plain afraid to get started. Grit your teeth because these moments will hurt. You can accomplish these urgings well only after reflectively meditating on this notion of "confronter," praying over it and incorporating it as part of your religious self-image.

Lastly, a spiritual director ought to possess the image of being an artist of ongoing faith. You are indeed one who delicately handles the most precious material possible — the actual elements of human lives. This material must always be respected; the abilities and experiences of each individual count as God's gifts to them. The finishing task of each is to discern his or her vocation, to learn love, truth, beauty and God's Mystery in concrete living. You are an artist of that discernment; your products are living "earthen vessels" of incredible beauty. I have often thought that one of the greatest mission fields of our age is to journey with someone through the jungles of modern culture and temptations, through the labyrinth of human motivations to the simple faith and love that confidently says "Yes" to God's Mystery. So be assured that you possess a truly artistic ministry of great worth.

These thoughts are sufficient for now. The ministry of spiritual direction holds a place of growing respect in the Church today, and you will be a part of that movement. I have shared so many of my thoughts and feelings with you on this subject because I want you to become the best possible director you can be. Your gifts will stimulate the growth of faith in many. Be courageous and hopeful.

Affectionately yours

Relationships in Spiritual Direction

James Gau, S.J.

For about eight years, I have been part of teams giving directed retreats and doing spiritual direction. Very early on in these team efforts the question arose about whether we would meet as a team, and what our meetings would consist of. There seemed generally to be several options: either to discuss in an abstract way the Spiritual Exercises, or different approaches to counseling and their relationship to direction, or the theological bases for direction, or to discuss very concretely particular cases we were actually dealing with. If we chose the latter, I would become uncomfortable in meetings which might seem to lack boundaries and scope. Still, there seemed much to be gained from a case-study approach. This question first raised for me the importance of *relationships* in spiritual direction. Our discussion of relationships in spiritual direction will proceed thus: 1) the purpose of spiritual direction, 2) the director/directee relationship, 3) the possible supervisor/director relationship, and 4) briefly, how the above two relationships reflect Jesus' relationship with us.

The Purpose of Spiritual Direction

A person seeks a spiritual director because he wants to become more responsive to the initiative of God's self-communication in his life; he wants to become more responsive to God's grace, to the God who acts in communicating Himself, first in creation, and then in His Son, Jesus. Because

This article originally appeared in *Review for Religious,* 38, July 1979, pp. 559-65. Reprinted by permission.

God created each of us as a center of consciousness, and because we see all of creation from the perspective of our particular consciousness, we come easily to believe that *we* have the initiative in our lives, rather than see our activity as a response to God's having acted first. The action of grace and the call of revelation invite us to break through the boundaries of our consciousness, to begin to see ourselves — and all creation — as God sees us. Thus, when a person first comes to spiritual direction, the director's concern will be to help him respond to the action of God's self-communication in his life. When a person first comes to spiritual direction, he may be unable to articulate this reality as the foundation of his life. The object of spiritual direction will be to bring this reality to experiential awareness.

In *Matthew 22:35-40* (par. *Mark 12:30; Luke 10:27),* Jesus tries to help a lawyer become more responsive to God when the lawyer asks, "Teacher, which is the great commandment in the law?" Jesus responds, "You shall love the Lord your God with all your heart, and with all your soul, and with all your mind. This is the great commandment." But Jesus, satisfying his question thus, did not stop: "And a second is like it. You shall love your neighbor as yourself." The directee seeks to become more responsive to God (the great commandment) and to his fellow human beings — and himself (the basic norm of the second commandment). The second is like the first because, as Paul does not tire of saying, the Spirit of Jesus dwells in our hearts:

> But you are not in the flesh, you are in the Spirit, if in fact the Spirit of God dwells in you. Anyone who does not have the Spirit of Christ does not belong to him. But if Christ is in you, although your bodies are dead because of sin, your spirits are alive because of righteousness. If the Spirit of him who raised Jesus from the dead dwells in you, he who raised Christ Jesus from the dead will give life to your mortal bodies also through his Spirit which dwells in you *(Romans 8:9-11).*
>
> I have been crucified with Christ; it is no longer I who live, but Christ who lives in me: and the life I now live in the flesh I live by faith in the Son of God, who loved me and gave himself for me *(Galatians 2:20).*
>
> And because you are sons, God has sent the Spirit of his Son into our hearts, crying, "Abba! Father!" *(Galatians 4:6).*
>
> To them God chose to make known how great among the Gentiles are the riches of the glory of this mystery, which is Christ in you the hope of glory *(Colossians 1:27).*

Since creation is God's self-communication and is continued in the incarnation of Christ Jesus, the Word of God for us is not so far that we need to look for someone to go over the sea or up to heaven to bring us His word that we may hear and do it. The word of God is very near; it is in our hearts and mouths so that we can do it *(Deuteronomy 30:11-14)*. God is much closer to us than we think. He is to be found in the very processes of creation, and in the very experiences of our lives.

The Director/Directee Relationship

How does the director help the directee become more responsive to God? How does he help him love the Lord his God with all that he is, and his neighbor as himself? How does the director help the directee open to God's grace and freedom?

He can do this directly and indirectly. He does this *directly* by listening for the spirit of God in the movements the directee experiences and, secondly, by paraphrasing, questioning, encouraging, instructing, confronting. The directee reveals himself to the director, and the director responds, depending on how and what the directee reveals. Of his thoughts, the directee is already more or less conscious, and he most likely is becoming increasingly aware of how his thoughts affect his feelings. He may not have been very conscious of these until he prepared for his direction-time, or even until he found himself saying certain things, but he is becoming conscious nevertheless. The director can make this consciousness even more emphatic by reflecting thoughts and feelings to the directee, helping him hear himself while even, perhaps, adding some clarity to what the directee said confusedly.

The director helps the directee *indirectly* by being aware that the directee will spontaneously and unconsciously reveal the way he relates to God and to others in his manner of relating to him.

When a directee enters a relationship with a director, he trustfully and freely gives him a position of influence in his life. To do this, the directee must know that the director cares for and loves him in a very fundamental way. For the director to love the directee thus, and to use the influence he has received appropriately, he does well to hold himself to a position of *objectivity,* even while responding personally. This position of objectivity can be a real safeguard and rock for the director, while being the best perspective from which to help the directee. For example, the director might not be more mature or holier than the directee, may be bothered himself by a temporary anxiety, may not be, in actuality, objective. But if he knows and understands his position as being objective, he may be able to put all these distractions aside, claim his position, and thus help the directee.

Then, as the directee relates to the director, the latter's position of objectivity contains the possibility of illuminating the directee's attitudes toward God and toward others. When the relationship between the director and directee is firm, the directee will, perhaps, choose to *change* or to *develop* his attitudes toward God and others as the director's objective position reveals these to him. As valuable as the directee's straightforward communication is, it remains only something that the directee *says* about himself, insofar as he understands and interprets himself, whereas the *way* he relates to the director reveals him as he is in action.

In light of the director's objective position, the directee might choose to *change* his attitudes toward God and others. For example, while the directee might not speak of it straight out to the director, he might actually be responding defiantly to the director as an authority-figure; suspiciously, because of what the director knows about him; fearfully, when he wants to speak, for example, of sexual feelings. Each of these responses — defiance, suspicion, and fearfulness — could be generalized to the director as stemming from painful experiences of excesses of force, of being betrayed, of hush-hush and punishment, for instance, in the family. If the directee communicates these attitudes toward the director, he most likely is maintaining the same attitudes also toward God and others.

The directee might choose to *develop* his attitudes toward God and others. For example, while the directee may not say it patently to the director, he might experience tenderness as he speaks about things of the heart; joy, as he speaks of newly discovered insights; determination, as he speaks of his hopes of success. Each of these responses — tenderness, joy, determination — could be generalized to the director from earlier pleasurable experiences of being loved, of having one's insights well-received by another, of feeling sure about one's self in the face of confrontation. If the directee communicates these attitudes to the director, he most likely also maintains the same attitudes toward God and others.

The director, however, could *provoke* such feelings of defiance, suspicion, and fear, or of tenderness, joy, and determination, by having lost his objectivity. Then, hopefully, he will see that the directee's responses are *not* generalized. Then, again hopefully, he will admit his fault, apologize, and be able to resume his position of objectivity.

The director thus gradually helps the directee bring to consciousness attitudes like defiance, suspicion, and fear, or tenderness, joy, and determination. Here, at this beginning stage, as all along the process, the directee may well block and resist his coming into consciousness of these attitudes and feelings because, when he does become aware of them, he experiences pain or vulnerability, begins to feel responsible for himself. After a time, the director-directee situation which occasions such attitudes in the directee might also begin to bring to the surface other situations when he also felt this way, until the causes and sources of such feelings begin to become clarified. At this point, the directee has the opportunity of knowing himself forgiven and healed by the Lord or of accepting gratefully and graciously God's gifts for His praise and glory. Proceeding in the fashion of "two steps forward and one backward," gradually the directee may begin to see, and want to change or develop his attitudes and behavior.

The attitudes proceeding from the above examples could begin to manifest the directee's *intentionality*, that is, his habitual way of perceiving God and others. For example, a suspicious person's attitude might regularly be some rendition of "If I surrender to God, He'll probably ask something really difficult of me," or, "If I share myself with this person, can I trust Him not to use what I tell Him against me?" A joyful person's attitude might regularly enable him to take delight in what appears to be a hopeless situation, like seeing the spark of the glory of God in a retarded person. Or his joyful attitude regularly enables him to meet new situations, despite the risk, with interest and excitement.

When the director becomes aware of the directee's "intentionality," he can begin to help the directee also to become aware of it by remaining objective, refusing to correspond with the directee's attitude and actions — even if they are directed toward him. Thus he remains like a balance at equilibrium, neither disapproving the directee's defiance, suspicion, or fear nor approving his tenderness, joy, or determination, but rather leaving it to the directee's decision to change or develop his particular intentionality. By maintaining a position of objectivity, the director hopes to illuminate for the directee his existential situation, thus helping the directee frame the dimensions of a decision. This process, however, often incites resistance, blocking, and perhaps even some disturbance in the directee, because the security of his world vision may be threatened. The directee came to direction because he wanted to grow in relationship with God and with his fellow human beings. In this process, he sees the possibility of putting off his own intentionality for the intentionality of Christ Jesus, of "putting off the old man to put on the new."

The Supervisor/Director Relationship

As the director tries to help the directee, so the supervisor tries to help the director. The director, though trained and experienced, is, of course, just a person, and he, like the directee, needs to grow in his relationship with God and with others. How does the supervisor help the director become more responsive to God? How does he help him "love his neighbor" as found in the directee? How does the supervisor help the director open himself to God's grace and freedom in his relationship with the directee especially? He can do this directly and indirectly. He does this *directly* by being attentive to the Spirit of God moving in the director-directee relationship as the director describes it; by reflecting, interpreting, challenging; by signaling where the director might be in correspondence, for example, with the directee's defiance by responding with force, with his suspicion, by responding with disdain, etc.; by admonishing the director about attributing the directee's growth to his direction rather than to the grace of God and the directee's own courage; or perhaps by assigning blame to the directee for the absence of any progress. Presumably the director truly is conscious of the dynamics existing between himself and the directee, since that is part of his responsibility, and can thus speak about them with good articulation. Still, the supervisor can engage the director in discussion about areas that might need expanding, others that might have been neglected, and can, perhaps, make suggestions about yet others.

The supervisor helps the director *indirectly* by being sensitive to the way the director relates to him, since this will often reveal the way the director is relating to God and to the directee.

When a director approaches another director to be his supervisor, most likely he is asking someone he respects to help him. For the supervisor to help the director, he also must maintain a position of objectivity. The supervisor may not be as skilled a director as the one coming to him for help, but this ought not be at issue. From his position of objectivity, the supervisor can throw into relief the director's attitudes toward God and toward the directee. If the relationship is objective (which does not mean impersonal), the director will have the option of *changing* or of *developing* his attitudes toward God and the directee as the supervisor's objective position reveals these to him. As valuable as is the director's understanding and interpretation of what he does in the direction situation, his manner of relating to the supervisor could be even more revealing.

In the light of the supervisor's objective position, the director might choose to *change* his attitudes toward God and the directee. For example, the director might respond defensively to the supervisor, as if he were a competitor; condescendingly, as if he were an intruder; apologetically, as if he were a taskmaster. All of these responses — defensiveness, condescension, apology — are most likely generalized to the supervisor out of the director's past, and may indicate the way the director relates to God and to the directee. The supervisor's role, however, is not to investigate the director's past but to examine whether and how he might be communicating these attitudes to the directee, thus preventing him from seeing the action of the Spirit in his life, and so impeding his growth in relationship to God and others.

The director might choose to *develop* his attitudes toward God and the directee. For example, the director might respond candidly to the supervisor as a friend; respectfully, as a mentor; confidently, as a peer. Each of these responses — frankness, respect, confidence — is also most likely generalized to the supervisor out of the director's past and may indicate the way the director relates to God and the directee. The supervisor's role will be to evaluate with the director the effect of such attitudes on his ability to perceive the action of the Spirit in the directee's life and on the directee's growth in relationship to God and others.

The supervisor, then, gradually helps the director bring to consciousness attitudes like defensiveness, condescension, apology, or frankness, respect, confidence. The director is likely to block and resist the coming into consciousness of such attitudes, because when he becomes aware of them, he might experience pain or the need to be more responsible. After a time, the supervisor-director situation which occasions such attitudes in the director might begin to illuminate some of the dynamics of the director-directee situation as well. At this point, the director has the opportunity of knowing himself forgiven and healed by the Lord, or of accepting gratefully God's gifts for His praise and glory. In this way the director may come to change or develop himself in the direction he gives.

The attitudes proceeding from the above examples — defensiveness, condescension, apology, or frankness, respect, confidence — as revealed in his relationship to the supervisor, could begin to manifest the director's "intentionality" toward God and toward others. For example, an apologetic director might have a tendency to take things back which he thought had come from the Lord when he is confronted by a directee, or to feel unworthy himself in the midst of so many other capable and talented directors. A confident director, on the other hand, might regularly depend on the Lord to give him what needs to be said to a directee, and regularly feel that he is competent in his work. Since each directee comes to direction with his own particular intentionality toward God and others, the director needs earnestly to know what his own intentionality is to be better able to empathize with the directee's view of the world and not seek to impose his own on the directee.

When the supervisor becomes aware of the director's intentionality, he can begin to help the director himself to become aware of it by remaining objective, refusing to correspond with the director's attitude. Thus, he remains as a balance at equilibrium, neither disapproving the director's defensiveness, condescension, or apology, nor approving his frankness, respect, or confidence, but leaving it to the director's decision to change or develop his particular intentionality. By maintaining a position of objectivity, the supervisor hopes to illuminate the existential situation of the director in his direction, thus helping him frame the dimensions of a decision. This process, however, often incites resistance, blocking, and perhaps even disturbance in the director, because the security of his world vision is being challenged. The director came to supervision because he wanted to become more sensitive to the Spirit moving in the directee. In this process, he has the possibility of putting off his own intentionality so as to perceive the intentionality of Christ Jesus growing in the directee.

In conclusion, the director-directee and supervisor-director relationships are reflections of Jesus' relationship with us. When the director (supervisor) responds from a position of objectivity to the attitudes and feelings of the directee (director), whatever they might be, he functions as Jesus did, the very Jesus whom he calls the directee (director) to meet in prayer (see, e.g., *Romans 3:21-26; 5:6-11; 12:14-21)*. The position of God in Jesus contains the possibility of illuminating our sinful and virtuous ways of relating to Him and to our neighbor, bringing them to consciousness, and affording us the opportunity of repentance and growth in faith. God-in-Jesus represents, not an intentionality, but the fullness of vision, one that refuses correspondence with our intentionality and our sinfulness. In Jesus, God Himself speaks. The inadequacy of our intentionality and our sinfulness clashes with His righteousness, thus revealing both Him and us.

PART THREE

The Practice
of Spiritual Direction

Good spiritual direction embodies two basic principles. The principle of uniqueness is the first — each person is unique, God's work in each person is unique, and each spiritual direction relationship is unique. The principle of development is the second — a person's relationship with God ordinarily develops through a series of distinct stages. Spiritual directors must never lose sight of these two principles.

A person's uniqueness is partially revealed through his or her sex, age, state-in-life, family and cultural background, education, occupation, and psycho-social maturity. God's unique guidance is manifested to some degree through the person's religious tradition, spiritual experiences, ways of praying and deepest longings. During their initial meetings, a director and directee review these areas to determine the possibility of their working together in spiritual direction and the general guidelines for their relationship.

As the spiritual direction relationship grows, the needs arising from the directee's stage of spiritual development gradually emerge. The needs of one recently converted to Christ will differ from those of a person who has been praying regularly for years; and these, in turn, may differ from those of a person experiencing the advanced stages of contemplation. An effective director is able to recognize and support the characteristic ways God works in persons during the various stages of the spiritual journey.

In this section, Shaun McCarty, Vilma Seelaus, and Louis Cameli discuss factors in the uniqueness principle; Rose Page and Antonio Moreno explore the principle of spiritual development. In addition, these articles offer some practical advice for the entire spiritual direction process.

On Entering Spiritual Direction

Shaun McCarty, S.T.

It was H.D. Thoreau who once said, "If you see someone coming to do you a good deed, run for your life!" I suspect similar sentiments in times past have made many wary of entering into the field of spiritual direction, either to give it or to receive it. Yet, more recently there seems to be renewed interest in and more of a felt need for this venerable ministry of individualized spiritual help. This article is an attempt to reflect on some of the questions and issues involved when one considers entering a spiritual direction relationship. I mean to deal with the topic more experientially than theoretically, that is, by using people more than books as my primary source.

Why the Current Interest?

There are a variety of reasons why people are seeking spiritual direction today. For some it has always been an expectation of the religious groups to which they belong. For others, it's the thing to do, a badge of belonging to an elite group of the "spiritually mature."

Yet for many people today the motivation seems more genuinely interior. It has for many been generated by deeply moving religious experiences occasioned by intense spiritual events like directed retreats and by participation in charismatic movements like *Cursillo,* Marriage Encounter and Charismatic Prayer Groups.

Younger religious today perhaps feel the need for spiritual

This article originally appeared in *Review for Religious,* 35, November 1976, pp. 854-67. Reprinted by permission.

direction as a result of more individualized programs of spiritual formation. Older religious have been led to a rediscovery of this value because of the ambiguities and ambivalences experienced in this post-Vatican II Church. Not a few have felt a sense of drifting rudderless in the stormy sea of "personal responsibility." People are seeking direction as a result of crumbling structures that once provided it. For example, in the Church today there are fewer specific regulations; a lower role for authority figures as dimensions of collegiality and subsidiarity develop; a decline in the frequent use of the sacrament of Penance; a shift in prayer patterns from common prayer forms and devotions toward less formal corporate prayer and more personal quiet prayer.

Whatever the reasons, I believe that the renewed interest in spiritual direction is indicative in many quarters that the Spirit is moving and that people are becoming more sensitive to His presence and power in their lives as well as more aware of how difficult it is to listen alone and unguided. And it is striking that this interest and need are not limited to religious and clerical circles. More than a few of the laity are sensing a call to a more profound spiritual depth and intimacy with the Lord.

Where Are the Resources?

At the same time, however, it appears that the resources for providing spiritual direction are not adequate to meet the needs. And there are reasons for this. The lack of availability of willing and able spiritual directors is a universal complaint. Those already active in this ministry are usually over-extended as it is. Unrealistic role expectations or job descriptions for the spiritual director which list a formidable array of qualities and qualifications necessary might make the Lord Himself hesitate to undertake the task! Such heroic and romantic expectations scare off many ordinary people who might well be apt helpers in spiritual growth for others. And ironically, these same grandiose job descriptions for spiritual directors sometimes attract self-styled "gurus" from whom it *would* be a good idea to "run for your life!" Add to these reasons for meager resources a lingering fear of the involvement demanded and dependency risked and it is little wonder that needs and resources do not always meet — not to mention the number of those "gun-shy" of direction due to bad past experience with distorted varieties of "spooky" phenomena mislabeled "spiritual direction."

In addition to those who *want* direction and can't find it, there are also those who *need* it and either won't look for it or won't accept it. In some instances, sound spiritual direction would mean the difference between staying with or leaving commitments.

In other cases, it may mean the difference between mediocrity and fervor. So many people allow passion to leave their prayer and their relationships and settle for lifeless loves. Ingmar Bergman's film "Scenes From a Marriage" is a chronicle of a commitment gone awry for want of passion in a love relationship between a man and his wife. How many commitments in and outside of marriage burn out for want of a bellows to fan the flame of passion that should energize a love relationship? How many relationships never survive the inevitable periods of disaffection? And how many pilgrimages of prayer die in the desert? I would submit that spiritual direction can be a bellows for one's fervor, an oasis in the desert.

What Is Spiritual Direction?

Before we can talk about entering into spiritual direction meaningfully, we need to know more precisely what it is we are entering into. But before saying what spiritual direction *is*, it might be helpful to consider some things it is *not*.

In a way both words, *spiritual* and *direction*, can be misleading. Spiritual direction is not "spiritual" in the sense that it is concerned with the life of the spirit or the life of the soul as somehow disengaged from mind and body. One's response to God is as one whole person. Body, mind and spirit are not separate parts or faculties of a person, but three different ways of looking at the same, integral person.

St. Paul expresses this integral unity of the person in a parting blessing to the Thessalonians when he says: "May the God of peace make you perfect in holiness. May he preserve you *whole and entire,* spirit, mind and body, irreproachable at the coming of our Lord Jesus Christ" (1 Thessalonians 5:23). A biblical use of the word "body" *(soma)* would suggest the person as viewed in his rootedness in and relatedness to this world, his solidarity with the rest of creation. "Mind" *(psyche)* would suggest the person viewed as being above the animal kingdom, as having the power of self-reflection, as having been called to a lordship and stewardship over the rest of creation. "Spirit" *(pneuma)* would suggest the person's outreach, his or her native openness to the transcendent, the point of a person's origin and contact with God. It is precisely under this aspect of one's openness to the beyond that a person has the ability to get in touch with something or Someone bigger than himself or this world.

In a person's day-to-day living there are resonances of one aspect of life in all the other aspects of that person's life. For example, when I have a headache, it is not just my body that aches. *I* ache and it has effects on my thinking and my prayer. Or if I have been wounded in spirit, it can lead to a cynical bent of mind and even a sour face!

This holistic view of person, so vital for sound spiritual direction, is helpful in that it enables one more easily to make distinctions without separation, and to maintain unity without confusion. Jacques Cuttat speaks of it:

> Greek as well as Oriental thought oscillates between two poles. Both are characterized on the one hand by a dualism which tends towards separation and, on the other hand, by a monism which tends towards fusion. The tendency that was predominant, first during the pre-Socratic era and later during that period of Christian thought when Stoic influences were strong, was that of uniting and even fusing fundamental dualities such as being-nonbeing, being-becoming, unity-multiplicity, intelligible world-sensible world, Logos-nature, knowing-known. Until the third century this monistic tendency marred the Christian philosophy of the Apologetic Fathers who sought chiefly to overcome Gnostic dualism. But from the time of the great ecumenical councils, especially those of Nicea (325) and Chalcedon (451) which defined the unity without confusion and the distinction without separation of the two natures in the one Person of Christ, we witness for the first time in the history of human understanding the dawn of a new form of thinking. It consists in "keeping together," that is, in "maintaining the tension" rather than resolving antithetic terms such as the one and the multiple, being and becoming, the same and the other, soul and body, spirit and nature.[1]

There is an interesting convergence of both biblical and these ancient conciliar understandings of wholeness with some contemporary psychological discourse that also stresses the unity of the human person. Perhaps the wheel has been rediscovered!

There are serious implications for spiritual direction which stem from a truly holistic conception of person. This, of course, does not mean that a spiritual director should be ready to function as physician, psychiatrist or even social secretary for anyone! Indeed, there *is* a focus on the "spiritual" dimension of the person, but with an awareness of and an attentiveness to the fact that other dimensions of the person's life can help or hinder growth in holiness.

Nor is spiritual direction "direction" in the sense of being overly directive. Of course its style will be fashioned by one's personality, training and demonstrated effectiveness. But the director does not tell people who they should be or what they should do. And this fact, if grasped, precludes fostering an unhealthy dependence of directee on director. Too often people in helping ministries, perhaps even unconsciously, tend to meet their own need to nurture more than the need of the person seeking their help.

Nor should a spiritual director impose on or coerce (however benignly) a person to a spirituality not his own. Of course it is true that there are some universal norms applicable to all the People of God, and there are even some common ones for members of a specific religious tradition, like Franciscans, Dominicans, Jesuits, Augustinians, Carmelites, and others. But most importantly of all, the form of a person's spirituality should be shaped by his own idiosyncrasy. His or her own uniqueness, as well as a freely chosen value system and an ordering of personal gifts, are the basis for fidelity. Each gives praise to the Lord best by being fully himself or herself, not by becoming a carbon copy of someone else (however holy) or by being shaped on someone else's pottery wheel — unless, of course, God is the potter!

Personally, I do not subscribe to an egalitarian notion of direction that would create a false and simplistic sense of equality between director and directee. This will become more obvious later when I describe some activities that a spiritual director actually does. The presumption in spiritual direction is that there is a certain "inequality" of experience, training, objectivity or whatever it is that urges one person to seek the help of another. Otherwise isn't there danger of the blind leading the blind? However, this relationship of inequality ought not be viewed as the inequality between superior and inferior. As a matter of fact (and I can testify from my own experience of helping others), the person helped may be more gifted, smarter, holier than the director. But *in the relationship of spiritual direction,* I do not see them as peers. This does not preclude the possibility of mutual ministry. What director has not been helped, edified, taught by those who come to him or her? I find it a salutary confrontation to be privy to another's burgeoning relationship with the Lord. In a word, I think a spiritual director should avoid either a condescending superior-inferior, or a one-sided helper-"helpee" relationship and try to experience the ministry more as a kind of traveling the road together, as being a gracious receiver as well as a generous giver!

Nor is spiritual direction co-terminous with the sacrament of Penance. Distinct, they are not necessarily separate. Though matter for healing may often emerge naturally in spiritual direction and even, at some point, be put within the context of sacramental absolution, I think it is helpful not to confuse the two operations. It has been the close connection between the two in the past that has been at least partly responsible for identifying the ministry of spiritual direction fairly exclusively with the priesthood. And I think this has led to some dysfunctional telescoping of two important means of spiritual growth, one sacramental and the other non-sacramental. When people are clear about the distinction and habitually differentiate the two, it seems easier to do both in the same setting.

Likewise it is important to maintain a clear distinction between spiritual direction and counseling. When the lines of distinction are fuzzy, this readily leads to the trivializing of one or both kinds of help. The focus in counseling is more on solving problems, of effecting better personal integration and adjustment in the process of human maturation. The focus in spiritual direction, on the other hand, is more on growth in prayer and in charity. It deals more explicitly with the faith dimension of human existence. It is true that some counseling does often occur in a spiritual direction relationship, but this is not the *focus* nor the basic orientation of the relationship.

What, then, *is* spiritual direction if not any of the above? There are almost as many definitions as there are people writing and talking about it. Jean Laplace is as concise and precise as any when he defines spiritual direction as "the help one person gives another to enable him to become himself in his faith."[2] Spiritual direction is a special ministry which involves certain gifts or charisms along with a set of skills which help to make the gifts operative. "A gifted presence to help a gifted self emerge" — that is how I see spiritual direction. This ministry of spiritual direction, then, calls for a reverence for the mystery of the other person and genuine hope for the "more to come" that is in him or her. Any genuine spiritual help should aid a person to be more open to the calls of the Holy Spirit in the events of life which summon that person to continued conversion and toward a deepening union with the Lord. Through the real presence of one to the other, the presence and power of the Spirit of God can be better discerned.

What Happens in Spiritual Direction?

Perhaps it is more realistic to deal with the activities proper to spiritual direction inductively rather than deductively, that is to say, by observing what actually does happen when people get and give direction, rather than by speaking about what should happen theoretically. I am not disdaining theory. As Kurt Lewin says, "There is nothing so practical as good theory." But "good theory" comes from reflection upon real experience, both good and bad! I think it is important to be habitually reflective about what we do and don't do so we can at least learn to make new mistakes, not the same ones over and over again. Some people think too much and get removed from reality into their ivory towers. But others act too much without thinking and get overwhelmed by a surfeit of the unprocessed data of experience. Both extremes are equally oppressive. As a piece of conventional wisdom expresses it: "Thinkers think and doers do. But until the thinkers do and the doers think, progress will be just one more word added to an already overburdened vocabulary of talkers who talk." With that word of advice in mind, let us proceed with observations of what actually goes on in spiritual direction. A variety of things happen at different times. They include:

(1) *Listening*. This is perhaps the most important skill (or art) needed: reverential listening to the unfolding mystery of another person's story — not just with the ears, but with the heart; not just to words, but to melody. Listening can do more to help a person clarify who God is and what God is asking of him or her than any other activity (or passivity) I know. This takes a big ear and a closed mouth. Sometimes it seems that the best we can do as spiritual directors is to stay out of the way of the Holy Spirit as He moves in another person's life.

Good listening helps clear the static so people can hear the Spirit speak.

(2) *Affirmation*. An important function of the director is his affirming the other person in his or her own giftedness. Many need help in identifying, developing and using their gifts. Often these gifts are buried beneath a crust of poor self-image so that people are not really in touch with the deeper level of their own unique giftedness. These gifts (charisms) are truly visible evidence of the Spirit in people's lives. A good director can help a person affirm such giftedness. There are few ministries more rewarding than that of helping a person in the search for his or her gifts. For it is "gift" that truly makes a person come alive from the inside out.

(3) *Confrontation*. Yet the discovery of gifts presumes not only affirmation, but testing for validation. Growth requires that each party keep honest in the search, that they unmask illusions which are often subtly deceptive. Angels of darkness often appear under the guise of angels of light. Keeping someone honest in his or her relationship with God and others — unmasking the demons — these are ways of describing an important task for the spiritual director. In order that a person be able to listen to the Spirit in an undistorted way, that person must be concerned with the issue of inner freedom. How open-handed is he or she before the Lord, how unshackled by self-concern, how ready for whatever God asks? A good director will help uncover areas of "unfreedom" and lead a person to an appropriate ascesis. For effective confrontation, however, the previous communication of loving concern and gentleness on the part of the director is presupposed.

(4) *Accountability*. Checking in regularly with a director can help a person avoid some of the pitfalls that come with "solo" assessment. It can prove difficult to persevere in self-evaluation for such reasons as being too busy, too tired, too unfocused. One can become easily discouraged when growth is not visible, or when one is too general and vague in setting goals or choosing means. Regular spiritual direction can provide the impetus for realistic specification, as well as concrete occasions to reflect on progress or regression.

(5) *Clarification*. A significant factor in growth is the ability to reflect upon the experience we have so as to gain insights from it. Someone has said that the unreflective life is not worth living. The experience of grace and of faith-life is always

going on, but it can stay on a relatively primitive level of unawareness or unconnectedness. A good director will be able to help a person bring his or her religious experience to the level of reflective awareness and get in touch with the trajectory of his or her past. To put it another way, for spiritual growth, a person needs to know his own story, to string the beads of past epiphanies so as to perceive the pattern of his relationship with God. This kind of activity, whereby a person can see more clearly the shape of his or her spiritual history, provides a touchstone against which to test the authenticity of a present decision or judgment. It helps the person to say with greater certainty "This is the Lord speaking" or "This anticipated response is an expression of the real me." Recently I received as a gift a little book of blank pages with the question on the cover, "How can I know what I know until I see what I say?" Perhaps a good director helps a person to see what he says so that he can know what he knows!

There is another area of clarification that needs attention. It is in reference to a person's value system. One grows to the extent that he lives consistently with his value system. This presupposes that the person is both identifying and ranking values for himself. For this ordering help is often needed. And as values get clarified there must be on-going challenge to make the values visible. A person realizes his values in the visibility that is given them. I use the word "realize" advisedly, meaning both to discover and to make real. It is important that the values be one's own and not those of the director. In developing a healthy Christian spirituality, of course, one's values ought to be continually confronted with Gospel values which should gradually correct, modify, undistort and ultimately lead a person really to put first things first.

One final area for clarification is that of clarifying who God is for the person under direction. The whole shape and orientation of a person's spirituality is deeply affected by the operative image of God in that person's life. Although professing belief in a personal, providential and compassionate Lord, many people tend to put God at a distance from their lives or are scared to death of Him. A director can help a person clarify that image.

(6) *Teaching*. Sometimes there are gaps in a person's understanding of issues related to growth. These gaps call for the help of one more learned and/or more experienced to instruct in the area of ignorance. Enlightenment is another factor that can free a person for further openness and growth.

But there is a mutuality of ministry here as elsewhere. The director ought to approach every teaching situation as learner as well as teacher.

(7) *Integration*. People's lives can become very scattered in the complexity of modern society, in the maze of renewal, in the frenetic activity of busy apostolic lives. They need to keep centering themselves, finding their "stillpoint" in Christ. With all the books and talks and workshops that have been part of renewal, some have tended either to tune out or to become passive. They listen somewhat attentively, take copious notes, but have difficulty in integrating into actual living what they hear and agree with. Things can remain in the idea stage rather than on the level, not only of hearing, but of evaluating and eventually owning. It is easy to get hooked on a "head-trip" whereby one thinks "renewal" comes simply from reading or talking about it. A director can offer the challenge, "What are you going to *do* about what you've heard or read?"

(8) *Counseling*. Even though it is important not to confuse counseling with spiritual direction, the fact is that a significant amount of counseling goes on in many spiritual direction relationships. Sometimes the Lord speaks to a person through a problem which is perhaps not explicitly related to prayer or faith-life. The element that makes such counseling compatible with spiritual direction is that it happens more by way of event rather than as the basic orientation of the relationship. The focus in an individual session may happen to be more of a counseling one, but the goals and the longer range dynamics in the relationship are those of spiritual direction. The basic orientation of the spiritual direction relationship is not problem-centered, but growth-centered. At some point in the relationship, perhaps at a later date, the person can be helped to see dimensions of the paschal mystery in a problem and not just helped to "cope" with it. It may be, too, that the activity of counseling may be more pronounced at certain stages of the spiritual direction relationship, especially at the beginning or at a time of crisis. But if the counseling needs become so strong as to affect the very orientation of the relationship on a more or less permanent basis, then it would be more honest to call it "counseling" rather than "spiritual direction," even if no referral is made. If professional therapy *is* needed, of course, referral is in order. Then continuing direction becomes a delicate matter of not working at cross-purposes with the

therapist.

(9) *Help Through the Desert.* I would like to make a distinction between dealing with a problem that calls for counseling and helping a person who is on spiritual pilgrimage through the desert. There are those special times for everyone seeking spiritual depth when he or she experiences the dryness of the desert, the apparent absence of God, perhaps the onslaught of the demonic. Nothing can get quite so boring and tiring and insipid or even frightening as spiritual growth. And there is nothing quite so painful as being broken open so the Lord can enter. A person's very efforts to become holy can lead to an "energy crisis." The recurring temptation for monks and other kindred spirits is *acedia,* that is, a distaste for spiritual things, an urge to "throw in the towel" when the going gets tough. This can very well be a part of the Lord's pedagogy in getting us to realize that sanctity is not a self-propelled enterprise by letting us experience such an energy crisis. Yet how many give up at this point either by "dropping out" or at least by "copping out" on spiritual depth and settling for a comfortable mediocrity for want of the right help at the right time to get through the desert?

(10) *Discernment.* Although much discernment in direction has been implied in what has been said thus far, the activities of the director should also be described under the explicit rubric of "discernment." That is to say, the spiritual director facilitates the process whereby the directee can examine the origin of movements within, often ambiguous and ambivalent, which are urging him toward or away from certain judgments and decisions. After living sometimes for years with clearly defined rules and with "black-and-white" clarity, many suddenly find difficulty in assessing particular situations and in clarifying motives involved in decision-making. It is not easy for anyone to choose between real and apparent goods. This aspect of the director's work is related very closely to keeping the directee honest and in touch with his genuine spiritual identity.

(11) *Prayer.* The final activity which goes on in spiritual direction, but by no means the least important, is prayer, both with and for the person coming for direction. The dynamics of grace are so much more at work than mere skills in direction. Often the mysterious workings of the Lord's presence are not susceptible to ordinary means of penetration. It is most ap-

propriate to pray with the person for the Lord's own guidance and help, especially at such times. It is also appropriate to begin and/or end each session with some explicit prayer which invites the Lord to be involved in the process and to send His Spirit to enlighten and to inspire, and later to thank Him for His help — though this should not become a mere ritual. As I mentioned previously, often it will be appropriate for the session to culminate in sacramental absolution if the director is a priest. But it should be clear that the sacrament of Penance and spiritual direction are not synonymous.

For Whom Is Spiritual Direction?

There is an old rule of thumb concerning the need for spiritual direction that says, "Always useful, sometimes necessary." I would think this holds true especially for those who give spiritual direction. To be truly effective in an ongoing way, a credible spiritual director is one who values it highly enough to be receiving it.

Spiritual direction is appropriate for all who are taking the spiritual life seriously, who are genuinely reaching for more. An important consideration in readiness for direction is where the person stands in relationship to making the fundamental religious act. Has the person made, or does the person want to make a decision to surrender to the Lord? Not just to become a self-actualized person. Not just to serve others. Spiritual direction implies at least the desire to reach beyond merely human or ethical growth to genuine religious growth.

Perhaps a further distinction should be made between those who *seek* spiritual direction and those who are *ready* for it. We may have to look more closely at what people are asking for when they say they "want a spiritual director."

Obviously many are looking for spiritual direction in the specific sense in which we have defined and described it thus far. Others may mean "direction" in the wider sense of any and all helps that will enhance their relationship with God and others — reading, friendship, classes, and so forth.

There are those who may be looking only for shared prayer and not for direction as such. There is a difference between getting together to pray and getting together to reflect on the experience of prayer. The two should not be confused. Direction has to do with reflecting on the process of prayer to see what is happening and what is not happening.

Some people are simply looking for a good confessor rather than a spiritual director. Again, that is a need that should be kept distinct, even if not separate from direction.

Others are more in search of a counselor. Again, even though this kind of help can aim at readiness for direction, the notions should be kept distinct.

There are also some who are just looking for a friend, a good, supportive relationship. Invaluable as it is, this is not the equivalent of direction. As a matter of fact, it can become problematic when the roles of friend and director are combined, though not necessarily so. For some aspects of direction, like affirmation, a good friend is eminently suited. But for others, like confrontation, objectivity can be somewhat hampered by friendship. In short, friendship can be a hazard as well as a help in spiritual direction.

Then there are those who don't express a desire for spiritual direction, but who have the *need* for it. Perhaps one of the challenges of this ministry is to find ways to help the objective need for spiritual direction become a felt need!

Who Is Suited for the Ministry of Spiritual Direction?

If we view spiritual direction as a ministry, then I would submit that the stress should be on identifying those who have the charisms necessary for it. This may be a practical alternative to constructing an overly-idealistic job description which may scare off many gifted people. Within the Christian community the Spirit brings gifts according to its need for ministry at a given time. So perhaps one approach in identifying spiritual directors should be one of testing and affirming those who "feel called" to be directors. Another of the obvious signs of such a call, I would think, is that of actually being sought out by others for such spiritual help. Whom are people asking for spiritual direction? They are not necessarily those who are hanging out shingles in a self-appointed ministry!

And the director obviously need not be a priest. There is no special character of the priesthood that marks him automatically or exclusively for this ministry. More and more men and women from non-clerical quarters are being sought out as directors. And a number of these manifest a hesitancy to

111

assume such a ministry before their own lack of help in developing the skills and acquiring the understanding that can make their gifts more operative.

Everyone called to be spiritual director need not be a living saint, but I would think there should be in himself or herself a deep desire to grow in the Lord. And there should be a basic equilibrium, together with an awareness of those areas of his life where he does not "have it quite together," so that he will be careful in guiding people in matters relating to such areas.

Group Spiritual Direction?

Some consideration should be given to the relative advantages and disadvantages of group, as opposed to individual spiritual direction. Some of the benefits of individual spiritual direction are: (1) a greater ease in communicating more deeply with a director; (2) less chance of evasion; (3) a more rapid getting to where the directee "is" in prayer and in their relationship; (4) a greater freedom and ability to talk when the right moment arrives. Some of the disadvantages of one-to-one spiritual direction are: (1) the danger of dependency; (2) undue influence by one person on another; (3) diminishing returns, perhaps, from one person.

Some of the benefits of group direction are: (1) a greater richness through diversity and the possibility of being affected by other people's prayer; (2) easier communication for some who have difficulty in relating one-to-one; (3) the benefits of communal experience; (4) less danger of dependency developing; (5) the impetus of group accountability. Some of the disadvantages of group spiritual direction might be: (1) a possible lessening of individual accountability through hiding within the group; (2) a greater threat to confidentiality; (3) the difficulty of self-disclosure in a group for some; (4) the practical difficulty of finding a time when all can get together regularly.

I am inclined to think it is not a question of the superiority of either individual or group spiritual direction. The style should be suited to individual need. But there will come moments, especially as people in a group progress in prayer at different rates, when each will need to meet with a spiritual director on an individual basis, even though that person be involved in group direction.

Negotiating Expectations

I think it is important that, as people enter into a spiritual direction relationship, mutual expectations be negotiated. Whether expectations are negotiated or not, they will be there to affect the relationship. Expressing and negotiating them tends to keep the more primitive ones from jeopardizing the relationship. Both potential and limitation should be faced realistically early in the process. Some of the factors that should be considered in this negotiation include:

(1) *Frequency and regularity of meeting.* There should be some kind of mutual commitment in terms of definite periods wherein direction will find the space and time to happen. There is good reason for setting regular times. When the reason to get together is not the result of a problem situation that has arisen, creating its own urgency, it is more likely that the growth process can be helped. Then, too, when fixed, the time (though flexible and adjustable to meet unforeseen contingencies) gets more priority in busy schedules on the side of both parties.

(2) *Clarification of specific areas that will be dealt with in future sessions.* As has been said already, a person will discover and deepen his values through the visibility that is given them. This visibility or specification of behavior in certain key areas like prayer, relationships in community, service to others, and so forth should be mutually agreed upon. It then becomes the basis of accountability in the whole process of spiritual direction. The accountability, of course, is not so much to the director as it is to God and to the individual himself.

(3) *Assessment provisions.* There should be some agreement to build in periodic evaluations of what is happening or not happening in the spiritual direction relationship. These evaluations offer the opportunity to consider new decisions about the direction, its continuance or the severance of the relationship. This provision may save spiritual direction from becoming pleasantly (or unpleasantly) insipid.

Even though provisions like these should be negotiated, I am hardly recommending that the relationship be overprogrammed or overstructured. Each successive session will provide its own agenda centering on what is happening in the life of the person and his or her response to the Lord. But it *is* helpful to try to focus the session somewhat each time so there can be some reflection in depth. Certain issues that recur can be tagged for future reference and explicit discussion. Ordinarily I would expect the here-and-now action of God in the person's life to constitute the heart of the agenda. Helpful in this regard is the practice of some kind of examen, that is, a habitual reflection on how the Lord has been speaking to me and calling me to conversion in the events of life and how I have or have not been responding.

(4) *Journal keeping*. For many, the discipline of articulating their spiritual autobiography has proven to be a valuable tool. It enables them to perceive the trajectory of the relationship they have had with the Lord and to discern the patterns of their dealings with Him. They are enabled to construct, as it were, a profile of their spirituality. It also enables a spiritual director to "tune in" more quickly on where a particular person has arrived in his spiritual growth as the relationship of direction begins. It is vital that each person know his own story so that he may live out its implications more authentically. There are several effective techniques in making and in keeping such a journal, none I know of more thorough than the *Intensive Journal* technique developed by Dr. Ira Progoff.

Some directors also find it helpful to keep a journal of their own by making notes after each interview. It is certainly an aid to memory and enables the director in retrospect to discern the rhythm and flow of the relationship over a period of time.

Conclusion

These, then, are some of the questions and issues to be dealt with in entering spiritual direction. There are certainly other questions and issues as well as other points of view. These observations are meant to be quite tentative and open to modification in the light of further experience. One cannot afford to be too absolutist or definitive in a helping ministry like spiritual direction. It calls for much awareness of human limitation as well as great dependence upon the Lord. As I indicated, the experience of being privy to people's dealings with the Lord is a humbling one.

In closing, I'd like to echo the thoughts of a kindred spirit whose experience has been that of psychotherapy. What he has to say might well be voiced by those of us involved in spiritual direction:

114

I want to conclude by saying very briefly what it means to me to be a psychotherapist. I feel like one of the more fortunate people. The men and women who come to see me entrust me with that which is most deeply meaningful in all their experience. They offer me the awesome privilege of participating in the very essence of their lives. When I am most authentic, I am most humble in my appreciation of this opportunity.[3]

What spiritual director can say less?

[1]J.A. Cuttat, "The Religious Encounter of the East and West," *Thought*, Vol. 33, No. 131 (Winter, 1958), p. 489.   [2]Jean Laplace, *The Direction of Conscience*. New York: Herder and Herder, 1967.   [3]James F.T. Bugental, *Search for Authenticity*. New York: Holt, Rinehart and Winston, 1965, p. 374.

New Approaches and Needs for Spiritual Direction of Women in the Catholic Church

Vilma Seelaus, O.C.D.

Changing cultural values, educational opportunities and life-styles in society have opened up even more opportunities for Religious women in the service of the Church.

In the case of the prayer life of the Church, two specific changes are noted: 1) the emerging prospect of women as spiritual directors for sisters, laity and priests; 2) the changing needs of women religious in their spiritual life and what this requires of priest directors.

This article examines in Part I the significance of women as spiritual directors in the light of history and points out the changes in religious life and cultures which brought modern women into this unique ministry. It offers specific suggestions for anyone choosing a director, whether priest or sister.

Part II speaks to priest directors, pastors and others who deal directly with religious women; highlights some general needs of sisters in various age levels; and notes some practical difficulties they may have. It also looks at the special needs of lay women in spiritual direction.

Part I — Women Directors: Significance & History

Today a person seeking spiritual direction might ask the question, "should I approach a sister or a priest?" A few years ago this option would rarely have been considered. Most books and manuals dealing with spiritual direction assumed the priest to be the one qualified to give spiritual direction. This is true not only of pre-Vatican II source material, but also of some very recent contributions. To cite a few examples: Guibert, the author of *Theology of the Spiritual Life* published in 1953 asks the question, "Is it necessary that the director be a priest?" To which he responds:

> Many authors unequivocally say Yes and the Code of Canon Law, canon 530, seems to support them. History does show that many who were not priests nevertheless acted as directors. Not only did the Fathers of the Desert do so, but also more recent saints such as Francis of Assisi, Ignatius of Loyola as a layman before his ordination in 1537, and even some women like Catherine of Siena and Teresa of Avila.[1]

But the author concludes:

> the office of director should ordinarily be reserved to priests because of the general economy of the supernatural order in which the priest is given the office of teacher; because the priest generally has a rounding in the theory and practice of the art of direction; because the Church does not look with favor on the custom of seeking direction from those who are not priests, aware as she is that such lay direction may easily have great disadvantages.[2]

Sacramentum Mundi shows the development of spiritual direction from the past and begins to deal with the need for a reappraisal of its nature and task. However, the author in describing the spiritual direction relationship writes "at the first meeting, the director, usually though not necessarily a priest, . . . etc."[3] This was published in 1970.

The Dynamics of Spiritual Self Direction by Adrian van Kaam was published in 1976. Van Kaam devotes some chapters to what he calls "private spiritual direction." He speaks of the need not only for an innate gift of prudence but also for wise preparation on the part of the director. In this context he says:

> any priest in good standing is implicitly approved as a spiritual director by his superiors as long as they do not object to his engagement in this task.[4]

Yet the experience of many people, especially sisters, indicates that priests also need special training. Seminary training of itself does not equip them for the ministry of spiritual direction. Some priests will admit of this themselves.

The paper prepared by the Committee on Priestly Life and Ministry of the NCCB, entitled *Spiritual Direction for Priests in the USA: The Rediscovery of a Resource,*[5] takes a more realistic approach. It deals not only with the need of priests for spiritual direction but also with the need for careful selection and formation of priests who are serving their fellow priests in this capacity. Its contents apply to spiritual direction in general and it complements what is considered in this article.

A New Phenomenon in the Church

If the assumption has been that a priest is the one to whom a person normally turns for spiritual direction, how are we to account for the many women in this ministry today? Perhaps one can say it was a natural and inevitable evolution. Women in general became more conscious of what it means to be a woman. Sisters also became more aware of themselves as Ecclesial Women and they began to reevaluate their role in the life of the Church. A broader vision opened up before them and contemporary needs called them forth. The desire to serve the Church out of the unique gift of their womanhood awakened the consciousness that masculine values had frequently been offered as the norm for their spirituality. For a long time women have worn these values as an ill-fitting garment. The inevitable consequence of women claiming the gift of womanhood is the fostering of a spirituality more in harmony with their deepest self.

For sisters, the women's movement has taken place within the ambience of the renewal of religious life. The process of renewal has contributed significantly to the number of sisters giving and seeking spiritual direction. In the early stages of the renewal chapters, the resource persons invited to chapters were usually men. It soon became evident that there was an increasing need for qualified women coming out of the same lived experience to share their expertise with their sisters. Superiors with vision began very early sending their sisters for advanced studies in theology, spirituality, and other related disciplines. Many sisters soon became recognized not only for competence in their field, but also for the womanliness and the spiritual vitality they communicated.

At the same time sisters in general were being faced with deep questions of meaning. Familiar and sometimes overly supportive structures were being changed or taken away; as a result of this it became evident that spiritual growth could not be measured by fidelity to externals. Changes which tended to foster responsibility as well as the opportunity for more personal and communal decision-making generated the need for a surer sense of direction from within. Directed retreats increased in popularity and for many sisters this was a step toward receiving on-going spiritual direction.[6] Sisters began to call forth their own sisters to journey with them as spiritual guides.

Sisters are also responding to the movement toward interiority in our culture. Some communities have Houses of Prayer to provide an atmosphere for a more intensive spiritual renewal for their sisters and many of these are local centers of prayer and sources for spiritual direction. Sisters are bringing the disciplines of Zen and Yoga to the service of Christian prayer. They are also having a significant role in establishing diocesan centers for spiritual development and they are contributing as well as benefiting from the charismatic renewal. Gradually, almost imperceptibly, the spiritual leadership in the Church has come to include sisters who have a unique gift to bring to this vital aspect of the Church's life.

Counseling and Direction, Two Different Things

It may be helpful at this point to distinguish between psychological counseling, spiritual counseling and spiritual direction. They are not the same, though all are concerned with the relationship between the inner and outer life of a person. Psychological counseling is primarily directed toward the psychological dimension of human growth. It normally leads toward greater consciousness and freedom. A person becomes more self-determining, better able to make decisions, and to assume responsibility for these decisions.

Spiritual counseling[7] provides a kind of spiritual guidance for someone who may or may not be praying but who has the desire to live in a manner pleasing to the Lord and to improve the spiritual quality of his/her life. Such a person might seek help in making difficult decisions or in dealing with problems in the apostolate, in community living, etc. Spiritual counseling can be a source of encouragement when prayer seems impossible for whatever real or imagined reason. It can be a lifeline for someone in psychological counseling whose energies are being consumed by the challenges of the moment. Someone in this position might find it difficult to sustain formal prayer at such a time. Spiritual counseling could help a person integrate psychological growth with the faith dimension of human living. This kind of integration leads to greater spiritual freedom.

Spiritual direction like psychological and spiritual counseling also leads to greater inner freedom. The spiritual director assists the individual to use his/her freedom in a manner harmonious with the individual's deepest self. Situating decision making within the context of prayer allows the Holy Spirit to guide one's life toward the genuine "liberty of the sons and daughters of God." Spiritual direction however is not only concerned with prayerful decision making. A person's prayer relationship with God affects every facet of daily Christian living.

The concept of spiritual direction has undergone considerable change in recent years. Today it is generally understood as a process whereby one person helps another to discover, express and achieve what God is asking in the life of the person seeking direction. It focuses on the desire to foster personal authenticity through a relationship with God in prayer. Spiritual direction enables one not only to discern the movements of God's life within but also to discover life's meaning and an inner orientation to channel daily activity. With the help of a spiritual director, a person is better able to discern the unique gift he/she can bring to the service of others. Spiritual direction nurtures therefore the whole of the Christian life. Today it is considered a pastoral ministry not to be exclusively identified with the priesthood and the teaching office of the Church. Seen in this pastoral perspective, it can now freely benefit from the contribution of religious women. This change in concept has opened to priests the complementary experience of receiving direction from sisters.

A contemporary phenomenon gaining momentum is that of women as spiritual directors. Already a significant number of women have achieved national recognition for their competence in this field. They are religious sisters from congregations which a few years ago were devoted exclusively to teaching or nursing. These sisters are contributing by their ministry of spiritual direction to the development of a deeper faith-life for many in the Church today. Some are also con-

tributing through articles and lectures to the growing understanding of the meaning of spiritual direction.

Should You Choose a Man or a Woman?

The question is asked, "Is it better to have a woman or a
man as a spiritual director?" This question will be pondered
by touching on some of the qualities needed in a good director.
These have been synthesized into six. Three are "anima" or
feminine qualities and three are "animus" or masculine
qualities. Here it is important to understand that both the
feminine and masculine dimensions are in woman and both are
in man. The feminine or "anima" predominates in the woman
and the masculine or "animus" predominates in the man.
Gentleness, intuition and receptivity are the three feminine
qualities to be considered. Strength, clarity and objectivity are
their masculine counterpart. Gentleness and strength, intuition
and clarity, receptivity and objectivity are to each other as the
"yin" and the "yan" of a whole or as two sides of the one
coin. They will be reflected on in their relationship to each
other.

The Need for Gentleness with Strength

If you ask someone with a good spiritual director to
describe the relationship, they will not infrequently say, "He
or she is very gentle." Gentleness is a quality often mentioned
first with feelings of deep appreciation for what its presence
means to the directee. A gentle person tends to be kind rather
than aggressive, harsh or rough. Patience and a soft spoken
manner often characterize such a person. Directors who are
gentle communicate a peaceful serenity which grows from living in the awareness of themselves and of others as precious to
the Lord. That which is precious is approached with reverence
and care, with gentleness.

Strength is the balance of gentleness. It is symbolized in the
scriptural passage, "The Lord is my rock." The kind of
strength here described is a familiar theme in St. Paul; it is an
inner power born of love, of God's indwelling Spirit of Love.
By firmly adhering to the Spirit within, the director is able to
be strong without being rigid or callous and is enabled to endure stressful situations with equanimity. A person strong in
the Lord communicates steadiness and a self-possession which

gives courage to the directee in difficult moments.

Gentleness and strength serve each other; one is not the antithesis of the other. To be truly gentle requires inner strength. Gentleness is not indecisiveness, nor is it a cover-up for the fear of hurting or being hurt. Honesty and straight forwardness are compatible with gentleness. A director who is strong yet gentle can challenge when this seems appropriate, for challenge is as necessary at times to the directee as wind and rain for hardy plant life. The presence of these two qualities helps to insure on the one hand, that the challenge is not experienced as destructive and on the other, that it is not so ineffective as to be unheard. Strength is the balance of gentleness as gentleness is the balance of strength.

The Place of Intuition and Clear Vision

The intuitive person possesses an inner eye which quickly perceives the heart of the matter. A director who is intuitive more easily comes to a comprehensive view of the spiritual life and is better able to see its various facets in their mutual relationship. Since intuition bypasses conscious reasoning to an immediate knowing, it gives direct, unreflected insight into a person or situation. The intuitive director therefore gets a kind of instinctual grasp of what the directee is trying to articulate. Intuition generates a kind of empathy between director and the person being directed. It leaves a feeling of being understood especially when the directee has been struggling to find words to describe what he or she wants to communicate. An intuitive sense, along with attentiveness to the spirit within, are especially needed at certain crucial moments in spiritual direction. Principles need to be applied with care and discretion, therefore the necessary training alone does not supply this inner intuitive grasp which prompts the director to one approach rather than another, to speak or to be silent, etc. Intuition has a wisdom of its own.

Intuition needs the companionship of conscious reasoning which makes for clarity. A person with a gift for clarity is able to reason soundly, can grasp the sense of another's remarks and can put them into proper context. Clarity is related to logical thinking in that it allows a person to see the necessary connection or outcome from what has gone before. A director thus gifted easily disengages the significant facts of a situation from the peripheral elements which create confusion and ambiguity in the directee. He or she is able to make clear and explicit what otherwise remains hazy and obscure. Clarity is as a welcome breeze which moves along a gathering of clouds, or like the rising sun which dissipates an early morning fog. It gives light to distinguish essentials from non-essentials and to perceive those things which may be diverting the directee from the issue.

Clarity however also needs the more comprehensive perception given by intuition. The clarity which comes from logical thinking can at times be very inadequate in the spiritual direction relationship. There are moments when the heart of another is giving messages which can only be perceived by an intuitive gaze into the depth of their being. The heart has its own logic which needs to be reverenced.

The Importance of Listening Objectively

The receptive director is a caring person who is able to put aside self-interest to be fully present to the directee. Receptivity is welcoming the directee into the sanctuary of the heart and there holding him or her with reverence before the Lord. It is an openness to receive; a capacity within the director to listen, to truly hear, and to draw in what is being communicated. It means accepting without judgment what is said, although making discriminating judgments (not moral judgments) has its appropriate place. Acceptance frees the person directed to move beyond his or her immediate experience to further growth. To be receptive of another's self-perception gives reassurance and communicates the feeling, "it is all right to be where I am." The grain of wheat needs time to "die" before new life appears. A receptive attitude helps the director be aware of urges to accelerate growth instead of waiting on the Lord. It enables the director to nurture within him/herself what has been received from the person directed until the appropriate moment to respond.

Just as receptivity enables the director to be fully present, to be as it were, one spirit with the one directed, objectivity makes it possible for the director to step aside from personal impressions, thoughts and feelings to see things in their own reality. The objective director is able to reach out to another's truth without bias or prejudice and is able to focus on the issue without becoming emotionally entangled. If the director is not objective, he or she will concentrate more on how things strike the director's mind rather than on the characteristics and significance of the thing itself in relation to the person being directed. Objectivity could make a director seem cold and aloof unless it is balanced by the warmth of receptivity. The ability to enter into another's experience without losing a sense of perspective is important in a spiritual director. Receptivity and objectivity create a delicate balance which allows the directee to perceive the genuine concern of the director while benefiting from the director's unbiased stance.

Having considered several of the balancing qualities needed in a spiritual director, some conclusions regarding woman vis-a-vis man in this kind of relationship can be offered. The important thing is not whether the director is a woman or a man, but rather the presence in the director of the necessary gifts and training for this ministry. Here I would like to share the reflections of a priest who has benefited from spiritual direction both from a fellow priest and then from a sister within a two-year period of time. He said:

> I actually found very similar qualities in both. They were both sensitive and understanding. Neither felt the need to deliver or rescue me, both let me have my own experience. They had an ability to be there in simple ways. I think at the time it was important to have Father B (a member of my community) as director. The following year it was helpful to have Sister A (someone outside the community) as director and to see my experience affirmed from this perspective. This had a "beyond the boundaries" effect and tended to broaden it. The main difference was the quality — not in the sense that one was better than the other — but that a feminine rather than a masculine coloring was present. To have had an affirming experience with Sister A was helpful — and recall that I had a high esteem for both.

How shall we understand the nature of this "feminine coloring" a woman brings to the spiritual direction relationship? A woman possesses the "anima-animus" qualities of gentleness and strength, intuition and clarity, receptivity and objectivity in her own unique way and a man in his. The "anima" qualities are normally more developed in a woman and these are the kinds of gifts invariably mentioned first in describing someone who is a good director. Women tend to be more gentle than men; our culture expects it of them. Their entire being is geared toward nurturing so they are usually more comfortable in expressing the affection and concern they feel for another person. Men are often inhibited in showing their affectionate feelings. Women are also considered more intuitive than men, although it does seem that men are becoming more aware that they limit their perception when they harness their intuition to the yoke of deductive thinking. What follows is the personal experience of a priest in his middle thirties who is receiving spiritual direction from a sister.

> When I first left the seminary, I went to a priest for spiritual direction. He helped me to see the value of service and to get involved in the apostolate. Recently I started going to a sister. She attracted me as someone whom I sensed could help me in my spiritual journey. She communicates a kind of inner strength which seems to come from rootedness in the Lord. At the same time, there is a gentleness about her that leaves me free to speak about things I've never looked at in myself before. When I had a priest as spiritual director, I found myself wanting to "measure up." We took more of an intellectual approach. The experience of being directed by a woman is putting me in touch with the affective side of myself. This sister challenges me, but in a way that has opened me more to being led by the Spirit. My decisions are not just thought out intellectually, they are discerned in prayer. I experience a greater harmony within as I become more at home with the "being" dimension of myself. My life is beginning to flow more from my center outward.

Sisters also have much to share with one another. Sisters are directing sisters and are bringing to the relationship the richness of their feminine approach to God and to life. A living spirituality more in harmony with their deepest self is usually the fruit of this experience. Having a sister as a director gives the directee a model and inspiration for her own life as a sister.

Women do bring a special gift to the ministry of spiritual direction. However, given the complementarity of the qualities described and the unique way they are present both in women and in men, at certain phases of growth it could be helpful to have a woman as spiritual director and at other times a man. A seminarian could benefit considerably from a woman as a spiritual director as part of his formation. The same is true for a priest at least sometime during his life. Women also can be strengthened and enriched by the complementarity of the masculine gift. A priest or brother who is a good spiritual director inevitably calls forth a woman's femininity as he guides her in her life with the Lord. Novices at least sometime during the novitiate training and older sisters who entered very young could be especially enriched by such an experience.

Part II — Priest Directors: Some New Directions

Priests are increasingly becoming aware of their personal attitudes and biases which are undesirable in a spiritual director. Chauvinism and superiority are unacceptable to women today. In a spiritual direction relationship these attitudes leave sisters with the feeling that they are not being taken seriously as persons. Some priests seem comfortable relating to sisters only in an authoritarian or paternalistic manner. They assume the role of decision making and thus deprive the directee of her rightful responsibility and of opportunities for growth. Unfortunately some sisters have been so scarred by priest directors with these attitudes that they are unwilling to try again even though there are excellent spiritual directors available today among priests.

Sisters themselves have fostered these attitudes in the past by putting priests on a pedestal. Some continue to do so and there are many reasons for this. It may be a manner of expressing reverence for the priesthood; it can also be an unconscious resistance to facing the painfulness of one's own truth. If a sister sees a priest as belonging to the "sacred," she need not accept him as part of the human experience. It is easy then to dismiss certain topics which need to be considered with the rationalization, "you do not talk about such things with a priest." Thus, areas important to human/spiritual growth such as negative feelings, sexuality, etc., will be left untouched. The director will be able to guide a sister toward greater freedom only if he himself has integrated personal identity with priesthood.

Sisters Are Different Today

Spiritual directors today are discovering that sisters of different age groups have different needs and these needs can often be identified with certain periods of life. Many young sisters are struggling with personal identity and are in process of claiming their own values while rejecting some they have taken on from parents or other authority figures. They are also in process of integrating personal identity with that of membership in a particular congregation. The legitimate desire for intimacy and how this can be realized and expressed within the framework of their celibate commitment can be an important issue in their lives. These issues cannot be ignored. Struggles in these areas inevitably affect their life of prayer. They need a lot of encouragement. The director can be encouraging only if he or she understands the significance of their struggle and what it means for human/spiritual growth. Sisters in their early years of religious life need an older person as spiritual director, someone who has already experienced and grown through many of the normal struggles of life. The director must be familiar with the road if he or she is to accompany another along the way. Experience is always important in a director; not only when guiding a person through the early stages of his/her journey with God, but also and most especially at certain crucial moments when the directee is being called to ways of prayer less travelled.

Sisters in their middle years are often exploring new dimensions of apostolic endeavors. This can be a time of anxiety as they learn new skills and begin to serve in untraditional ways. These sisters need encouragement to use fruitfully the years ahead and affirmation to better appreciate life already lived. It is a time for building trust and deepening faith in the Lord's fidelity. Sisters in their middle years come to a moment in life when they are faced with deep questions of meaning. This is frequently a time when the "being" dimension of human existence cries to be heard. This yearning for greater interiority can be interpreted as a call to join a contemplative community, when in fact it is usually an invitation to integrate a more contemplative stance into daily activity. The apostolate then becomes not something a person does for others but something a person *is* for others. A sister's very being becomes apostolic by the totality of her surrender to the Lord. She is being transformed into an apostle by God Himself so that all she does flows from the center of her being where she is united with Him. When a person is thus rooted in God, all that she does is fruitful for the Church.

Older sisters deserve support in the ways of prayer that for so long have been a source of enrichment for them. At the same time they may need help to find freshness in these familiar ways. Sisters no longer able to serve others actively can feel very useless. They need to value their being and to realize the apostolic dimension of prayer and suffering.

Discussing Some Practical Problems

Many expectations are placed upon sisters today in their apostolates. Because of inner and outer pressures, it is often difficult for them to claim time for prayer. Now that the responsibility for personal prayer is rightfully theirs, many sisters are torn and they find it difficult to establish priorities and a balance between apostolic activity and their prayer relationship with the Lord. The apostolic dimension of prayer itself is often outside of their awareness. In a supportive spiritual direction relationship, sisters are able to prioritize their values and make better practical decisions regarding their time. They are also better able to find support in living with the consequences of their decisions. A "yes" to one thing almost always involves "no" to something else.

Finding a suitable place for prayer is another contemporary problem. Apartment living provides little room for privacy. Unless a Church is close by, it is difficult for some sisters living in small apartments to find a place for personal prayer and reflection. This creates tension and needs to be faced with honesty and discernment.

The variety of prayer forms acknowledged today has been liberating for some sisters and binding for others. If one of these forms becomes "the way" of praying, a sister can be closed to growth. For example: a sister with a facility for shared prayer who finds much satisfaction in this way of praying, may find herself gradually needing time just to be quietly present to the Lord. If her prayer group puts pressure on her to share or if she feels guilty thinking this quiet presence to be a waste of time, her anxiety can stifle prayer. Spiritual direction helps a person recognize and value God's unique gift of prayer as it unfolds through the different phases of the inner journey.

Special Importance to Lay Women

The universal call to holiness reaffirmed by Vatican II has not fallen on deaf ears. Lay women, married and single, are discovering what it means to live in Christ Jesus. This discovery has put them more in touch with their own contemplative dimension and they are feeling the need for guidance and help in integrating this dimension with the other facets of their life. They need support in finding a rhythm of prayer compatible with their specific reality as professional women or mothers of families. They often need help in recognizing the guilt feelings which come from the unrealistic expectations they tend to place upon themselves. As spiritual direction brings women more in touch with their own experience, many are surprised and encouraged by the richness of the inner life already developed within them.

Where Do You Find a Woman Director?

Some dioceses in the country today have a Diocesan Center for Spiritual Development. These Centers are often staffed by a team of sisters and priests. Some congregations of sisters have Centers for Spirituality connected with their provincialate or former novitiate buildings. Giving retreats and spiritual direction is the primary apostolate for some congregations such as the Cenacle sisters. Houses of Prayer sponsored by apostolic congregations usually have sisters available as spiritual directors. Contemplative monasteries of nuns are also possible sources for spiritual direction. Good spiritual directors have a way of becoming known without any advertising on their part; people who have benefited by their guidance tend to spread the news.

Some Conclusions

A good spiritual director is one who has the necessary gifts and training and who has been called forth by the confidence of others to this ministry. What usually attracts is a kind of spiritual depth and vitality which is communicated in the very being of the one called forth. He or she is recognized as a person of prayer. A director who does not pray is like a guide accompanying another through territory unfamiliar to both; thus, a director needs experience not only in prayer but also in receiving spiritual direction. The director may be a man or a woman. There are times when it is advantageous for the director to be a man, and times when it is advantageous that the director be a woman. This may seem an obvious and simple conclusion, but in the light of the historical development presented in the beginning of this paper, its significance cannot be overlooked. What would have been theory a few years ago is now a reality. There are many women, mostly sisters, who have been called forth by their own sisters, by priests, and by lay men and women to minister as spiritual directors. This phenomenon is quietly yet persistently changing the traditional concept of the priest as spiritual director. Because the feminine qualities of gentleness, intuition and receptivity are especially important in fostering the directee's life with God, and women more often live out of these gifts, it seems likely that the number of women called to minister in this important dimension of the Church's life will continue to increase. The quality of the Church's spiritual leadership is being enriched by their presence in this field and it offers the hope that women's contribution will find its rightful place in every facet of the Church's life.

[1]Joseph de Guibert, *The Theology of the Spiritual Life,* p. 159. [2]*Op. Cit.,* p. 159-60. [3]Karl Rahner (ed), *Sacramentum Mundi,* Vol. VI, p. 166. [4]Adrian van Kaam, *The Dynamics of Spiritual Self Direction,* p. 390. [5]National Conference of Catholic Bishops, *Spiritual Direction for Priests in the USA: The Rediscovery of a Resource,* 1977, Washington, DC, US Catholic Conf. [6]Sandra Schneiders, "The 'Return' to Spiritual Direction," *Spiritual Life,* Winter 1972, p. 263 ff. [7]I am indebted to Sr. Kieran Flynn, Center for Religious Development, Pawtucket, RI, for this distinction and other helpful observations.

Spiritual Direction for Priests in the USA: The Rediscovery of a Resource

Louis J. Cameli, S.T.D.

Part I — Introduction

Dying to self and rising with the Lord, therefore, takes place in the myriad interactions between the priest and his world, his people, his friends, and the Lord. There is no way for spirituality to be fostered except in appropriate interactional activity in all these areas of priestly existence. The spiritually mature priest is one who is constantly growing according to the different stages of his life through these interactions.

To speak in a practical fashion, however, other persons are the facilitators of all interactional activity, whether on the outer rim of meeting one's culture or the inner circle of contact with the Lord. Other persons give me the stimulus and the power to participate in life; they are the vehicles of God's grace to me.

For this reason we propose that the spiritual renewal of the American priesthood base itself on the principle of interaction. We are suggesting in an appendix some concrete ways in which this interaction is exemplified.

Spiritual Renewal of the American Priesthood,
page 64

One possible interaction not mentioned in the *Spiritual Renewal of the American Priesthood* (SRAP) appendix but indicated throughout the text itself is spiritual direction.

This article appeared in 1977 as a booklet with the same title from the Publications Office of the United States Catholic Conference. It is reprinted here with permission of the USCC. The booklet may be purchased separately from the Publications Office, United States Catholic Conference, 1312 Massachusetts Avenue N.W., Washington, D.C. 20005.

The present paper takes up the invitation of SRAP to explore new possibilities and reacquaint ourselves with traditional resources, as we search for a deeper and more authentic spirituality for American priests. This paper is addressed mainly to bishops and those with them who are charged with the responsibility of helping priests grow in spiritual life. The paper aims to be a resource sheet. If programs and helps are to be offered to priests, decisions must be made. If decisions are to be made wisely, background information is needed. This paper attempts to be helpful by offering some background on one possible area of help.

A Ministerial Spirituality and Spiritual Direction for Priests

Following in the footsteps of Vatican II's *Decree on the Ministry and Life of Priests,* SRAP develops a ministerial spirituality for priests. The key feature of any spirituality is the unity of life in God's Spirit. SRAP sees the unity of the priest's life of prayer and ministerial activity in sharing the Paschal Mystery, the dying and rising of the Lord Jesus. The renewal of priestly spirituality centers on sharpening the unity of priestly ministry and life, and also responds to the urgent needs for developing specific means to help priests personally achieve a unifying spirituality.

The need for means enables us to review elements of our tradition: to see a need for prayer experiences, a need for discernment, and a need for reflection on integrating ministry in prayer life. These needs suggest the process of spiritual direction as a beneficial resource. For spiritual direction draws together a number of dimensions which serve the priest's unity of life. The priest today is also more and more seen as a director and discerner of the spiritual life of his people. The renewal of the sacrament of reconciliation makes this abundantly clear as well as work with charismatic prayer groups and a style of administration which discerns the gifts of the community. Their own experience in the spiritual direction process could enhance priests' ministerial work.

The present paper explores ways in which spiritual direction might contribute to the ministerial spirituality of priests. It does not claim to be a detailed treatise on the spiritual life or on the process of spiritual direction or a full elaboration of a

132

ministerial spirituality. Rather, it introduces spiritual direction as a resource for priests personally and for the expanded effectiveness of their ministry.

The sections which follow take up the general notion of spiritual direction (part two), which is then applied to priests (part three). Finally, observations are made concerning the practical and, specifically, the programmatic planning aspects of spiritual direction for priests (part four).

Part II — Spiritual Direction in General

Introduction

At times the name "spiritual direction" evokes a negative reaction among people who found it unproductive and unhelpful in their seminary or novitiate experience. The very term "direction" seems to imply a binding of the spirit, a narrowing of another's freedom. A better term more reflective of the reality could well replace spiritual direction, but "spiritual direction" is the term in use by custom.

Traditionally, spiritual direction involves a relationship between two people centering on specifically spiritual matters. Today, dimensions of spiritual direction may be found in groups, in counseling, and in theological reflection. The description offered here focuses on the traditional "one-on-one" sense of spiritual direction, while not, of course, excluding or minimizing the value of other forms.

Spiritual Direction in General

When we speak of spiritual direction in general, the talk is liable to become very abstract. Different schools of spirituality and different traditions have left their imprints on the way of "doing" spiritual direction. For our purpose, it may be best to note a set of contrasts which highlight what is new or newly emphasized in spiritual direction today. Even this approach will be somewhat abstract, but it will be supplemented by a specific study of spiritual direction for priests.

Contrasts between old and new do not mean opposition nor mutual exclusion. The issue is rather one of nuance, of shading, and of emphasis. So, for example, the purpose of spiritual direction as it might have been considered a few years ago was to provide a refueling for the individual, a time for seeking support for the application of self to the tasks of life. The task of spiritual direction today emerges more clearly in the word "integration." More than refueling for work, spiritual direction provides the avenue of seeing some *unity* between what happens in one's inner life of prayer and conviction and the pattern of one's outer activities. Thus, two fundamental areas for discussion in spiritual direction are prayer and its extension into action, mortification as identification with the Lord and its extension into an asceticism of practice, work, and involvement.

The process of spiritual direction in the past accented a didactic approach, perhaps even some sort of preset program or agenda. Today, while the element of teaching ought not to be entirely absent from spiritual direction, spiritual directors feel more comfortable with a tone of mutuality. Both director and directee are open to hearing the word of the Lord in the life of this individual. Parenthetically, this renewed appreciation of mutuality underlines the weakness of terms such as "direction," "director," etc. Beyond a tone of mutuality, spiritual dialogue today allows the agenda to set itself, that is, the material for discussion comes not from a preset program, but from the ways that the Lord seems to be working in this person's life and at this time and in these ways. Thus the tone of spiritual direction today highlights mutuality and existential concerns.

Spiritual direction in the past has focused on problems and accountability. A spiritual director helped directees to solve problems of prayer, vocation, and community relationships. The director also provided an index of accountability especially with regard to pious exercises. Today, spiritual direction does not abandon problem solving nor accountability but accentuates more sharply the positive growth elements of spiritual life.

What can spiritual direction offer? It can offer a relationship centered on a dialogue about prayer and life. It can offer an opportunity for growth in the spiritual life by freeing the person to love and to serve more generously, more consistently, more integrally. Spiritual direction — in perhaps elevated but real terms — means movement into the mystery of the Lord who calls us.

Part III — Spiritual Direction for Priests

An Example of the Process

The idea of spiritual direction presented above represents a rather general and abstract process. To specify things, we can examine the concrete spiritual direction process of a priest. The example which follows is exactly that — an example. Many approaches are possible. A single illustration, however, can help us to understand the dynamics more clearly.

When Fr. X approaches Fr. Y for spiritual direction, it is very much a meeting of two Christians sharing the same search to discover the way of the Lord. The first natural and right thing is simply to get to know each other. The directee with help from the director begins to give a sketch of his life, including family circumstances, education, interests, etc. The personal history of the directee then shifts to the more specifically spiritual dimension. Together the director and directee attempt to see how the directee's relationship to the Lord has grown by tracing his developing image of God, an image which is reflected in the type and quality of prayer at different stages of his life. They will also trace — as best as they can — other significant religious developments, for example, growth of moral conscience, stages of vocational decision, devotional practices, influential reading, etc. However much time Frs. X and Y spend on this history, it is time well spent, because it will provide a common understanding of past experience which will set a context for their future dialogue.

In the next phase Frs. X and Y touch on a subtle and important moment of the spiritual direction process. Together they try to determine what Fr. X wants, what is the desire, what is the intent that draws him to spiritual direction. This clarification of intent has obvious importance for facilitating the spiritual direction dialogue by clarifying expectations. More importantly, Frs. X and Y try earnestly to search out the desire and intent, because this dynamism is a way in which the Lord draws us to Himself. The attraction or drawing which we experience will take different shapes — as the multiple experiences of the saints attest. Frs. X and Y surely do not comprehend the entirety of the Lord's design at this time. Some basic indications lay a foundation to which they will periodically return.

The discovery of intent and desire helps Frs. X and Y to see the "direction" which the Lord is giving. At the same time, when Fr. X accepts this direction, he commits himself to growth or moving toward the fulfillment of that desire and intentionality implanted in him by the Lord. The commitment to growth or movement forward immediately raises questions concerning certain obstacles and resistances to growth. It may be at this point that Fr. Y the director who also has some psychological counseling skills, sees certain emotional or relational issues which must be resolved, so that the pursuit of a deeper spirituality can take place. In that case, appropriate help is given either within their relationship but now on a slightly different level or with the assistance of an outside psychological consultant.

Dealing with history, intent, and resistances sets the context for what becomes the basic ongoing pattern of Frs. X and Y's spiritual direction process. That pattern has two movements which Frs. X and Y will choose as they judge best: (a) from self to the Gospel; (b) from the Gospel to self.

(a) In the "a" movement (from self to the Gospel), Fr. X speaks of the events, experiences, and relationships in his life both in a ministerial and non-ministerial context. He speaks of his prayer both personal and liturgical. He notes the experiential resonance of that prayer — what it generates, whether it leads to peace, challenge, questioning, joy, pain and purification, etc. Frs. X and Y join in a shared process of discernment, trying to note the patterns, the lines of action and direction. Referring to the Gospel and Fr. X's history, they attempt to clarify and interpret what is happening.

(b) In the "b" movement (from the Gospel to self), Frs. X and Y read Scripture together and pray together. They engage in an intense listening process, trying to hear the challenge of the Gospel, letting its message inform their ministry and life.

These are two movements which do not go in opposite directions. In the course of a spiritual direction meeting, Frs. X and Y may use both.

Frs. X and Y meet on a regular basis. They maintain a flexibility in the format of their dialogue. The regularity insures that their meetings are not simply problem-centered or scheduled when Fr. X feels "down" and needs a lift.

In brief, the relationship between Fr. X and Fr. Y is a fraternal one — two pilgrim brothers walking together, discerning the very way they are to walk.

Analysis of the Process

The example cited above provides one picture of the spiritual direction process for priests. It may be helpful to summarize some essential "events" which take place in that process and contribute to the priest's spirituality.

1. In spiritual direction the priest articulates his inner and outer experience. He puts into words what he sees, feels, perceives to be happening in his life and in his ministry.

2. In a conversation which poses questions and seeks clarification, the priest comes to a clearer vision of himself and how God is at work in his life, among his people, and through his priestly ministry.

3. The perception and the vision of the Lord at work leads to a clarification, a sorting out, a setting of priorities and directions. At times, there may be no clarification but simply an experience of being drawn more deeply into infinite mystery. The appropriate response at that time is silence.

4. When the Lord's "lines of action" emerge in a clarification and a vision of the situation, an enabling freedom allows the priest to act more effectively and responsively to the issues of personal life and public ministry. The immobilizing complexity that seems to afflict so many priests breaks down into manageable possibilities for the future.

5. In the atmosphere of freedom, vision and clarification, some of the needed elements of a priest's life emerge: encouragement, affirmation, demands, and challenge.

6. The spiritual direction process seeks throughout the unifying and integrating dimensions of the priest's ministry and life in his relationship with the Lord. As a result the sensed closeness and presence of the Lord and sharing in the Paschal Mystery ought to grow.

Benefits of Spiritual Direction for Priests

Some of the benefits of spiritual direction for priests are self-evident in the example and the analysis given above. Here we focus on five benefits, two of which enhance the ministry of the priest to others and three which primarily affect the priest in a personal way. The purpose of listing benefits matches the scope of this paper, that is, to provide bishops and others with background for making practical decisions concerning programs for priests.

1. *An increased communication capacity.* To understand the first benefit, recall that the process of spiritual direction involves a personal articulation of the priest's faith experience. This will have its effect in the priest's heightened capacity to speak warmly and personally about faith in the public forum. In one sense, he has undergone spiritual direction as an exercise which will enable him to speak the word of God *to the hearts* of men and women. This capacity stands in contrast to the rather shy approach which is maintained in talking to people about faith, a shyness which often retreats into cold theory or theology or psychology. The need for this sort of warm and personal discourse on faith is evident in the appeal of the charismatic renewal for many people, which has become perhaps our only wide-ranging forum for speaking about personal faith with some feeling.

2. *Development of skills in spiritual direction.* A priest's involvement in spiritual direction yields not only self-understanding but an understanding of the process itself and its dynamics. Having experienced spiritual direction as a directee, he can transfer many of the same values and dynamics into his own role as director in the sacrament of reconciliation, pastoral counseling, etc.

The benefits of an increased communication capacity and development of skills in spiritual direction touch mainly on the ministry of the priest. The following have to do more with the personal enrichment and development of the priest.

3. *A better self-awareness for growth.* Through spiritual direction a priest can come to real appreciation of *growth* in his life. He can picture himself more clearly as a pilgrim in a pilgrim Church. The effect of such self-awareness is a lessening of the explosive and destructive guilt which is a present occupational hazard for priests. We reason to ourselves: "I am not perfect. Therefore, I am bad." To recognize honestly and humbly that we must grow spiritually takes the edge off of any practical angelism that may plague us.

4. *Sense of self-worth.* As an extension of the self-awareness spoken of above, spiritual direction leads to a healthy reappraisal of the particular self-worth of the priest. This is not simply the same as healthy psychological self-esteem. Rather, we are dealing here with a deep recognition that in God's plan I as a priest have a particular role, a special vocation, indeed, a unique destiny and design that belongs to

me alone.

5. *Meeting the developmental needs of priests*. Spiritual direction should not simply be problem-centered; nonetheless, there are some critical moments or phases in the life of a priest when spiritual direction can be helpful. Below are cited four critical points in the life of a priest as presented by Msgr. Giovanni Colombo ("La direzione spirituale del clero diocesano," in *Problemi attuali della direzione spirituale,* Rome, 1951, pp. 197-234). These critical points serve as an example of problem issues which could be met very well in an ongoing spiritual direction process.

a. Newly ordained: this is the critical time of transit from seminary to full priestly ministry. Perhaps the emphasis in the USA on the diaconate as the time of ministerial initiation has made us less aware of the post-ordination period as a critical moment. We presume that the rough edges have been honed away. In fact, they have not.

b. Early 30's: the priest who has made the adjustment from seminary to priestly ministry enjoys a true and deep optimism concerning the possibilities for his ministry in the early years. This optimism can quickly vanish as a number of disappointments appear on the scene, as his own personal limitations and the limitations of structures become apparent. Thus, there is a radical shift from optimism to pessimism. There is a need to make a transit from optimism through pessimism to realism.

c. Mid 40's: this, too, is a critical period. A number of basic questions arise concerning meaning in and of one's life. For the priest, the question of celibacy is especially urgent at this time — not so much the felt need for intimacy as the need to generate, to experience paternity.

d. Late 50's and above: the aging person can move in two directions, and the priest is not exempt from these possibilities. The aging person can grow in wisdom with an accompanying serenity that is born from a life-long experience that knows enough to recognize the relative and to fix one's eyes on what is truly absolute and important. The aging person, on the other hand, can become more and more isolated with an accompanying kind of paranoia and distorted perception of reality. It is when a priest accepts this second possibility that devastating effects occur. It is sad for the aging person, but it also has a demoralizing effect on the younger clergy and the Church community at large. To experience an unwise, unhappy, or jealous priest who looks suspiciously on life and, implicitly, on God and the Church is tragic.

These are some critical developmental periods in the life of the priest. Each phase which involves intensely personal issues can be facilitated through a process of spiritual direction.

Part IV — Practical Aspects

Introduction

These reflections tell us that spiritual direction is indeed a valuable resource, one which can be worth the effort of development and promotion. A set of reflections such as these can remind us of the usefulness and possibilities of a traditional resource. Yet, at the same time, there are so many possibilities and so many voices calling for attention that an economy of energy investment must prevail, and a selection must be made.

Spiritual direction ought to be counted among a number of resources that are possible for priests. Its peculiar value is in the individual attention that is given to the priest and the possibilities of posing and raising questions that might never be raised in another forum, such as group discussion or even psychological counseling.

The value of spiritual direction for priests implies that those responsible for the ministry and life of priests ought to give consideration to making this asset available to priests. This involves planning and programs. Immediately, a whole set of practical questions arise. These must be addressed, even if a general lack of experience in the area of wide-scale spiritual direction for priests permits us only to formulate tentative responses.

There have been a few diocesan-wide programs making spiritual direction available to priests. Some basic practical information emerges from those experiences. Significantly, priests react with initial indifference to spiritual direction. They do not perceive its value nor its usefulness. Once a few begin to take advantage of this resource, however, spiritual direction usually finds wide acceptance. Practically, this means that a bishop ought not to wait for a request from the priests of the diocese for spiritual direction. Once it is offered, it will attract many priests.

The Selection and Formation
of Spiritual Directors for Priests

A truly perplexing question concerns the selection and formation of appropriate directors. Who are the people who can capably exercise the ministry of spiritual direction for priests? Before noting the specific qualities of a spiritual director for priests, four general observations are in order.

(1) A process of natural selection takes place even now in those instances when a priest seeks counsel or direction. Those people who are helpful and give evidence of a genuine spiritual life draw others to themselves. Some people are naturally and supernaturally gifted for spiritual direction. This becomes evident, even if at times the gift must be encouraged and perhaps publicized.

(2) At times it may be appropriate and helpful that a person other than a priest be a director for a priest. That person, however, ought to be very much aware of the ministerial dimensions of the priest's life which give shape to the way his spirituality grows (cf. SRAP). The situation comes to mind of St. Teresa of Avila who counseled priests and did so in light of her own extraordinary experience of inner life and outer apostolic activity.

(3) The traditional wisdom of allowing for two forums, one internal and the other external, best translates into the spiritual direction situation for priests by not associating the spiritual direction with the administration of the diocese. The issue here is not simply confidentiality, which is presumed, but a freedom from institutional agendas, which may prejudice the spiritual direction process.

(4) The formation and qualification of a spiritual director need more study and elaboration than is possible here. We are, quite frankly, working with an incomplete theoretical and systematic framework which would describe the exact function of a spiritual director today. It is unwise, however, in the face of that lack to fall prey to a tendency that wants to "mystify" the work of the spiritual director, or to limit the possibility of such work to a very few extraordinary persons. The priest-spiritual director, who has a number of years of theological and personal formation in his background, is fulfilling a part of his ordinary ministry of caring and facilitating growth in faith for others but in a special way and in a special forum.

With these observations noted, three sets of qualities suggest themselves as essential to the task of spiritual direction: (1) the personal spiritual experience of the spiritual director; (2) a capacity to listen well; (3) knowledge.

(1) *Spiritual experience.* The spiritual director ought to be a person in touch with the Lord, a person with deep spiritual experience which has been gratefully received, carefully reflected upon, and manifested in a practical wisdom. It is good to remember that great spiritual people of our tradition were deeply rooted in the real world. Spiritual experience and common sense blend in these people to form persons who are not only close to the Lord but who also can draw others to Him.

(2) *Capacity to listen well.* The spiritual director ought to have the capacity to listen in a non-projective way. The Spirit like the wind blows where it will. Consequently, it is important that the directee be allowed and encouraged to grow in the unique way that is fashioned for him by the Spirit. That requires attentive listening.

(3) *Knowledge.* The knowledge of the spiritual director ought to be primarily a practical wisdom. Specific understanding will also prove necessary at times, especially in the areas of theology-spirituality, ministry, and psychology. The spiritual director's theological-spiritual knowledge ought to include some appreciation of the Christian experience in Scripture and in the history of the Church. A certain "economy" of knowledge is important here. It is, for example, important that a spiritual director for priests be well versed in a contemporary and authentic theology of priesthood and ministry, a theology which is in dialogue with the richness of the Catholic spiritual tradition. Furthermore, the spiritual director ought to have some practical understanding of priestly ministry and the many forms that it takes. If the spiritual director is to accompany the priest in his search to integrate and to fructify his ministerial experience with his personal inner experience of the Lord, then it becomes clear that the spiritual director cannot be unfamiliar with the meaning of priestly ministry and its many practical implications. Finally, the spiritual director of priests should be in possession of some psychological knowledge. The spiritual director is not a psychologist. An awareness of common patterns of emotional life, of development and behavior, however, can sensitize the spiritual director to discern the difference between a movement of the Spirit

142

and a movement of the spirit. The relationships between psychology and spirituality — convergence, difference, complementarity, etc. — are yet to be explored in a satisfactory systematic fashion. The exact background in psychology needed for effective spiritual direction forms part of the question that must be researched.

Questions of Programmatic Planning

Finally, the last practical question: how can a bishop begin or initiate a process of spiritual direction for his priests? How can he and those with him who are responsible for helping priests of a diocese offer this resource?

Several avenues of approach are possible. The two major possibilities are: (1) to call in resources from outside the diocese; or (2) develop resources within the diocese.

Drawing on resources from without the diocese may mean engaging the time and talents of religious priests — a team, for example — to initiate the tradition of offering spiritual direction to priests of the diocese. Gradually, over the course of time the work of the religious can be supplemented with priests from the diocese.

Development of resources from within the diocese is, of course, more difficult but certainly possible. Priests who have the esteem of their colleagues and who witness to lives of fruitful and holy service might be asked to serve their fellow priests. Some form of preparation seems advisable. In the future, institutes specifically designed to prepare spiritual directors of priests may be established regionally throughout the country by bishops — perhaps at a few major seminaries with facilities and faculties available for such a course.

A number of institutes of spirituality and spiritual formation already exist in the United States. If a bishop seeks information on the training programs of these institutes, he may contact the office of the National Organization for Continuing Education of Roman Catholic Clergy (NOCERCC).[1]

Conclusion

A bishop faced with many needs in his diocese may find it difficult to respond to a central task which belongs to him — to provide for the spiritual care of his priestly co-workers. It is especially important that he reflect on ways of *providing resources* for his priests. In this way, he exercises his "ministry to the ministers." The present paper on spiritual direction for priests has offered some reflections on a potentially fertile agent for helping priests grow in spiritual life and in their capacity to be spiritual leaders. In this context, spiritual direction for priests partakes of the *nova et vetera*. It is a tried and proven means of growth in life in the Spirit. It is also new as a resource offered on a wide scale. Thus, this paper which is the result of a number of committee discussions is entitled "The Spiritual Direction of Priests: The Rediscovery of a Resource." It has been offered with the hope of providing a stimulus for reflection and action.

[1]NOCERCC, 5401 South Cornell Avenue, Chicago, IL 60615, (312) 752-8849.

Direction in the Various Stages of Spiritual Development

Rose Page, O.C.D.

The quality of being a long-term, often a lifelong relationship distinguishes spiritual direction from other forms of counseling or guidance. Spiritual direction can continue through times of joy and sorrow, confusion and light, fullness and emptiness. But this distinctive quality of spiritual direction pertains less to its continuity than to the very nature and goal of this unique helping relationship.

The counselor is concerned with problem resolving and once the client has resolved his problem through acceptance, altered behavior or an altered self-image, the counseling relationship is terminated. The spiritual director deals with a more extensive goal and a far broader agenda. Jesus established the goal when He prayed: "As thou Father art in me and I in Thee, so also may they be in us . . . that they may be as we are, one."

Therefore all the dimensions of human personhood and all aspects of life must be integrated with God's life within until there is "total and permanent union according to the substance of the soul and its faculties" (John of the Cross). This is of course a lifelong task and so also the role of the director.

To maintain that spiritual direction is by nature a long-term relationship implies that the director will be guiding the directee through various stages of growth. Each stage has its own particular problems, challenges and tasks. Advice and direction that is suitable to one stage may not be so for others, may even be harmful as John of the Cross maintains in *The Living Flame*. So it

This article first appeared in *Contemplative Review*, 12, Fall 1979, pp. 11-18. Reprinted by permission.

would seem that in order to be truly helpful as a director it is necessary, not only to understand the basic process of direction, but also to be able to apply it to the various stages of spiritual development.

The Stages of Spiritual Development

To divide the spiritual life into a number of stages can seem arbitrary. However, if we consider the spiritual life as the gradual conversion of the whole human personality, we then have the basis for our division. Each stage represents the struggle of a specific human power or faculty for conversion, for union with God. Beginning with the more external consciousness and continuing to each successive stage of depth until the total person has been absorbed and integrated into the life of the Spirit at the deepest center of the soul, the process is one of ever deepening cycles of self-awareness, surrender and union. Such a division no longer seems arbitrary. It provides the director with guidelines for evaluating the development of the directee's spiritual life and for helping directees understand their experience. It also provides insight as to what efforts and ascesis are needed to face the particular challenge of each stage.

I would divide the spiritual life into eight stages: Awareness, Assimilation, Commitment, Conscious Integration, Fidelity, Absorption, Penetration and Transformation or Final Integration.

AWARENESS: The first stage is marked by the newly awakened personal awareness of spiritual reality. It is more than an intellectual acceptance of truth. It seems to encompass more of the person and is usually accompanied by emotions of joy and consolation or fear and dread. This awareness has its source in experience. The experience might come from an encounter with a religious person or book. It might be a numinous experience of nature or of a religious ceremony. What is important is that it makes the truth of spiritual reality hit home. Probably for the first time in their life, persons in this stage are faced with the option of taking religion seriously.

ASSIMILATION: This is a time of touching and verbalizing the meaning of religious experiences. What is it saying to me about God, about myself, about life? The "facts" of the experience are reflected on and their implications regarding the personal past, present and future are sorted out. (Will the seed fall on rock or on fertile soil?) It is a time when reflection comes naturally either through a system of meditation or more likely in our culture, through reading and study. Prayer is likely to have many emotional overtones and sometimes much effort is made to recreate the conversion experience.

COMMITMENT: Faith is more than an assent to ideas. It is a commitment to an attitude, a stance about life. As St. Paul says, "Put on the mind of Christ." Accepting faith is always a leap into the indefinite, the infinite realm of meaning. Commitment is the decision to take that leap. For many, this stage is a time of vacillation and anxiety. For some this stems from a need for intellectual certainty, for others, from a kind of faintheartedness in facing the implications of conversion or from a keen awareness that they will never again belong to themselves but to the Other.

CONSCIOUS INTEGRATION: "What good is it to profess faith without practicing it? Faith that does nothing in practice is thoroughly lifeless" (James 2:12). The challenge in this stage is to adjust one's way of life to one's commitment. This involves efforts at the elimination of sinful or unchristian behavior and the adoption of religious practices which will fortify the life of faith and the relationship with God. It is a time when the need for discerning the will of God in one's life is strongest. What does God want of me? What does He want me to do with my life?

FIDELITY: When we first turn to God we experience emotional satisfaction in our religious practices. We are carried along by our fervor and it takes little effort to pray, to meditate, to be good. But in time this emotional fervor dries up. Prayer, meditation, attentive participation at liturgy takes so much effort. Also the nastier side of our character, which we thought had been conquered, seems to reemerge. It is a time of desireless desire, of dry will, of naked fidelity.

ABSORPTION: "Be still and know that I am God." The development of the will which is the work of fidelity breaks our dependence on our emotions and sensibilities in relating to God. It releases the deeper positive aspects of the unconscious to participate in our spiritual life. This results in greater creativity and less self-centeredness. In our prayer, it opens the way to the beginning and development of contemplative prayer, the intuitive loving knowledge of God. This stage is marked by a growing capacity for absorption in prayer. There is greater sensitivity to God's subtle action within the deeper reaches of our being.

PENETRATION: This period is traditionally called the Dark Night of the Soul. Absorption of the psyche in contemplative prayer at times leaves the more conscious part of the psyche in a kind of limbo of inactivity. Naturally, persons experience anxiety when they realize that their memory, intellect, will and sense perceptions are not functioning properly. The problem is compounded by the fact that contemplative prayer has reached such depth that it is often imperceptible. The person seems caught in darkness, emptiness and void.

Also, as the positive unconscious power is activated through contemplative prayer, the negative aspects of the unconscious are also activated and at times with great force. The id and superego (in the form of temptations to excessive pleasure and comfort, to lust on the one hand or scrupulousness, guilt and depression on the other) can have a field day since the ego (rational powers) has seemingly lost its control of the unconscious forces. All the human unconscious desires that motivate us in our religious life have been exposed and found wanting. The contemplative experience of God has taught the soul that He will not, cannot, satisfy these self-centered desires. We have reached the limits of human motivation and exhausted the human capacities for believing, hoping and loving. This darkness alternates with the light of infused faith, hope and charity. It is through these alternating periods of light and darkness that transformation is gradually brought about.

TRANSFORMATION: "I live now, not I, but Christ lives in me." In transformation persons know themselves to believe, hope and love, not through their own power but through the deeper power of the Spirit within. There is a continual awareness of the presence and action of the Trinity, of oneness with God. They have discovered their own soul and they are now aware of the deepest contemplative activity that was previously hidden in darkness. Also through a gradual acclimatization, contemplative activity can now go on without causing reverberations throughout the psyche (ecstasy) or blindness and absorption of the conscious faculties. Rather than being left aside for prayer, the rational and sensible faculties can now participate and cooperate with the soul in its love and knowledge of God, in its prayer. This effects the integration of the whole person in God and in itself.

The Process of Spiritual Direction

The first four stages deal with the conversion of the conscious powers. Through the religious experience, the emotions and feelings are turned toward God. The powers of reflection and imagination follow suit in assimilation as do the intellect and will in commitment and integration. Since it is impossible to use one of these faculties without the others being involved at least to some degree, it would seem inaccurate to assign separate stages for them. But this is valid in that there is more emphasis on one or another during these different stages of development.

These four stages also present us with a model for the process of spiritual direction:

1) enable the directees to verbalize, recount and identify their experience,

2) help them explore the "feelings" and "meanings" of the experience,

3) provide the strength and support which enables them to make the commitment to which their inner meaning is calling them,

4) help them to develop alternatives for concrete faith action, to choose among the alternatives and then to evaluate their performance and results.

Different aspects of this process will be emphasized according to the stage of development and the needs of the directee. It would be wrong to push for specific choices or even commitment when persons are overwhelmed with experiences or on the other hand to demand detailed accounts of conversion experiences when directees are faced with having to make concrete choices. But the process is integral to each stage. The experiences, challenges and choices are different at each stage but there is always experience, challenge and choice to be dealt with.

Should the spiritual director be "non-directive"? In the counseling process the non-directive approach might be the most effective and the director should have no qualms about using non-directive techniques for exploring experiences, feelings and meanings. And certainly, the non-directive approach insures our not pushing persons into premature commitments and choices. But beyond the counseling role, the director should be prepared to offer instruction in prayer, meditation, ascesis and to recommend background reading in Scripture, theology and spirituality. With self-awareness and a good measure of respect and empathy for the directee, the director can integrate this dual role of counselor and instructor.

Direction Beyond the Conscious Stages

Direction is essentially a conscious process. But as in psychotherapy, conscious process can be used to explore the subconscious, unconscious and superconscious, or to put it more simply, to broaden the area of self-awareness. The basic process of direction developed above is therefore appropriate to the stages of fidelity and beyond.

In *fidelity* the experience of repeated failure and inadequacy needs to be shared and accepted. The fear of having lost touch with God must be explored. But what is most important, the person needs help in understanding the meaning of all this, that it is actually a call to a deeper relationship with God and reassurance that all is not over, that God does not break the bruised reed and that He is a God of mercy and compassion. Reassurance comes, not from hammering home these truths to the directees but from helping them to discover the truth or Truth within themselves. Instruction in quieter forms of prayer will often be more effective than rationales about the happy state of a soul in darkness. The directee will need the strength and support of the director to accept this path of dry fidelity and to persevere on it.

In the stage of *absorption* we can expect little from a catharsis of feeling. First of all, through the development of the deeper will in the stage of fidelity, overidentification of the self with emotional feelings has been broken. Rather than enabling them to verbalize their emotions and depending on the degree of absorption of the faculties, persons have to be at times reminded that their emotions are still operating as they tend now to be unaware of them. This is done not to again center them on their emotions but to keep the emotions at a conscious level rather than allowing them to escape into the unconscious as repressions. This would be unhealthy and create even more difficulties during the Dark Night of the Soul. Also reminding them of their emotions helps them to preserve a certain sense of healthy humanness (humility) and reality. In cases of intense absorption, the director may also have to be something of the guardian of the physical health of the directees, reminding them to eat properly, get enough sleep, etc.

The director should create an accepting atmosphere within which persons can share their contemplative experiences. Meaning should center on the simple awareness of the knowledge and love of God, not in an analysis of the distinct elements, forms, figures or ideas. Analysis at this stage leads to a centering on the peripheral and the self rather than on God. For this same reason, journal keeping is usually not advisable for persons who are habitually in the contemplative state. The whole thrust should be on the simple awareness of the Other, not the self. Decision making is also different now. Rather than developing alternatives for concrete action taking, we should now be trying to discover ways of cooperating as fully as possible with the action of the Spirit within and of eliminating whatever interferes with that action.

In *penetration,* the difficulties are twofold, the emergence of the negative unconscious material and the experience of the dark void. The process for dealing with each is somewhat different.

The directee should be encouraged to speak about obsessions, anxieties, fantasies, all the content surfacing from the negative unconscious. In so doing the infinite character of unconscious material becomes limited, defined. Here catharsis of feeling is important, though difficult. At this time the director should not be afraid to take on a strong directive role. Directees now need to "borrow" the ego strength of the director. This enables them to use their own rational powers (their ego strength) to analyze and cope with their situation. These powers which were converted and strengthened in the earlier stages of the spiritual life now can become a strong ally in controlling these unconscious forces.

Rather than allowing directees to languish in self-pity, self-hate or anxiety, the director should help them to develop specific will exercises for controlling their seemingly wild thoughts, emotions and sensations. However, in evaluating the results, the director should keep in mind that what is important is the effort not the success or failure. It is in persevering effort that we find the reassurance that the personality is not disintegrating. The director should not be afraid to suggest the use of distractions and recreation, that is, any physical or psychological help that will counteract and/or dissipate the force of the negative unconscious.

"Who can see God and survive?" In dealing with the painful void we must keep in mind that this is a form of contemplation. It is often experienced as an unspecified agony. The person is at a loss to know if the pain is physical, psychological or spiritual. Efforts to analyze will only increase the agony and create more confusion. Rather than analyzing the pain to discover the heart of the problem, they should be encouraged to enter into the experience, thereby searching out the very subtle presence of God that is contained in the experience. The greater the crisis, the closer they are to the underlying intuition that "one is all right in God." The crisis is being caused by the intensity of the contemplative light in the depth of the soul. When they are unable to cope any longer they should be encouraged to distract themselves, not to run away, for they would be running away from God, but to gain strength to endure.

In the beginning stage of *transformation* the directees might need reassurance that the use of the faculties, especially the memory, intellect and will, no longer interferes with the action of God but that now these faculties cooperate with that action. Their own experience, though, would in time provide this assurance. They may need some help in integrating their reawakened faculties into their spiritual life, in adjusting to the lack of drama and emotional fervor and in choosing suitable apostolic endeavors for their spiritual energies. But in time the Guide within suffices. For the most part, a spiritual director is no longer needed. As St. Teresa says in her final spiritual testimony, "I no longer have any need to seek out learned men or tell anyone anything." What is appreciated now is a spiritual friend, who, recognizing the great work that has been done in the soul, praises God for it.

Contemplation According to Teresa and John of the Cross

Antonio Moreno, O.P.

St. John of the Cross, in *The Living Flame of Love,* discusses at length a problem of spiritual significance today, for there are now many who are interested in contemplation. Many spiritual masters, he says, do much harm to souls because of their ignorance regarding the nature and properties of contemplation.

> Although this damage is beyond anything imaginable, it is so common and frequent that scarcely any spiritual director will be found who does not cause it in souls God is beginning to recollect in this manner of contemplation.[1]

The damage done is great because

> the affairs of God must be handled with great tact and with open eyes, especially in so vital and sublime a matter as is that of these souls, where there is at stake almost an infinite gain in being right and almost an infinite loss in being wrong.[2]

Perhaps these directors err with good will, because they do not know any better. Not for this reason, however, should they be excused for the counsels they rashly give, without first understanding the road and spirit a person may be following.[3]

What these directors do not understand and have the obligation to know is the way of the spirit. Consequently, they cause the souls, as often happens, to "lose the unction of these delicate ointments, with which the Holy Spirit anoints and prepares them for himself."[4] These masters do a great injury to God by intruding with a rough hand where he is working, for "it cost God a great deal to bring these souls to this stage."[5] St. Teresa, too,

This article first appeared in *Review for Religious,* 37, March 1978, pp. 256-67. Reprinted by permission.

in her *Interior Castle,* says that the shortcomings of half-learned men cost her very dear, and she advises that one consult learned persons, "for even if they have not themselves experienced these things, men of great learning have a certain instinct to prompt them, as God uses them to give light to His Church."[6]

The saints' complaints concern primarily the ways of contemplative prayer in general and the differences between meditation and contemplation in particular:

> They are not aware that those acts they say the soul should make, and the discursive reflection they want it to practice, are already accomplished, since the soul has already reached the negation and silence of the senses and of meditation and has come to the way of the spirit, which is contemplation.[7]

The worst damage a master can do is to insist on the practice of meditation, which is good for beginners but not for those souls already introduced by God into the state of contemplation. Meditation leads to contemplation. The spiritual growth of the soul follows a process of maturation that is characterized by steps that it has to go through in order to reach the high state of divine union.

St. John of the Cross emphasizes the connection between grace and nature. Grace does not destroy nature nor does Christian life destroy men; rather, it elevates them. Hence, although the degree of perfection of the Christian soul depends primarily on its growth in grace, it also depends on its human nature. There is always a psychological transformation underlying the growth of sanctifying grace which affects deeply the cognitive and the appetitive powers of man. This is the reason why the Spanish mystic says that God works on the soul

> with order, gently, and according to the mode of the soul. Since the order followed in the process of knowing involves the forms and images of created things, and since knowledge is acquired through the senses, God to achieve His work gently and to lift the soul to supreme knowledge, must begin by touching the low state and extreme of the senses. And from there He must gradually bring the soul after its own manner to the other end, spiritual wisdom, which is incomprehensible to the senses.[8]

This principle is crucial to understand the action of God in the soul. God respects the nature of man; He acts on man in conformity with the nature He Himself has created. And since the intellect depends upon the apprehension of the senses, which is always material, the object of the intellect is also in a sense material, namely, the nature of material beings. This knowledge based on material beings renders difficult our knowledge of God, for as God is spirit, He cannot be known directly by the intellect, but only through analogy. Hence the natural and spiritual growth of man evolves from the material to the spiritual, from the senses to the intellect, and from the passions to the will.[9]

Thus God, following the natural growth of the soul, brings a person to the supreme spirit of love by first instructing him through forms, images, and sensible means according to the individual's own manner of acquiring knowledge. The practice of beginners is to "meditate," to make acts of discursive reflection with the help of the imagination. This step is well-known to spiritual directors, but they do not know the second step, namely, contemplation; here the action of God in the soul is very delicate and mysterious.

> When the appetite has been fed somewhat, and has become in a certain fashion accustomed to spiritual things, and has acquired some fortitude and constancy, God begins to wean the soul, as they say, and place it in the state of contemplation. This happens when the soul's discursive acts and meditation cease, as well as its initial sensible satisfaction and fervor. The sensory part is left in dryness because its riches are transferred to the spirit, which does not pertain to the senses.[10]

God often anoints a contemplative soul with some delicate unguent of loving and peaceful knowledge, far withdrawn from the senses and imagination. As a result, the spiritual person cannot meditate nor reflect on anything earthly. But this is exactly what the spiritual master does not know, as John laments:

> Then a spiritual director will happen along who, like a blacksmith, knows no more than how to hammer and pound with the faculties. Since hammering with the faculties is this director's only teaching, and he knows no more than how to meditate, he will say: "Come, now, lay aside these rest periods, which amount to idleness and a waste of time; take and meditate and make interior acts, for it is necessary that you do your part; this other method is the way of illusions and typical of fools.' "[11]

The damage done to the soul is immense, for it blocks the action of God in the soul, and, according to the Spanish mystic, these directors shall not go unpunished corresponding to the harm they caused:

> God becomes extremely indignant with such directors and in Ezekiel promises them chastisement: "You ate the milk of my flock and you covered yourself with their wool and did not feed my flock; I will, he says, seek my flock at your hand" (Ezekiel 34:3, 10).[12]

When Meditation Should Be Abandoned

The practice of meditation should not be abandoned sooner, nor later, than is required by the Spirit. "Just as it is fit to abandon [meditation] at the proper time that it may not be a hindrance in the journey to God, it is also necessary not to abandon this imaginative meditation before the due time so that there be no regression."[13] Thus, to help the director, St. John delineates some signs which the person must observe within himself.

In the *Ascent,* the first sign is the realization that one can no longer make discursive meditation nor receive satisfaction from it as before.[14] In the *Dark Night,* this sign is third. "The third sign for the discernment of this purgation of the senses is the powerlessness, in spite of one's efforts, to meditate and make use of the imagination, the interior sense, as was one's previous custom."[15] The reason for the impossibility of meditation is that the person has already been granted all the spiritual goods which it is possible to obtain by way of meditation. Hence the lack of benefit derived by the spirit from this exercise.[16]

This explanation, which is rather a negative one, is complemented in the *Dark Night* by a positive reason which suggests the different cognitive process that is proper to contemplation.

> God begins to communicate Himself through pure spirit by an act of simple contemplation, in which there is no discursive succession of thought. The exterior and interior senses of the lower part of the soul cannot attain to this contemplation. As a result the imaginative power and phantasy can no longer rest in any consideration nor find support in it.[17]

Let us see now the second sign, which is a sequel of the first in the *Ascent.* The second sign to discontinue meditation is an awareness of a disinclination to fix the imagination or sense-faculties upon other particular objects, external or internal.[18]

156

In the *Dark Night,* this is the first sign. "The first sign is that as these souls do not get satisfaction or consolation from things of God, they do not get any from creatures either."[19]

These pious persons are very much in love with God, but even the images that concern God — those which are more conformable to this love — fail to satisfy them. Much less, therefore, the images of creatures.

> This dryness and distaste proves that it is not the outcome of newly committed sins and imperfections. For when the appetite is allowed indulgence in some imperfection, if this were so, some inclination or propensity to look for satisfaction in something other than the things of God would be felt in the sensory part. For when the appetite is allowed indulgence in some imperfection, the soul immediately feels an inclination toward it, little or great, in proportion to the degree of its satisfaction and attachment.[20]

In other words, habits and dispositions of the soul are formed by repetition of acts. Evil acts would form a vicious habit that would incline the person to commit sins. Such is not the case here, for souls in this state are not attracted by creatures or earthly goods at all.

Let us now describe the last sign. In the *Ascent,* the third sign for discontinuing meditation, and the surest one, is that the soul likes to remain alone in loving awareness of God, without particular considerations, in interior peace, quiet and repose.[21] This loving awareness is sometimes anguished, for "the memory ordinarily turns to God solicitously and with painful care, and the soul thinks it is not serving God but turning back."[22]

It appears that St. John of the Cross contradicts himself, for if the soul remains alone in loving awareness of God it should not, it would seem, think it is not serving God. However, this happens because in the beginning the light of contemplation is so recondite and delicate, so spiritual and interior, that the soul does not perceive it or feel it as before in meditation. As a consequence the contemplative soul may think it is not serving God properly.

> Since the individual lacks the feelings of the sensitive part of the soul by not possessing these particular ideas and concepts which the senses and intellect are accustomed to act upon, he does not perceive this knowledge. For this reason: the purer, simpler, and more perfect the general knowledge is, the darker

it seems to be and the less the intellect perceives. On the other hand, the less pure and simple the knowledge is in itself, the clearer and more important it appears to the intellect, since it is clothed, wrapped, or commingled with some intelligible forms apprehensible to the intellect or the senses.[23]

The lower part of man — his senses, imagination and passions — has little share in the initial act of contemplation. The soul is aware of a loving presence of God, of peace, of interior repose, and of joy. But this experience is new, removed from the senses, and the beginner in contemplation may believe he has been deceived.

God transforms the operation of the spiritual person little by little from the senses to the spirit. And since the sensory part of the soul is incapable of appreciating the goods of the spirit, it remains deprived, dry and empty. While the spirit is tasting, the flesh tastes nothing:

> If in the beginning the soul does not experience spiritual savor and delight, but dryness and distaste, it is because of the novelty involved in the exchange. Since its palate is accustomed to these other sensory tastes, the soul still sets its eyes on them. And since, also, its spiritual palate is neither purged nor accommodated for so subtle a taste, it is unable to experience the spiritual savor and good until gradually prepared by means of this dark and obscure night.[24]

Although in the beginning the soul is unable to experience the full spiritual savor of contemplation, the spirit, however, does feel the strength and the energy to work, even though it may not experience savor. Even without the savor, this contemplation produces in the soul an inclination to remain alone and in quietude.[25]

This supernatural communication is called a "general and loving knowledge," and affects both the cognitive and appetitive part of man. For just as it is imparted obscurely to the intellect, so too a vague delight and love is given to the will without distinct knowledge of the object loved.[26]

All these reasons and signs should be weighed in deciding to discontinue meditation and to start contemplation.

Some Considerations on the Nature of Contemplation

Contemplation is indeed a complex phenomenon which affects souls differently according to their individual characteristics and their degree of holiness. For purposes of this article, however, we only wish to explain and describe in schematic fashion the beginning of contemplation in order to see its difference from meditation.

In the *Dark Night,* St. John of the Cross defines contemplation as a "secret and peaceful and loving inflow of God, which, if not hampered, fires the soul in the spirit of love."[27] This descriptive definition emphasizes some of the effects produced by contemplation in the will, that is, love and peace, but the cognitive element is lacking. A better definition is found in the *Living Flame.* "Contemplation is one act by which God is communicating light and love together, which is loving supernatural knowledge."[28]

Contemplation consists essentially in a special illumination of the intellect, a divine wisdom which fires the will with love. This special illumination affects the higher part of man, the spirit. But it is impcrtant to note that this illumination, this knowledge, is not the abstract knowledge of theology and science, but a knowledge which is experimental, intuitive, and concrete. It presupposes the intellectual apprehension of something which is already present in the soul, the Trinity, which dwells in the center of the soul through grace.[29]

Contemplation, therefore, is a simple gaze on divine Truth; it is a judgment of faith infused by charity regarding God, and perfected by the gifts of the Holy Spirit. There is no discourse in contemplation. There is only the simple intuition of God present in the center of the person. It is therefore easy to understand why meditation, which entails discourse and abstract knowledge, should eventually give way to contemplation. St. Teresa says:

> This is a prayer that comprises a great deal and achieves more than any amount of meditation on the part of understanding. . . . In these periods of quiet, then, let the souls repose in its rest; let them put their learning aside.[30]

The preparation for contemplation depends on the person's generosity and detachment. The exercise itself of contemplation, however, is beyond our own possibility. It depends on God, who freely and when He wishes bestows this gift upon the soul.[31] The principal agent and mover, therefore, is God, who quietly and secretly inserts in the intellect and will a loving wisdom that these faculties passively receive, as St. John of the Cross says in the *Dark Night*. St. Teresa writes in the *Interior Castle*: "In reality the soul in that state does no more than the wax when a seal is impressed upon it — the wax does not impress itself . . . it surely remains quiet and consenting."[32] This passivity is an important trait of contemplation, for, as she says, it is a gift received in the soul when the spirit of God blows and not when we wish:

> [Contemplation] is a supernatural state, and, however hard we try, we cannot reach it for ourselves; for it is a state in which the soul enters into peace, or rather in which the Lord gives it peace through His presence.[33]

Not only is God the principal agent of contemplation, He is also the guide and director of these chosen souls. Only God knows the ways by which He leads them to the summit of holiness. God guides them in mysterious ways, beyond the possibility of human understanding. This requires strong faith, for "God acts as the blind man's guide who must lead him by the hand to a place he does not know how to reach [to supernatural things of which neither his intellect, will, nor memory can know the nature]."[34] Blind faith, docility to His grace, and trust in God's mysterious ways are necessary qualities of any contemplative soul.

Therefore, the spiritual master must take heed and remember that the principal guide and mover of souls in this matter is not himself but the Holy Spirit who never abandons His care of them.

> Thus, the director's whole concern should not be to accommodate souls to his own method and condition, but he should observe the road along which God is leading them. And if he does not recognize it, he should leave them alone and not bother them.[35]

Anthropomorphism and ignorance distort speculative theology, but they are even worse with regard to mysticism, where the action of the Spirit is mysterious, ineffable, and impossible to communicate.

The Prayers of "Recollection" and of "Quiet" in Contemplation

Contemplation is difficult to understand and to communicate, especially to those who have never had experience in it. For it begins to touch the supernatural and this, as St. Teresa notes, is difficult to explain. "When the Lord begins to grant these favors, the soul itself does not understand them, or know what it ought to do . . . for, although I have read many spiritual books which touch upon the matter, they explain very little."[36] St. John of the Cross explains the nights of the soul, but St. Teresa better describes the psychological states of the soul which characterize the prayers of contemplation. The power of introspection of this Spanish woman is unique and her imagination vivid: water, fountains, rivers, bees, castles, shepherds, flowers, and many other Castilian images are used continuously to illustrate her description of contemplation. With them she gives a masterly analysis of this obscure and mysterious phenomenon. We shall try to summarize her doctrine regarding the first two prayers of the contemplative soul: the prayer of "recollection," and the prayer of "quiet."

St. Teresa calls the first supernatural prayer "recollection" because in this prayer the soul collects together all its faculties and enters within itself to be with its God.[37] To describe this prayer, St. Teresa recalls first the words of St. Augustine in his *Confessions* about his seeking God in many places, and eventually finding him within himself.[38] What happens, then, to the soul is described by St. Teresa in the *Interior Castle:*

> It is the form of recollection which seems to me supernatural, for it does not involve remaining in the dark or closing one's eyes, nor is it dependent upon any thing exterior. A person involuntarily closes his eyes and desires solitude; and, without the display of any human skill there seems gradually to be built for him a temple in which he can make the prayer already described; the senses and all external things seem gradually to lose their hold on him, while the soul, on the other hand, regains its lost control. It is sometimes said that the soul enters within itself, but I cannot explain things in that kind of language, for I have no skill in it.[39]

The soul finds itself so near the fountain that, even before it has begun to drink, it has its fill. In this way, the person remains alone with God and is thoroughly prepared to become enkindled. God begins to illuminate the soul in a passive and mysterious fashion known only by the individual who receives this gift. At that instant meditation is left behind, and contemplation begins to dawn. St. Teresa analyzes the differences between contemplation and meditation in the following way:

> When we are seeking God within ourselves [where He is found more effectively and more profitably than in the creatures] it is a great help if God grant us this favor. Do not suppose that the understanding can attain to Him merely by trying to think of Him as within the soul, or the imagination, by picturing Him as there. This is a good habit and an excellent kind of meditation, for it is founded upon a truth — namely, that God is within us. But it is not the kind of prayer that I have in mind, for anyone can practice it for himself.[40]

In other words, Christians know in faith that God is within the soul, and we can meditate upon this truth by using our imagination, picturing Him there and thinking about it. This is not contemplation but a simple meditation, for everything depends on the free activity of our cognitive powers. The contemplative prayer of recollection is also founded on the truth that God is within; but the psychological and spiritual processes which pertain to it are totally different from the meditation of that same mystery. In meditation we think and imagine the mystery, in contemplation we experience and intuit it. Thus, St. Teresa explains how the same truth is known through contemplation:

> What I am describing is quite different. These people are sometimes in the castle before they have begun to think about God at all. I cannot say where they entered it or how they heard their Shepherd's call: it was certainly not with their ears, for outwardly such a call is not audible. They become markedly conscious that they are gradually retiring within themselves; anyone who experiences this will discover what I mean: I cannot explain it better. I think I have read that they are like a hedgehog or a tortoise withdrawing into itself; and whoever wrote that must have understood it well. These creatures, however, enter within themselves whenever they like; whereas with us it is not a question of our will — it happens only when God is pleased to grant us this favor. For my own part, I believe that, when His Majesty grants it, He does so to people who are already leaving the things of the world.[41]

This first contemplative prayer recollects the powers of the soul. But it is chiefly the intellect that God captures by this prayer. God illumines the soul's knowledge to a much higher degree than any we can attain by ourselves. The intellect is led into a state of absorption in which, without knowing how, it is much better instructed than it could ever be as a result of its own efforts. The only wise thing to do by those favored with this prayer is to keep silence and to accept God's action gently and peacefully. For "in such spiritual activity as this, the person who does most is he who thinks least and desires to do least."[42]

The effects of recollection are explained by St. Teresa with her usual skill:

> It is clear that a dilation or enlargement of the soul takes place, as if the water proceeding from the spring had no means of running away, but the fountain had a device ensuring that, the more freely the water flowed, the larger became the basin. So it is in this kind of prayer; and God works many more wonders in the soul, thus fitting and gradually disposing it to retain all that He gives it. So this gentle movement and this interior dilation cause the soul to be less constrained in matters relating to the service of God than it was before and give it much more freedom.[43]

This prayer of recollection is considered the first contemplative prayer of the soul. Many spiritual writers, however, emphasize the prayer of "quiet," in which God captures not the intellect but the will. The will is united to Him, and consequently, this prayer affects chiefly the appetitive part of man rather than his cognitive powers. St. Teresa describes this prayer in *The Interior Castle, The Way of Perfection,* and the *Life.*[44] The best description of this state is perhaps found in the *Life,* although the distinction between recollection and quiet is not so clear there as it is later found in the *Interior Castle.* For St. Teresa, this prayer is the beginning of all blessings when the Lord begins to communicate Himself to the soul.

> This state is a recollection of the faculties within the soul, so that its fruition of the contentment may be of greater delight. But the faculties are not lost, nor do they sleep. The will alone is occupied, in such a way that, without knowing how, it becomes captive. It allows itself to be imprisoned by God, as one who well knows itself to be captive of Him whom it loves. . . . Everything that now takes place brings the greatest consolation, and so little labor is involved that, even if prayer continues for a long time, it never becomes wearisome. . . . His Majesty begins to communicate Himself to the soul . . . and this is true joy.[45]

163

The effects of the prayer of quiet are chiefly peace and joy, which are sequels of charity. In these souls, so much loved by God, the virtue of charity informs all the rest of the virtues:

> This quiet and recollection in the soul makes itself felt largely through the satisfaction and peace it brings to it, together with a very great joy and repose of the faculties and a most sweet delight. As the soul has never gone beyond this stage, it thinks there is no more left for it to desire and, like St. Peter, it wishes that it could make its abode here. It dares not move or stir, for it thinks that if it does so this blessing may slip from its grasp: sometimes it would like to be unable even to breathe.[46]

The will is in union with God; the intellect and imagination, however, are not necessarily recollected and they may wander away from God busying themselves with earthly things. The important thing here is not to lose the union of the will with God. If the soul tries too hard to bring these powers into submission it runs the risk of losing the prayer of quiet altogether. For, although the will is not yet completely absorbed, it is so well occupied, without knowing how, that whatever the distractions of the understanding and imagination, they cannot deprive it of its contentment and rejoicing.[47]

> The other two faculties help the will so that it may become more and more capable of enjoying so great a blessing, though sometimes it comes about that, even when the will is in union, they hinder it exceedingly. When that happens it should take no notice of them but remain in its fruition and quiet; for, if it tries to recollect them, both [faculties] and the will will suffer.[48]

Contemplation consists in a passive reception of the love of God by means of prayer. As was said before, it is a gift which God bestows upon the soul when He pleases. Therefore, if the faithful in their eagerness try to force God with their actions rather than await its passive reception, the effect is the opposite of what was intended, and contemplation is lost.

> This quiet and recollection — this little spark — it proceeds from the spirit of God . . . it is not a thing that can be acquired, as anyone who has had experience of it must perforce realize immediately; but this nature of ours is so eager for delectable experiences that it tries to get all it can. Soon, however, it becomes very cold; for, hard as we may try to make the fire burn in order to obtain this pleasure, we seem only to be throwing water on it to quench it. . . . What the soul has to do at these seasons of quiet is merely to go softly and make no

noise. By noise I mean going about with the understanding in search of many words and reflections with which to give thanks for this benefit. . . . Let the will continue in the fruition of that favor, and be as recollected as the wise bee, for if no bees entered the hive and they all went about trying to bring each other in, there would not be much chance of their making any honey.[49]

These principles and descriptions explain why, as St. John of the Cross and St. Teresa explain, after a certain period of meditation God brings the soul gradually to contemplation. Meditation and discursive reasoning have been left behind, and from now on God Himself takes special care of these souls in ways only known by His divine wisdom. Not only should a spiritual guide not hinder this divine action, but he should encourage the soul to receive it with faith, docility, and trust.

[1]St. John of the Cross, *Living Flame of Love*, Stanza 3, n. 43. *The Collected Works of St. John of the Cross*, Trans., K. Kavanaugh O.C.D. and O. Rodriguez O.C.D. (Washington, 1973).   [2]*Ibid.*, n. 56. See n. 53.   [3]*Ibid.*, n. 56. See n. 62.   [4]*Ibid.*, n. 31.   [5]*Ibid.*, n. 54.   [6]St. Teresa of Jesus, *Interior Castle* (New York, 1961), Trans., E. Allison Peers. "Fifth Mansion," ch. 1, p. 100. See *Ibid.*, *The Life of Teresa of Jesus* (New York, 1960), Trans., E. Allison Peers, ch. 13, p. 146.   [7]*Living Flame of Love*, Stanza 3, n. 44. See n. 45.   [8]*Ascent of Mount Carmel*, II, ch. 17, n. 3.   [9]Thomas Aquinas, *In Boethius de Trin.*, q. 6, a. 2. Aquinas says that with regard to divine things we can use the senses and the imagination as the beginning of our knowledge, but not as its end, for we cannot judge divine things to be such as what the senses and imagination apprehend. See *Summa Theol.* I, 87, 7; I, 84, 7 ad 3.   [10]*Living Flame*, Stanza 3, n. 32. See n. 62. See also nn. 31, 36, 53.   [11]*Ibid.*, n. 43. See nn. 32, 33.   [12]*Ibid.*, n. 60. See nn. 56-57, 62.   [13]*Ascent of Mount Carmel*, II, ch. 13, n. 1.   [14]*Ibid.*, n. 2.   [15]*Dark Night*, I, ch. 9, n. 8.   [16]*Ascent of Mount Carmel*, II, ch. 14, n. 1.   [17]*Dark Night*, I, ch. 9, n. 8. In the *Ascent of Mount Carmel* II, ch. 14, n. 2, St. John of the Cross adds another reason for this sign, which has been the foundation for the much debated doctrine of acquired contemplation that is held by some Carmelite schools: "The second reason for leaving meditation is that the soul has acquired the substantial and habitual spirit of meditation. The purpose of the acts of meditation is the acquisition of some knowledge and love of God by means of repetition of acts regarding particular ideas. Now this has been converted into the habitual and substantial general and loving knowledge. This knowledge is neither distinct nor particular, as the previous one."   [18]*Ascent of Mount Carmel*, II, ch. 14, nn. 2 and 3.   [19]*Dark Night*, I, ch. 9, n. 2.   [20]*Ibid.*, I, ch. 9, n. 2.   [21]*Ascent of Mount Carmel*, II, ch. 13, n. 4. See n. 2.   [22]*Dark Night*, I, ch. 9, n. 3.   [23]*Ascent of Mount Carmel*, II, ch. 14, n. 8.   [24]*Dark Night*, I, ch. 9, n. 4.   [25]*Ibid.*, n. 6.   [26]*Ascent of Mount Carmel*, II, ch. 14, n. 12.   [27]*Dark Night*, I, ch. 10, n. 6.   [28]*Living Flame*, Stanza 3, n. 49. See nn. 38, 43.   [29]Jn. 13:14; 1 Cor. 3:16-17: "Do you not know that you are the temple of God and that the Spirit of God dwells in you? If anyone destroys the temple of God, him will God destroy; for holy is the temple of God, and this temple you are." See 1 Cor.

6:19; 2 Cor. 6:16; 2 Tim. 1:14. For the nature of this experimental knowledge see: Antonio Moreno, O.P. "The Nature of St. Thomas' Knowledge *Per Connaturalitem.*" *Angelicum* (Rome) 47 (1970), pp. 44-62.   [30]St. Teresa, *Life*, ch. 15, pp. 158-159.   [31]St. Teresa, *Interior Castle,* Fourth Mansion, ch. 3, p. 89: "Let us try, without forcing itself or causing any turmoil, to put a stop to all discursive reasoning . . . but it should not try to understand what this state is, because that is a gift bestowed upon the will. The will, then, . . . should not labor except for uttering a few loving words."   [32]*Ibid.,* "Fifth Mansion," ch. 3, p. 109. See *Living Flame,* Stanza 3, nn. 32, 33, 36; *Dark Night,* II, ch. 23, n. 2.   [33]St. Teresa, *The Way of Perfection* (New York, 1964), Trans. E. Allison Peers, ch. 31, p. 200.   [34]St. John of the Cross, *Living Flame,* Stanza 3, n. 29. [35]*Ibid.,* n. 46.   [36]St. Teresa, *Life,* ch. 14, p. 151. See *Interior Castle,* Fourth Mansion, ch. 1, p. 72.   [37]*The Way of Perfection,* ch. 28, p. 185. See *Interior Castle,* Fourth Mansion, ch. 3, p. 85.   [38]St. Augustine, *Confessions,* Bk. X, ch. 27: "Thou wert within and I was without. I was looking for thee out there. . . . Thou wert with me, yet I was not with thee." See *The Way of Perfection,* ch. 29, p. 191.   [39]*Interior Castle,* "Fourth Mansion," ch. 3, p. 85. See *The Way of Perfection,* ch. 28, p. 187; ch. 29, p. 193.   [40]*Interior Castle,* Fourth Mansion, ch. 3, p. 86. See *The Way of Perfection,* ch. 28, pp. 186-187.   [41]*Interior Castle,* Fourth Mansion, ch. 3, p. 87.   [42]*Ibid.,* pp. 87-88.   [43]*Ibid.,* pp. 90-91.   [44]*Interior Castle,* Fourth Mansion, ch. 1 and 2; *Life,* ch.14 and 15; *The Way of Perfection,* ch. 31.   [45]*Life,* ch. 14, pp. 149-150. See ch. 15, p. 162; *The Way of Perfection,* ch. 31, p. 202; *Interior Castle,* Fourth Mansion, ch. 3, p. 83. In the *Interior Castle,* "Fourth Mansion," ch. 3, Teresa calls the prayer of quiet "spiritual consolations" which have their source in God, to distinguish it from "worldly joys" which have their source in our nature and end in God. In spiritual consolations the soul is "at the source of the water and fills without making any noise . . . for the water flows all the time" (p. 81).   [46]*Life,* ch. 15, p. 154. See *Interior Castle,* Fourth Mansion, pp. 81-82.   [47]*Life,* ch. 15, p. 155.   [48]*Life,* ch. 14, p. 149. See *The Way of Perfection,* ch. 31, p. 207.   [49]*Life,* ch. 15, pp. 156-157. See *Ibid.,* p. 159; *The Way of Perfection,* ch. 31, p. 202.

PART FOUR

Spiritual Direction and Christian Tradition

The Church from its beginning has always tried to help Christians respond fully to the inner guidance of the Holy Spirit. Evidence of this may be seen in the New Testament, the Church's liturgy and each era of Christian history. Moreover, spiritual direction throughout the centuries has been practiced by the entire Church: men and women, laity and clergy, members of religious orders.

The articles and recommended readings for this section convey both the continuity and diversity of spiritual direction in Christian tradition. Their chronological arrangement allows you to observe its practice in New Testament times, the Middle Ages, the Reformation period, and the Twentieth Century. More importantly, the readings reflect the whole Church's involvement in the ministry of direction — men and women like Teresa of Avila and John of the Cross; laity and priests like Catherine of Siena and Thomas Merton; Benedictines, Franciscans, Carmelites, Dominicans, Jesuits and many other religious communities have all made their distinctive contributions.

Those who enter spiritual direction today, whether as directors or directees, thus draw upon an ancient heritage rich enough to suit every modern taste and to discern every movement of the Spirit. Drawing continually upon this heritage, the contemporary ministry of spiritual direction continues to serve the most exciting of all Christian mysteries — God present in His people drawing each person to divine union.

Discernment of Spirits in the New Testament

John H. Wright, S.J.

The current and continuing interest in the discernment of spirits manifests a very real and deeply felt need. Many accustomed ways of doing things are changing and persons eager to do God's will are often unsure of what course to take. The problem may be expressed in this way: among the many impulses to act that we experience, which are good and correspond to God's intentions, which are finally evil and opposed to God's will? The problem area is not that of manifest moral choice, where the alternatives are clearly good or evil. No discernment process is necessary to decide whether such things as paying your debts or spreading slanderous gossip are proper or improper courses of action. The problem area is that of the intrinsically permissible, of courses of action that are not in themselves clearly commanded or forbidden: what is my vocation in life? What work should we undertake? What advice can I give someone who has come to me?

A concrete, individual situation frequently cannot be adequately understood and evaluated simply in terms of universal principles and laws. When all these have been applied, it may still not be clear which of the many possible avenues really furthers the design of God. But it must be possible somehow to discover this, otherwise it is useless to think and speak of the will of God in this particular situation.

There is no need here to suppose that among many possible courses of action there can be only one that accords with

This article originally appeared in *Communio: International Catholic Quarterly*, 1, Summer 1974, pp. 115-27. Reprinted by permission.

God's will. There may be several genuinely good possibilities which are almost equally capable of advancing the Kingdom of God: it is important to choose some one of these and to avoid significantly inferior or ultimately detrimental choices. But which of the equally good choices is made is not greatly important. It is much more important to make one of them and to get on with it. Of course, it can also be that one of several possibilities is actually the unique choice to which God is moving us through His Spirit, or the one to which He draws us with special urgency.

The teaching of the New Testament on the discernment of spirits is particularly important, not only because the New Testament is the Holy Spirit's enduring gift for the guidance of the Christian community, but because the problems confronting the New Testament Church are remarkably like our own. The older structures and prescriptions of Judaism offered some helpful models for liturgy, discipline, and church organization; but the new wine could not be put in the old wine skins. How should the believers in Jesus work out the details of their organization? In what direction and with what speed should they proclaim the gospel of the dying and rising of Jesus? To what degree were they still bound by the law given through Moses? How could they speak their message to Gentiles, who had no understanding of the Old Covenant between God and Israel? It was a problem of change and continuity, of proclaiming something new while preserving the lasting values of the old, of announcing the unfailing faithfulness of God in a new idiom and in reference to new events.

Of course, the differences between the situation of the apostolic Church and the modern Church are as important as the similarities. They announced a new Covenant, a new revelation of the Father's love, a new invitation to faith, a new creation in Jesus Christ the Lord, and a new people of God. We do not find our situation changed on these points. Our continuity here is essential and inviolable. But individually and collectively we today, like the early apostolic community, must face questions of life-style, vocation, missionary activity, discipline, exercise of authority, manner of worship, and a host of other more personal matters without finding sufficient guidance in the practice of the immediate past.

169

Two other features of the life of the New Testament Church make our situation similar to theirs, and their teaching important for us: a certain tendency to confusion and disorder, and the appearance of false teachers. St. Paul speaks of both these things in a context of the discernment of spirits. His most extensive treatment of the gifts of the Spirit is found in the First Letter to the Corinthians, chapters 12-14. At the end of this section he gives directions for the preservation of order in the Christian assembly. He says that when prophets speak to the assembled brethren (and no more than two or three should do this), the others are "to judge the worth of what they say" *(1 Corinthians 14:29)*. The community, thus, is to exercise a function of discernment with regard to the charismatic contributions of its members. He concludes this section by directing, "Set your hearts on prophecy, my brothers, and do not forbid those who speak in tongues, but make sure that everything is done properly and in order" *(1 Corinthians 14:39-40)*.

It was a situation in the same community at Corinth that drew forth Paul's words of warning about false apostles. He fears that the pure faith of the Gospel may be corrupted by these men *(2 Corinthians 11:1-6)*. He points to the unselfishness of his own life as evidence of trustworthiness *(7-12)*. He then speaks directly of his rivals: "Such men are false apostles. They practice deceit in their disguise as apostles of Christ. And little wonder! For even Satan disguises himself as an angel of light. It comes as no surprise that his ministers disguise themselves as ministers of the justice of God. But their end will correspond to their deeds" *(13-15)*. In our days, as in his, it is necessary to penetrate disguises and to discover who are sincerely and honestly announcing the word of salvation, preaching not themselves but the Gospel of Jesus Christ.

It is sometimes said that for the emergence of the Spirit and the creation of the just society all we need do is remove the oppressive structures that stifle us. But when existing structures are removed (and this may often be quite necessary), many impulses are released, and it may just as well be the demonic as the charismatic that emerges. The experience of the New Testament Church illustrates this, as well as almost every revolution in history. For nearly every successful overthrow of tyranny has finally resulted in the imposition of a new tyranny.

Thus, not every force released by the disappearance of an out-moded structure is an impulse from the Holy Spirit. We need to discern, to distinguish the spirits.

The New Testament does not provide us with any easy rules of thumb enabling us automatically to determine the will of God. We are never in the position of somehow compelling God to reveal Himself. We are always under the grace of God, receiving His gift as gift. The effort to discern the movement of the Holy Spirit is part of our endeavor to receive His gift, to accept His mercy, not some kind of manipulation of God which makes Him communicate information to us. Our consideration of the New Testament data will fall into four sections: 1) a brief word about the New Testament stress on doing God's will; 2) the foundation for discerning the will of God and the motion of the Holy Spirit; 3) the general noetic principle of discernment given in the Gospel; and 4) the manner of applying this principle to particular situations.

1. Doing God's Will

Doing God's will or (what is the same thing) following the guidance of the Holy Spirit is a brief summary both of the life of Jesus and of the ideal that He proposes to us. The Letter to the Hebrews places these words on Jesus' lips as He comes into the world: "Sacrifice and offering you did not desire, but a body you have prepared for me; holocausts and sin offerings you took no delight in. Then I said, 'As it is written of me in the book, I have come to do your will, O God' " *(Hebrews 10:5-7)*. Jesus assures us in the Gospel according to John: "Doing the will of him who sent me and bringing his work to completion is my food" *(John 4:34)*. Finally, as He confronts His passion and death He prays to His Father in His agony: "Abba (O Father), you have power to do all things. Take this cup away from me. But let it be as you would have it, not as I" *(Mark 14:36)*.

In the prayer that Jesus taught us — the prayer that is daily on the lips of Christians throughout the world — we say, "Your Kingdom come, your will be done on earth as it is in heaven" *(Matthew 6:10)*. Later, when Jesus described those who belong to Him, He said, "Whoever does the will of my heavenly Father is brother and sister and mother to me" *(Matthew 12:50)*. St. Paul sums up the meaning of our sonship in the words, "All who are led by the Spirit of God are sons of

God" *(Romans 8:14)*. As these words of Paul indicate, doing God's will means moving in a certain direction under the guidance of the Spirit, rather than accomplishing some particular works, though it may at times require this.

2. Foundations of Discernment

The word which best summarizes the New Testament teaching on the foundation of all discernment of spirits is *wisdom*. St. Paul describes the wisdom in the *First Letter to the Corinthians 2:6-16*. He has just exposed the bankruptcy of all merely human wisdom, but acknowledges that among the spiritually mature he does proclaim a wisdom that God has prepared for those who love Him *(cf. 2:6-9)*. This wisdom comes to us from the Holy Spirit, who alone searches the depths of God. He helps us "recognize the gifts He (God) has given us" *(2:12)*. A natural man, not living by the Spirit of God, cannot understand this at all; it is foolishness to him *(2:14)*. The spiritual man "appraises everything" *(2:15)*, for through the Spirit he has "the mind of Christ" *(2:16)*. Thus, only the spiritual man, possessing a kind of divine wisdom, can recognize God's gift, can judge of things with the mind of Christ.

A little later in the same epistle, St. Paul explicitly mentions the discernment of spirits among the gifts God gives different individuals as a "manifestation of the Spirit . . . for the common good" *(1 Corinthians 12:7)*. "Prophecy is given to one; to another power to distinguish one spirit from another . . ." *(1 Corinthians 12:10)*.

In the Captivity letters, there is further mention of wisdom as the way to know God's will: ". . . we have been praying for you unceasingly and asking that you may attain full knowledge of His will through perfect wisdom and spiritual insight" *(Colossians 1:9)*. In the opening hymn of Ephesians, the apostle thanks God because He "has given us the wisdom to understand fully the mystery, the plan he was pleased to decree in Christ" *(Ephesians 1:9)*. Further on he exhorts his readers: "Do not continue in ignorance, but try to discern the will of God" *(Ephesians 5:17)*. The word translated "ignorance" means more than the simple absence of knowledge; it describes one who is the opposite of a sensible, thoughtful, prudent, wise person. (The Greek word is *aphron,* the opposite of one who is *phronimos.)*

When we seek a deeper insight into this wisdom, it seems to involve two principal elements, one an attitude, the other an experience. The attitude was indicated by St. Paul when he wrote that God had prepared this wisdom for those who love Him *(1 Corinthians 2:9)*. It is basically the antecedent willingness to do God's will, whatever it may be. One who seeks to know God's will with the intention of afterwards deciding whether he will do it or not, will never come to know it. Jesus pointed out that this willingness is what enables a man to know whether the word he proclaims is from God or not: "My doctrine is not my own; it comes from him who sent me. Any man who chooses to do his will will know about this doctrine — namely, whether it comes from God or is simply spoken on my own" *(John 7:16-17)*. St. Paul sees the ability to judge what is God's will as the fruit of complete dedication to God and of renewal of mind: ". . . offer your bodies as a living sacrifice holy and acceptable to God, your spiritual worship. Do not conform yourselves to this age, but be transformed by the renewal of your mind, so that you may judge what is God's will, what is good, pleasing, and perfect" *(Romans 12:1-2)*.

The experience which belongs to this wisdom seems to be most fundamentally the peace which God alone can give and no one can counterfeit. Doing God's will means accepting His Kingdom into our hearts and lives. St. Paul reminds us: "The Kingdom of God is not a matter of eating or drinking, but of justice, peace, and the joy that is given by the Holy Spirit. Whoever serves Christ in this way pleases God and wins the esteem of men. Let us, then, make it our aim to work for peace and to strengthen one another" *(Romans 14:17-19)*. In another passage, St. Paul indicates how both the peace of God and the God of peace are with those who direct their efforts toward what is according to His will: ". . . God's own peace, which is beyond all understanding, will stand guard over your hearts and minds, in Christ Jesus. Finally, my brothers, your thoughts should be wholly directed to all that is true, all that deserves respect, all that is honest, pure, admirable, decent, virtuous, or worthy of praise. Live according to what you have learned and accepted, what you have heard me say and seen me do. Then will the God of peace be with you" *(Philippians 4:7-9)*.

This experience of peace is the awareness that we are moving toward Him, that we are being guided by the Spirit, that His

Kingdom is being established in our minds and hearts. It is a kind of taste of His presence. When we consider different courses of action, we are able from this experience to discover this taste where He is present, where His spirit leads, and thus to recognize where His will is drawing us. The Latin word for wisdom is *sapientia*. It is derived from the verb *sapere,* meaning to taste or to relish. Thus the *sapiens* or wise man is one who relishes the truth, one whose taste enables him to judge prudently and discreetly. The same root is present in the Greek *sophos* "wise" and *sophia* "wisdom." The Hebrew verb meaning "to be wise" is *hacham,* which in turn seems to be related to *hech* "tasting" from *hanach* "to taste."

3. The General Principle of Discernment in the Gospel

The most general principle for the discernment of spirits comes to us from the teaching of Christ as given in *Matthew 7:15-20.* The context is the Sermon on the Mount, and Jesus is warning His disciples against false prophets. He is telling them how to distinguish false prophets from true prophets. This was a problem that arose with special urgency in the Old Testament. Prophecy in the time of the monarchy had become institutionalized to a large degree. Groups of men attached to the royal court were designated as prophets and charged with the task of delivering the word of the Lord to the king. The prophet Jeremiah met great hostility from these men, when he prophesied the fall of Jerusalem. When they contradicted him and tried to discredit him, Jeremiah warned the people about false prophets, men who predicted peace, when strife truly awaited them. "From of old, the prophets who were before you and me prophesied war, woe, and pestilence against many lands and mighty kingdoms. But the prophet who prophesies peace is recognized as truly sent by the Lord only when his prophetic prediction is fulfilled" *(Jeremiah 28:8-9).* He is reflecting a similar teaching given in Deuteronomy 18:21-22: "If you say to yourselves, 'How can we recognize an oracle which the Lord has spoken?' know that, even though a prophet speaks in the name of the Lord, if his oracle is not fulfilled or verified, it is an oracle which the Lord did not speak. The prophet has spoken it presumptuously, and you shall have no fear of him."

Jesus now frames His own teaching in very similar fashion: "Be on your guard against false prophets, who come to you in sheep's clothing, but underneath are wolves on the prowl." He then announces the basic principle of discernment: "You will know them by their fruits." He elaborates on this by illustrating it from nature, saying that we don't gather grapes from thorns nor figs from thistles, and that sound trees and decayed trees are easily distinguished by the fruit they bear. He concludes: "You can tell a tree by its fruit" *(Matt. 7:15-20)*.

Jesus Himself applies this principle to a particular case, the unbelief of the Pharisees. After a series of miraculous healings culminating in the cure of a man who was blind and mute, a group of Pharisees charged that Jesus was expelling demons by the help of Beelzebub, the prince of demons *(cf. Matthew 12:22-24)*. Jesus first showed the absurdity of this explanation, supposing as it did that evil was fighting against itself *(12:25-30)*, and then went to the root of their unwillingness to believe: the rejection of the light, a sin against the Holy Spirit, unforgivable because the sinner refuses thereby to take the first step to which God calls him *(12:31-32)*. Then He once again announces the principle of discernment, which both validates His action and condemns theirs: "Declare a tree good and its fruit good or declare a tree rotten and its fruit rotten, one or the other, for you can tell a tree by its fruit. How can you utter anything good, you brood of vipers, when you are so evil? The mouth speaks whatever fills the mind. A good man produces good from his store of goodness; an evil man produces evil from his evil store" *(Matthew 12:33-35)*.

4. Method of Applying to Particular Situations

Jesus tells us that we are to judge a tree by its fruit. We are to discern the motions of the Holy Spirit from impulses that are ultimately from the Evil One by what comes of them. But what in particular are we to look for? Several passages in the New Testament give us very helpful indications of the kinds of fruit that enable us to judge in this matter.

Perhaps the most significant of these is given by St. Paul in his letter to the Galatians. The main theme of his letter is denunciation of a restrictive legalism that the Pharisaic or Judaizing party among Christians was trying to impose upon the newly baptized. St. Paul sees in this a failure to grasp the essential meaning of Christ's work, canceling out the liberty and freedom that He gained for us. Paul begins his concluding exhortation with the words: "It was for liberty that Christ freed us. So stand firm, and do not take on yourselves the yoke of slavery a second time" *(Galatians 5:1)!* But a liberty that rejects a new imposition of law can easily become libertinism, a pretext for every form of selfishness. Living in freedom does not mean doing whatever you please. Hence, he says further on, "My brothers, remember that you have been called to live in freedom — but not a freedom that gives reign to the flesh" *(Galatians 5:13).* With these words, St. Paul introduces a favorite theme of opposition: flesh/spirit. Reading this out of a tradition of Greek philosophy we might be tempted to think of this as a body/soul distinction; but that is not Paul's point. The "flesh" means the weak, creaturely, mortal, self-centered being, cut off from God by the refusal to allow His love to transform his life. It includes what we would call both body and soul. The "spirit" means sometimes the Holy Spirit given to us as a principle of new life, and sometimes the human spirit energized and guided by the Spirit of God.

St. Paul first encourages his readers to renounce all selfishness: "Out of love, place yourselves at one another's service. The whole law has found its fulfillment in this one saying: "You shall love your neighbor as yourself" *(Galatians 5:13-14).* He then gives the general direction: "My point is that you should live in accord with the spirit and you will not yield to the cravings of the flesh" *(5:16).* He explains the conflict that is going on and its consequences in our lives: "The flesh lusts against the spirit and the spirit against the flesh; the two are directly opposed. This is why you do not do what your will intends" *(5:17).* Our good resolutions crumble under the all-pervasive drag of selfishness. But release is possible, and it means true freedom from the law as well: "If you are guided by the Spirit, you are not under the law" *(5:18).* There can be no mistaking the results of following the "flesh," of yielding to merely self-centered drives: "It is obvious what proceeds from the flesh: lewd conduct, impurity, licentiousness, idolatry, sorcery, hostilities, bickering, jealousy, outbursts of rage, selfish rivalries, dissensions, factions, envy, drunkenness, orgies (and in case he has forgotten anything, he adds), and the like" *(5:19-21).* He ends this list by warning "those who do such things will not inherit the Kingdom of heaven" *(5:21b).*

Following the Spirit leads to very different results: "In contrast, the fruit of the spirit is love, joy, peace, patient endurance, kindness, generosity, faith, mildness, and chastity" *(5:22-23)*. And Paul, as if to settle the objections of those who had been insisting on the Mosaic observances, adds: "Against such there is no law" *(5:23b)!*

Therefore, no matter how good or desirable or justified a course of action may at first appear, it must finally be judged by what it actually produces. The lead of the spirit will not produce the works of the flesh; nor will the flesh yield the fruits of the spirit. No amount of rationalization can change the facts: if dissension, rivalry, envy, bickering, and such result from the path chosen, then the Holy Spirit is not guiding. And if love, generosity, joy, and peace are present, then it is not human selfishness that has brought it forth, but the Spirit of God.

Tucked away in Paul's extended treatment of charismatic gifts in the First Letter to the Corinthians is the brief well-known description of the characteristics of love or *agape,* a description which likewise provides an excellent indication of the difference in fruits produced by the good and evil trees. For Paul, love is the effect of the Spirit's presence in us *(cf. Romans 5:5),* it is His greatest gift *(1 Corinthians 12:31; 13:13)*. Hence when he tells us what love does and does not do, he is telling us how to discern the guidance of the Spirit from evil and misleading inclinations. "Love is patient; love is kind. Love is not jealous, it does not put on airs, it is not snobbish. Love is never rude, it is not self-seeking, it is not prone to anger; neither does it brood over injuries. Love does not rejoice in what is wrong but rejoices with the truth. There is no limit to love's forbearance, to its trust, its hope, its power to endure" *(1 Corinthians 13:4-7)*. This can be read as a portrait of Jesus, who was led by the Spirit during His life *(Luke 4:1; 4:14; 4:18),* and handed Himself over to death for love of us *(Galatians 2:20)*. It likewise serves to indicate those courses of action that come from His Spirit, and are the fulfillment of His command that we are to love one another as He has loved us *(cf. John 15:12)*. This suggests that one way to describe the different movements of spirits is by the adjectives *loving* and *unloving.* The former indicates the inspirations of the Holy Spirit; the latter, the temptations of the Evil One.

St. John agrees with St. Paul on love as the principle of discernment. It both enables the world to tell who belong to Christ, and it enables the Christian to know that he is truly living the life of Christ. Jesus tells His followers: "This is how all will know you for my disciples: your love for one another" *(John 13:35)*. And in John's first letter we read: "That we have passed from death to life we know because we love the brothers. The man who does not love is among the living dead" *(1 John 3:14)*.

But St. John has an additional concern. An incipient Docetism had appeared among Christians, affirming that Jesus only appeared to be a man. Details of that early heresy are wanting, but it is clear that John saw here an error aimed at the essential meaning of Christianity. However much a person may claim to speak under the spirit of God, not all spirits are to be believed: "Beloved, do not trust every spirit, but put the spirits to a test to see if they belong to God, because many false prophets have appeared in the world. This is how you can recognize God's Spirit; every spirit that acknowledges Jesus Christ come in the flesh belongs to God, while every spirit that fails to acknowledge Him does not belong to God" *(1 John 4:1-3)*. The principle implicit in this teaching of John remains valid for us today: a tendency to reduce, distort, or explain away the mystery of God's redeeming love revealed to us in Jesus Christ comes from "the spirit of the anti-Christ" *(cf. 1 John 4:3b)*. No doubt we need to reinterpret that mystery continually so that it may speak to men and women of every age; but our reinterpretation cannot be a destruction and still claim to come from the Spirit of Truth *(cf. John 16:13)*.

The Moment of Discernment

How does the moment of discernment actually take place? How does the person seeking to do and to know God's will actually decide how the Spirit of God is leading him? The New Testament itself gives no clear indications in this matter. But St. Ignatius Loyola in the *Spiritual Exercises* suggests three times for making this decision. They are three manners or methods of choosing according to the will of God, and they are often combined together in various ways. The first is a moment of insight, as unexpected perhaps as St. Paul's conversion on the road to Damascus, that God is calling us to a certain course of action. The conviction is given to us, complete and sure, without argument and with no more possibility of doubt than the certainty of our own existence. This does not, of course, preclude subsequent reflection, testing, and confirmation. But basically the matter is settled and we know it.

The second manner of choosing according to the will of God is to reflect upon the various reactions we experience within us as we contemplate each of the possible lines of action. Where do we find the peace and joy that resonates with the experience of the total giving of ourselves to God and with the peace that that brings? Where do we discover movements of jealousy or envy or impatience drawing us to act in a certain way? One who sincerely wants to do the will of God whatever that may concretely involve may well be able to discover in these reactions a sure sign of the attraction of the Holy Spirit or of a temptation to evil, even under an appearance of good.

The third manner of choosing is to consider all the reasons that can be thought of for or against the different possible choices. This consideration continues until you see that one or more reasons are actually decisive in this situation. This is not a simple matter of weighing and balancing objective values; it is taken for granted that this has been done but that the results are ambiguous. Rather, the examination of reasons goes on until the desire to do God's will discovers what it is seeking in the reasons on one side or another. It simply becomes clear that one set of reasons should be operative in this situation. At the end of discernment in all three methods the choice is offered to God for confirmation by His peace which "surpasses all understanding."

There has never been a time in the history of the Church when we could afford to neglect this earnest seeking to know the will of God. But it can hardly be questioned that today's uncertainties impose this quest upon us with special urgency.

The Rule of 1223:
A Franciscan Model
for Spiritual Direction

Louis Davino, O.F.M.

There has been some discussion lately among Franciscan scholars as to whether the Rule of St. Francis is a spiritual document or a legal statement in regard to the life of the Brotherhood. Without going into the whole argument of the spiritual versus the legal nature of the Rule, this paper will concern itself with the spiritual attitude Francis attempted to instill in his friars so that they would achieve a sound relationship with God the Father. I have therefore chosen to portray Francis as a spiritual father concerned with the individual friar's ability to follow the Gospel, or, as the Rule of 1221 states, to follow "the teaching and the footsteps of our Lord Jesus Christ" (ch. 1).

In his role as founder of a new Order, Francis establishes a relationship with his friars based on individual freedom in living out the Gospel rather than on authoritarian decree. Because of this attitude, Francis becomes *"pater* in the full spiritual meaning of the word."[1] Thirteenth-century figures writing about Francis often refer to his relationship with his friars as a father-son relationship. Jacques de Vitry writes in his second sermon on the friars, "For Saint Francis was our spiritual father"; and in the same sermon he states that the Poverello's "sons thus multiplied throughout the world."[2]

Odo of Certonia, in a sermon dated 1219, used the word *son* in a parable concerning the friars and their relationship to Francis:

This article appeared in *The Cord,* 26, October 1976, pp. 288-95. Reprinted with permission from *The Cord,* A Franciscan Spiritual Review, published by The Franciscan Institute, St. Bonaventure, NY 14778 USA.

When Brother Francis was asked who should feed his brethren since he was accepting so many (without careful scrutiny), he replied: A certain king once fell in love with a peasant woman living in the woods, and she gave birth to a child. After she had nursed him for some time, she went to the king's palace to request that the king feed his child from then on.

When this was reported to the king, he said in reply, "There are many worthless and wicked people eating food in my palace; it is only fair that my own son dine with them."

Francis explained the story by saying that he, himself, was that woman whom the Master, by His teaching, made fruitful and that he, Francis, brought forth spiritual sons.

Accordingly, since the Lord feeds so many wicked men, it is not to be wondered at that he should feed his own sons along with the others.[3]

Francis' care and concern for his friars as their father is also mentioned in the different thirteenth-century biographies about him. Thus Brother Bernard "was sent to other regions by obedience to his kind father" (2 Celano 10:24); and Francis "spoke indeed not as a judge but as a tender father to his children" (Legend of the Three Companions 14:59). The Legend of Perugia (17) says, with reference to the Testament, that "here [are] the words that our Father left His sons and His brothers as He was dying."

Francis' biographers and commentators see within him the love of a father toward his children: "Francis follows his friars step by step on their way through the world, admonishing and exhorting with fatherly concern."[4] Throughout the development of the Rule, Francis never lets go of this relationship. He uses words and provides a method in the Rule that leave no doubt that he is conscious of his role as spiritual leader, adviser, and father. He is a true "abba" to his disciples.

A spiritual father, from the time of St. Anthony of the Desert, has been described as one who totally surrenders himself to the will of God and guides his disciples to the same goal. This total surrender is based on prayer and the meditative reflection on the word of God in Scripture and on discovering the heart by concentrating on the Incarnate Word as the totally selfless person. I will now proceed to describe these same characteristics of a spiritual father as manifest in St. Francis through his Rule of 1223.

181

The Word of God

The spiritual father (or director) provides an atmosphere in which the word of God is confronted by the disciples and thus becomes a challenging adventure for those seeking God's will while continuing the journey *(in via)* toward perfection, the Kingdom of God. St. Francis provides this challenge for his friars by stating in his Rule of 1223 that the life of the friars is to follow Christ by living the Gospel: "The Rule and Life of the Friars Minor is this, namely, to observe the Holy Gospel of our Lord Jesus Christ" (ch. 1): and ". . . we may live always according to the poverty, and the humility, and the Gospel of our Lord Jesus Christ" (ch. 12). Francis quotes from Scripture throughout his Rule and often refers to the necessity of living the Gospel. "Throughout his life, his response is to the texts of Scripture before anything else."[5]

It is through Scripture that Francis discovers his vocation and way of life. This manifests Francis' openness to God's word and his docility in allowing that word to act within him. Francis directs his friars to have the same type of openness to God's word; and he guides them in being receptive to the word in their daily lives. In other words, he is conscious of the workings of the Holy Spirit within himself and desires his friars to be explicitly aware of the same Spirit working within them. "They should realize . . . that the only thing they should desire is to have the Spirit of God at work within them" (Rule of 1223, ch. 10).

Because of the freedom of the Spirit working within each person, Francis does not set down black and white legislation in his Rule; rather, he presents general principles of behavior, leaving details to be worked out by the individual friar. He "left the actual details of behavior largely uncontrolled, so that each might be at liberty to make his service as the Holy Spirit moved him."[6] Francis believed deeply in the workings of God in his own life, and he directs his friars to be open to God's inspiration in theirs: Only "if any of the friars is inspired by God" should he ask permission to go among the Saracens (Rule of 1223, ch. 12). So sensitive is Francis to the Spirit working in the friar that in chapter 10 of the same rule he commands the ministers not to make demands upon any friar that may be against "their conscience and our Rule."

The emphasis on Scripture and the working of the Holy Spirit leads Francis to sacrifice his own will and put total trust and confidence in God. To instill this same trust and dependence upon God in his friars, Francis states in his Rule that the friars are to be "as strangers and pilgrims in this world, who serve God in poverty and humility" and "beg alms trustingly" (ch. 6). Francis believes that all good things come from God's providence: ". . . and in the words of the Gospel they may eat what is set before them" (Rule of 1223, ch. 3). Implied in this statement is the belief that God will take care of His sons if the Gospel is lived faithfully. Francis sees this providence not only in terms of material need, but also as active in the very beginnings of his Order: "When God gave me some friars . . ." (Testament).

Complete trust in God's providence allows Francis and his friars to dwell on the workings of God in everyday experiences by not uselessly worrying about the future. In the *Scripta Leonis* there is an interesting story in which Francis tells the cook not to prepare many vegetables in case some remain left over for the next day; thus, following the Gospel injunction of not concerning oneself with tomorrow, they will be attentive only to the present.[7] Francis directs his friars to discover in everyday life the workings of God and the inspiration of the Holy Spirit. And this discovery can take place and bear fruit only if the friars remain dependent upon God in living out the ideal of Franciscan poverty.

Discover the Heart

Francis' total surrender to the will of God naturally leads him to let go of his false self and to unmask the self-deceptions that keep him from the Father. The attitude of childlike trust and abandonment to the Father permits the individual to discover who he is in his relationship with the Father.[8] To let go of one's selfishness, which is no less than the practice of poverty, allows the person to come into contact with his own heart: "Their poverty should become . . . the means to honest self-knowledge and self-criticism."[9] Francis also desires that his followers be able to realize that self-deception is enslaving and prohibitive to the free workings of the Spirit within: ". . . each should rather condemn and despise himself" (Rule of 1223, ch. 2). To be able to root out the ego, the friar must be aware that all things come from God: "The subjects . . . should remember that they have renounced their own wills for God's sake" (*Ibid.*, ch. 10).

Because Francis can recognize and experience the workings of God within him, he can also accept and live more easily with his own past: "He stripped himself completely naked before all"; he can be sensitive to God's will in the present: "He seeks now so to despise his own life"; and he can look forward to a future in conformity to God's will: "And that meanwhile only the wall of flesh should separate him from the vision of God" (1 Celano 6:15). This peace with, and knowledge of, oneself can be achieved by the friars, but only if they are honest in living the Gospel. Dishonesty in living the Gospel seems to irritate Francis. There is a recorded incident in which Francis, who has the ability to discern falsity in his friars, dismisses one of them for not living up to the Gospel ideal of work: "There was a certain Brother among them who prayed little and did not work. Considering these things, St. Francis knew through the Holy Spirit that he was a carnal man. So he said to him: 'Go your way, Brother Fly.' "[10]

Francis values honesty with self in "following in the footsteps of our Lord Jesus Christ," and he provides a method for continuous self-appraisal in this area. In chapter 6 of the Rule of 1223, he tells his friars, as members of the same family, not to hesitate to let others know their needs. I believe that this statement implies both material and spiritual needs. He uses the analogy of a mother's love for her son: "For if a mother loves and cares for her child in the flesh, a friar should certainly love and care for his spiritual brother all the more tenderly." What Francis is directing his followers to do is to express to one another their minds, their feelings, so that all may grow in the love of God and one another.

Revealing one's mind seems to have been a common practice with Francis and his friars. Celano gives an account (1, 12:30) of a meeting among the first companions of Francis after they returned from a missionary journey:

> They then gave an account of the good things the merciful Lord had done for them; and if they had been negligent and ungrateful in any way, they humbly begged and willingly received correction and punishment from their holy father. For thus they had always been accustomed to act when they came to him, and they did not hide from him the least thought or the first impulses of their hearts.

This account gives a good model for direction: (1) the friars were sent out into a particular situation from which to learn;

(2) they returned to share experiences among themselves and with Francis; (3) they were honest with one another and with their spiritual father in that they did not hide anything from one another but spoke openly; and (4) they accepted correction and advice from Francis. The friars themselves wish to grow spiritually within the Brotherhood. They seek to be honest with one another; they seek directions from one another and from their spiritual leader; and they willingly open themselves to discover whether what they do is God's will or self-gratification. In one "legend," the friars are gathered together at the Portiuncula. There, they speak openly of their vocation:

> And calling to himself those six friars of his, in the woods near the chapel of St. Mary of Portiuncula, where they often went to pray, he said to them: "Consider, dear brothers, our calling that God has mercifully given us: not only for our own but also for many others' benefit and salvation."[11]

Francis most likely wants his ministers to have the same type of relationship with the brothers. Chapter 7 of the Rule of 1223 states that friars who fall into sin are to go to their ministers, and the ministers are to "be careful not to be angry or upset." And in chapter 10, the ministers are exhorted to receive their subjects "kindly and charitably, and be sympathetic towards them as friars." For Francis, the ministers are servants to the friars, just as Francis himself seeks to serve them: "That is the way it ought to be; the ministers should be the servants of all the friars."

Prayer

A spiritual father or director guides his disciples in prayer. Through prayer, the will of God is made known. Francis himself desires his friars to pray privately and together so that their hearts are made free to receive graces from God. Thus he encourages them to pray to the Holy Spirit "unceasingly with a heart free from self-interest" (Rule of 1223, ch. 10). Whenever anything important is to be decided, Francis prays:

> They all conferred together as true followers of justice whether they should dwell among men or go to solitary places. But Francis, who did not trust his own skill, but had recourse to holy prayer before all transactions, chose not to live for himself alone, but for him who died for all (1 Celano 14:35).

Francis and his friars pray for guidance and then share with one another the outcome of their prayer. Only after this is done is a decision made. Francis does not fear consultation; rather, throughout his life he seeks the advice of others. When the Order is in crisis, he goes to Rome and asks for a Cardinal Protector. Even in the Rule of 1223, St. Francis makes provision for his followers to seek advice: "If they ask for advice, the ministers may refer them [those who wish to enter the Order and are to dispose of their goods] to some God-fearing persons who can advise them how to distribute their property to the poor" (ch. 2); and "if any of the friars is inspired by God to go among the Saracens or other unbelievers, he must ask permission from his provincial minister" (ch. 12).

What Francis leaves his friars in the Rule is a statement of spiritual values he wishes each friar to possess. He, as *forma minorum,* leaves a model to his followers on remaining firm in Gospel living and achieving Brotherhood. The Rule is a model that frees the person in order to recognize within himself the workings of the Spirit: "The Rule is of prime importance in shaping and guiding the whole spiritual life and mental outlook of the Franciscan."[12]

The elements, as found in the Rule of 1223, that serve as basic foundations for spiritual direction among the Franciscans can be summed up as follows: (1) meditative reflection on Scripture, (2) providing situations in which the Gospel is confronted and the friar is challenged, (3) sharing experiences to discern the true workings of grace within each friar, and (4) seeking guidance through consultation and prayer, both private and communal. This model of Franciscan direction is experiential since Francis himself thought in the concrete, everyday experiences of his own life. Through this approach, it would seem, the Franciscan spiritual father is able to lead his disciples to the discovery of the true self which, in effect, would be a conformity "to the prudence of the spirit and the wisdom of God and the Spirit of the Lord."[13]

[1]K. Esser, *Origins of the Franciscan Order* (Chicago: Franciscan Herald Press, 1970), p. 59. [2]*Analecta Ordinis Minorum Capucinorum* 19 (1903), pp. 150-51. [3]*Archivum Franciscanum Historicum* 2 (1929), p. 585. [4]K. Esser, "The Definitive Rule of the Friars Minor," *Round Table of Franciscan Research* 34 (1969), p. 41. [5]M.D. Lambert, *Franciscan Poverty* (London: S.P.C.K., 1961), p. 53. [6]Rosalind Brooke, *Early Franciscan Government* (Cambridge: University Press, 1956), p. 57. [7]Rosalind Brooke, ed. & tr., *Scripta Leonis*

Oxford: Clarendon Press, 1970), pp. 197; 94-95 (= "Legend of Perugia," §4, *Omnibus*, p. 980).   ⁸Cf. William Doheny, *Selected Writings of St. Teresa of Avila* (Milwaukee: Bruce, 1950), p. 251.   ⁹K. Esser, "The Definitive Rule . . . ," p. 34.   ¹⁰R. Brooke, *Scripta Leonis*, 196 ("LP," §62; *Omnibus*, 1038).   ¹¹*Legenda S. Francisci Anonymi Perusini*, in *Miscellanea Francescana* 9 (1902), pp. 39-40.   ¹²I. Brady, tr., *The Marrow of the Gospel* (Chicago: Franciscan Herald Press 1958), p. 106.   ¹³*Ibid.*, p. 199.

St. Catherine of Siena's Principles of Spiritual Direction

Benedict Ashley, O.P.

Among Dominicans of the past from whom we can learn about Dominican spiritual direction, St. Catherine of Siena (1347-80) is a valuable source. She both received direction and provided it for others. Her writings offer us examples of, and guidelines for, counseling others in their journeys of faith. She was, moreover, a remarkable saint, deeply immersed in the mystery of grace and gifted with the ability to speak eloquently about it.

Catherine was not a religious but a member of the lay division of St. Dominic's order of preachers.[1] Around her in Siena, she gathered a group of followers who liked to call themselves "The Family" or "The Beautiful Band" (Bella Brigata).[2] This surprisingly diversified community of men and women called Catherine their "Mamma," although she lived to be only thirty-three. Among her "family" were priests, religious, theologians, hermits, nobility, parents (including Catherine's mother who originally opposed her daughter's chosen way of life), and politicians.

In more than 380 extant letters we can see very concretely how Catherine guided many of these friends towards the heights of the spiritual life, sharing with them her own experiences. From these letters one might reconstruct her method of guidance given both personally and through conferences which she preached to her "family." What is most evident in these letters is her deep love of her friends, her willingness to

This article first appeared in *Spirituality Today,* 33, March 1981, pp. 43-52. Reprinted by permission.

suffer for them, her sensitivity to their problems, and her constantly hopeful and encouraging attitude toward each and every one. Some, like the poet Neri di Landuccio, who suffered painful depressions, needed such support badly.

In the present article, however, I will not attempt to analyze Catherine's letters but will comment on the little treatise on spiritual direction which is contained in her one book, the summary of all her doctrine, *The Dialogue of Divine Providence.* [3]

Three Degrees of the Light of Faith

Chapters 88-96 of the *Dialogue,* subtitled "Tears," deal with the affective experiences of spiritual growth. Then comes a section, chapters 98-109, on "Truth." In a transitional chapter (97), Catherine in prayer begs God, the Eternal Father, to answer two troubling questions about her responsibilities as a spiritual guide to those who consult her. She fears that she herself may go astray. She first apologizes for wearying the Lord with so many questions, since she knows that He loves "few words and many deeds." Then she asks her two questions. First, what is she to say to those who ask her counsel? Is it her duty to pass judgment on their spiritual condition or not? Second, by what signs can she judge that they are moving along the right path? Is it not possible that what seems growth in virtue is really disguised self-love?

Because Catherine's questions are so much to the point, God is quick to reply. But He cautions her that His answers can be understood only by those who really yearn to hear the truth and open themselves to hear it. Divine truth is light itself to the eye of human intelligence, but the pupil of that eye is faith, without which the eye is blind. In Baptism every Christian has been illuminated by the light of faith, but this light shines with three different degrees of clarity.

The first degree is common to all Christians and leads them to begin their spiritual journey (98). [4] By this light they see the dignity of the human person created in God's image, but they also must recognize the vanity of all human ambitions, the depths of their sinfulness, and the struggle between spirit and flesh within them. "Your sin consists simply in loving what I hate and hating what I love," the God of Love says to Catherine (98).

The second degree of faith is found in those who realize

that, as pilgrims, they cannot tarry on their way to God but must make haste (99). Spiritual growth involves two processes. On the one hand, no progress can be made without the consistent practice of ascetic discipline to break through selfishness and open the self to the true love of God. On the other hand, the greatest discipline is not self-imposed but comes from the humble, patient, and persevering acceptance of the trials of life permitted by God's providence. Here, as throughout the *Dialogue,* Catherine insists, on the basis of her own experience, that although asceticism is absolutely necessary for spiritual growth, it must always be used as a means and never as an end in itself.

The third and brightest light of faith begins to shine when the Christian is ready to accept the will of God with gratitude and praise (100). To do so is to enter a state of union with God in which all selfishness is burnt away in the fire of love, so that one lives wholly for others in obedience to the Father as Jesus Himself lived — one lives in the sacrificial love of Christ. Such Christians have wills overflowing with love of God and neighbor, memories filled always with God's presence, minds illuminated by the vision of God's providential plan for His creation. These enlightened ones no longer judge others but only feel compassion for their sufferings, while they are convinced that whatever they themselves suffer is God's purifying love at work in them. Although they still have not reached their journey's end in ultimate peace and glory, they already receive a pledge of that victory in the deep inner peace they now experience. In this world they are like Christ on the cross, "whose flesh was sad and tormented, but His soul was happy because of His union with the divine nature."

Reflecting on these chapters we note that they provide the fundamental general principle, or rule, of spiritual direction, as Catherine understood and practiced it, namely, that the first responsibility of the director is to see that the person under guidance is properly instructed in the great central truths of the Christian faith and that they are motivated by love of God and neighbor. Without this foundation, no true Christian spiritual life is possible.

In the following chapters the Eternal Father provides Catherine with three specific rules of direction.

Three Specific Principles

The first of these principles (which answers the first of Catherine's original two questions) is "Do not judge" (Matthew 7:1-5) (102). The Father warns Catherine that it is all too easy for directors to set themselves up in judgment over those whom they counsel. Only God can judge anyone's true spiritual state. Unless directors have the humility to dwell in self-knowledge, accepting those they counsel without judging them, they will soon be deceived by the devil and become blind guides. If, however, directors refuse to judge, simply encourage their clients to grow in virtue, and point out the paths which lead to futility, then clients will soon learn to trust their directors. "When you think you discern vice in others, put it on your own back as well as theirs, acting always with true humility. Then if the vice is truly there, such people will change their ways all the sooner, seeing themselves so gently understood" (102). Those familiar with the modern theory of counseling will immediately recognize that Catherine had already discovered that the counseling relation is based on a trust engendered by the counselor's unconditional acceptance of the client.

The Father next turns to Catherine's second question about how to ascertain whether those she counsels are on the right path, but in answering it He gives her a second and a third rule. In explaining the second of these He takes it for granted that directors should pray constantly for those they direct, so that they may be sensitive to their feelings and states of mind (103). Hence, sometimes a director will realize that one client is experiencing a time of light and joy, while another struggles in darkness, loneliness, and great confusion. Nevertheless, directors should not make the mistake of thinking that the former are doing well and the latter badly. The process of spiritual growth requires such periods of trial and apparent absence of God. "I make the person who is praying for this soul feel the pain as well. I do this because of the gracious love I have for the soul who is being prayed for, so that the one who is praying may help disperse the cloud that hangs over that spirit" (103).

We might formulate this rule by saying that directors should encourage and support those who are struggling. They should not judge their progress merely on the basis of subjective experiences, but rather on their realistic growth in humble self-knowledge and the other virtues. Modern counselors also recognize that healing and growth do not take place in clients who are unwilling to face the pain of "working through" their problems and who refuse to tolerate apparent regression in order to progress.

Another aspect of Catherine's second question is answered by a third rule which the Father explains (104-5). Everyone is led by God's providence along his or her own unique path. Some directors themselves practice severe penance (as Catherine did) and have seen some of their clients profit by similar practices; they are tempted to enforce such practices on all. This is a bad mistake because not all people have the same kind of bodies, the same temperaments, or the same conditions of life. What helps one, harms another. Ascetical practices, since they are only means and not the goal of the spiritual life, must be proportioned to the needs and stage of progress of the individual.

The Father then qualifies this rule by reminding Catherine of the Christian duty of fraternal correction *(Matthew 18:15-18)* which arises when a director sees that a client is falling into behavior that is objectively seriously sinful. Then it is necessary to confront the client with the norms of the Gospel, first privately, then, if necessary, before two or three other Christians. If this admonition fails, then the Christian community should insist that its members live by its moral standards. The *Dialogue* again and again returns to the theme that Christians live in the Christian community and have responsibility for it.

Signs of Progress

After giving these three specific rules of direction, the Father turns to the final part of Catherine's second question: What are the signs of true progress? (106-7). In an earlier part of the *Dialogue,* the Father had already told Catherine about the sign of spiritual progress which He now describes as "the gladness and hunger for virtue that remain in the soul after My visitation, especially if she is anointed with the virtue of true humility and set ablaze with divine charity" (106). Catherine, however, has noticed that sometimes this sign is ambiguous, consequently, the Father explains it.

God tells Catherine that when humans are in love with something, they tend to lose their ability to judge it objectively. Consequently, when they experience some spiritual pleasure, they very humanly incline to immerse themselves in it and cling to it as if it were the reality they are seeking, mistaking the shadow for the reality. When they fall into this trap, they abandon serious prayer and find themselves under the direction of an "angel of light" who is really the devil. The only remedy is to seek, not the experience of God, but God Himself.

The best proof that a Christian is truly seeking God is growth in humble knowledge of self and practical service of God and neighbor. Pleasant spiritual experiences sought for their own sake will soon fade and leave behind only "pain and the pricking of conscience, without any desire for virtue" (106). False joy is really an expression of selfish love, while true joy is the fruit of the service of God and neighbor. It is an overflow from that service, not an end in itself, for God alone is our goal.

The Father concludes His answer to Catherine by encouraging her and those she may guide to persist courageously in prayer: "I do not spurn my servant's desires. I give to those who ask, and even invite you to ask. And I am very displeased with those who do not knock in truth at the door of Wisdom, my only begotten Son, by following his teaching. Following his teaching is a kind of knocking that calls out to me, the eternal Father, with the voice of holy desire in constant humble prayer. And I am the Father who gives the bread of grace through this door, my gentle Truth" (107; cf. Matt. 7:7-11). Thus Catherine could not doubt that the call to the heights of holiness is given not only to an elite but to all.

So delighted was she to hear this that she concludes this part of the *Dialogue* with an ecstatic prayer of praise and thanksgiving (108). Why has God condescended to flood her with such light? "What moved You to this? Love. For You loved me without being loved by me. O fire of Love! Thanks, thanks to You, eternal Father." She prays that she may keep to the straight path shown her. Then at once she begins to pray for the priests of the church, especially those who are of her "family," including in particular her own two spiritual guides (probably Tommaso della Fonte and Raymund of Capua) that they may be true pillars of the church. Finally, she begs for still deeper understanding that she may be able to work, not only for the renewal of her "family" and her order, but for the reform of the whole Church and the salvation of the world (109).

The general themes of this treatise are in no way original. They reflect the classical tradition of spiritual direction which goes back to the Desert Fathers. The practical application of the Gospel to the guidance of ascetics made by these hermits and cenobites was probably known to Catherine through the *Lives of the Desert Fathers,* translated into Italian by Dominic Cavalca (d. 1342) of nearby Pisa,[5] as well as through Dominican preaching and, perhaps, William Flete, the English Augustinian. This tradition was later to receive a new and powerful formulation by St. Ignatius Loyola in his *Exercises.* [6]

What, then, is Catherine's originality, if any? I believe it is to be found in certain themes familiar to her from childhood from the preaching in her home parish of San Domenico — themes into which she achieved a profound, personal insight through prayer and meditation. In Catherine's day, the thought of St. Augustine and St. Bernard still dominated Dominican preaching, as we can see from Cavalca's popular works.[7] The Scholasticism of St. Thomas Aquinas is still not prominent in the *Dialogue,* although Catherine refers to him with pride (158), and there is little in her teaching with which a Thomist can find fault.[8]

For both Thomas and Catherine the holiness which is the goal of spiritual direction is a transformation, not a destruction, of human nature. This transformation is also a restoration of the image of the Trinity according to which we were created. Holiness consists in a union with God in faith, inspired by hope, and achieved by love, a love which is nothing less than a share in God's own love for His creatures. Such love can flourish only if supported by all the other virtues. We can grow in love only by the service of our neighbor, in obedience to God. Such obedience is a cooperation with God's own loving, providential care of the world. We cannot, however, obey God by our own strength, but only by His grace, for which we must continually pray. God has given us all grace through Christ crucified, the Word incarnate. We live in Him only when we also live in His body, the Church, the living witness of His hidden presence.

Thus Catherine would not have dared to direct others, if she had not been entirely ready to be directed herself by the Church. Nor did she seek to direct them by any other principles than the Gospel which she had heard preached and on which she had daily meditated. What she heard in ecstasy from the

Eternal Father was the same message, only deeply understood by one who had learned to listen in the deep humility of self-knowledge achieved by constant prayer and much suffering. Catherine was original, therefore, only in her practical appropriation of the Gospel truth, which is ever new.

Catherine's principles for spiritual guides can be summed up conveniently as follows:

1. *General Principle:* Be sure the one you are to counsel is well instructed in the Catholic faith, and that he or she is motivated by a desire to grow in the love of God and neighbor.
2. *Specific Rules:*
   a. Dò not judge, but accept and encourage your client to follow Christ in daily living.
   b. Do not measure a client's spiritual progress by his or her subjective experiences, pleasant or unpleasant, but by steady growth in humble self-knowledge and practical service of God and neighbor.
   c. Help your clients to achieve a disciplined way of life and prayer suited to their individual needs.
3. *Signs of Progress:* True obedience to God brings an abiding joy and peace, but feelings of joy and peace are not to be trusted unless they are accompanied by growth in self-understanding and unselfish service of neighbor.

[1]The best biographies of St. Catherine in English are: Johannes Jorgensen, *Saint Catherine of Siena,* trans. Ingeborg Lund (New York: Longmans, Green and Co., 1939), and Arrigo Levasti, *My Servant, Catherine,* trans. Dorothy M. White (Westminister, Md.: Newman Press, 1954). The main source of *Leggenda Maiore* of Raymund of Capua is also available in English: *The Life of Saint Catherine of Siena of Blessed Raymund of Capua,* trans. George Lamb (New York: P.J. Kenedy, 1960). Unfortunately none are in print.   [2]I have made use here of an unpublished paper, "La Famiglia: The Fellowship of the Disciples of St. Catherine of Siena as a Model of Evangelical Community," by Vivian Gilbreth.   [3]The best edition is that of Giuliana Cavallini, *II Dialogo* (Rome: Edizioni Cateriniane, 1968), which has been translated by Suzanne Nofke in the Classics of Western Spirituality series (New York: Paulist Press, 1980).   [4]The numbers in parentheses here and in the following pages refer to the chapters of the *Dialogue.*   [5]I hope soon to publish a paper on Cavalca. See the brief article by I. Colosio in *Dictionnaire de spiritualité,* vol. 2, cols. 373-74.   [6]A very helpful study on the sources of St. Ignatius's theory of spiritual direction is Piet Penning de Vries, *Discernment of Spirits according to the Life and Teachings of St. Ignatius Loyola* (New York: Exposition Press, 1975).   [7]Cavalca's work *The Mirror of the Cross* is typical of Dominican preaching of this time. It probably influenced St. Catherine.   [8]The most commonly cited difference is that Catherine uses the Augustinian triad memory-intelligence-will to explain the image of the Trinity in the soul, while St. Thomas *(Summa theologiae,* I, ques. 93, art. 7), teaches that the most proper analogy is to be found in the acts of knowledge and will as they proceed from the soul.

Spiritual Direction According to St. John of the Cross

Joel Giallanza, C.S.C.

Spiritual direction is fast becoming a very important ministry in the Church. Not that direction has been neglected within the history of the Church, but the plethora of materials available and workshops offered in recent years is evidence of the emphasis placed on this ministry as a true support to growth in the spiritual life. Indeed, it could almost be said that spiritual direction is becoming something of a science, not in the sense that a multitude of rigid norms are necessary to it; but rather, that some competencies are essential to the process of assisting someone along the road to union with God.

It seems obvious that one such competency is familiarity with the spiritual doctrine of the great mystics. Even more specifically, the teachings of such saints as Teresa of Avila and John of the Cross should hold a place of priority for anyone engaged in this ministry.

With this in mind, these present reflections are offered. In *The Living Flame of Love,* stanza 3, paragraphs 30 to 62, St. John speaks of the impact that spiritual directors have on the persons with whom they work.[1] The immediate context of this section is founded on the truth that "God is the principal agent in this matter, and that He acts as the blind man's guide who must lead it by the hand to the place it does not know how to reach" (29).[2] No obstacle, therefore, should be placed on the road along which God is leading an individual. But, says St. John, "there are three blind men who can draw if off the

This article originally appeared in *Contemplative Review,* 11, Fall 1978, pp. 31-7. Reprinted by permission.

road: the spiritual director, the devil, and the soul itself" (29). It is with the first of these "blind men" that these reflections will be concerned.

Rather than commenting on this section of St. John's work in an expository way, it may be more helpful to identify some principles which seem to be operative throughout it. Hopefully, these principles will be held as primary values by those in the ministry of spiritual direction.[3]

1. Directors must be personally committed to growth in the spiritual life.

At the very outset of this section, St. John delineates the qualities necessary for this ministry; namely, "besides being learned and discreet, a director should have experience" (30). Even though these three are listed, priority is clearly given to experience. Directors may be very learned and discreet, but without experience they will not be able to lead a person to spirit "nor will (he) even understand it" (30).

St. John maintains this priority on experience throughout this entire section. However, his method of maintaining this priority is somewhat surreptitious; that is, St. John speaks less directly about the necessity of experience itself and more directly about the hindrance to growth that inexperienced directors can be. His imagery is graphic; directors who do not understand the stages of prayer beyond discursive meditation are like "a blacksmith, (who) knows no more than how to hammer and pound with the faculties" (43). Therefore, when the Lord is bringing a person into simple contemplation, directors can be an obstacle to spiritual growth by "not understanding souls that tread the path of quiet and solitary contemplation, since they themselves have not reached it and do not know what it is to part with discursive meditation, and think these souls are idle" (53).

Personal commitment to growth in the spiritual life challenges directors, not only to know something of what the Lord is doing in another's life, but also to have experienced it to some degree. Such experience comes from fidelity to prayer. Admittedly, one's own experience will not exactly parallel that of another person, but the specific point on which St. John is speaking here — moving beyond discursive meditation — will be the same for both directors and directees.

The importance of the other qualities — learning and discretion — can be seen in light of this. Learning is more pervasive than mere book knowledge. Surely those engaged in the direction ministry must be familiar with the wisdom to be found in this history of Christian spirituality. Even a casual reading of the *Life* of St. Teresa of Avila reveals the frustration she experienced at the hands of directors who did not understand higher stages of the spiritual life. Learning, for St. John, goes beyond academic knowledge. In *The Ascent to Mount Carmel* and *The Dark Night,* he speaks of the foundational place that self-knowledge holds in the spiritual life. Indeed, the scientific exactitude with which he speaks about different stages in the spiritual life is utilized precisely to give his readers clear insights into the activity of the Lord in their lives. Therefore, spiritual directors must have a discipline of self-reflection through which they progress to an increasingly clear understanding of their own spiritual development.

Self-knowledge, then, is an essential part of the learning that constitutes the experience of directors. Further, it is upon this self-knowledge that authentic discretion rests. Discretion is not simply a virtue exercised by directors; rather, it is the attitudinal frame of reference within which the entire process of direction takes place. That is, discretion is the way of proceeding in this ministry based on one's learning, both academic and self-discovered, and experience. Above all else, discretion places a priority on what the Lord is doing in the life of a directee. And that priority will be maintained because learning and experience have taught directors to respect the unique process of growth through which the Lord is leading others.

This first principle for spiritual directors from St. John of the Cross illustrates three important points. First, personal commitment to growth challenges directors to be aware of the importance of their own spiritual experience. Within that experience will be valuable information without which their ministry will be less intense. Second, commitment to the spiritual life demands that directors have a progressive and personal knowledge of spirituality. That is, a growing knowledge founded on the wisdom of the masters and the insights drawn from disciplined self-reflection. Third, such a commitment sensitizes directors to the respect necessary in discerning what the Lord is doing in the life of the directee.

Anything less is to confine the Lord, and the person in direction, to one mode of operation.

2. Directors must realize that the principal guide is always the Holy Spirit.

It is almost hoped that this principle needs little elaboration. The fact that it is listed second does not indicate a lack of importance — truly this is the first principle of spiritual direction. Rather, in St. John's writing, it flows logically from what has been said thus far. The realization of the Spirit as the Director comes about through a life of commitment to personal growth in the spiritual life. Therefore, "directors should reflect that they themselves are not the chief agent, guide, and mover of souls in this matter, but that the principal guide is the Holy Spirit, who is never neglectful of souls, and that they are instruments for directing them to perfection through faith and the law of God, according to the spirit God gives each one" (46).

The failure of some directors to realize this prompts St. John to call them "blind men." Directors that do not take seriously the importance of disciplined self-reflection "may thus be an obstacle to the guidance of the Holy Spirit" (62). Truly, this is the most serious indictment that could be levelled against a spiritual director. And so, St. John makes no apologies when he is compelled to say that such directors should not be excused since they are "rudely meddling in something they do not understand" (56). And even more forcefully he says they "will be punished; since this is their duty, they are obliged to be careful and understand what they are doing" (62). Admittedly, this is strong language; nevertheless, the only alternative is for directors to remain in that blindness which comes from an insensitivity to what the Spirit is doing in the directee's life.

This principle has a very practical application. It can never be assumed that a particular director is the only one that could ever guide a particular individual. St. John puts this in the form of a question: "Is it possible . . . that you are so perfect the soul will never need any other than you?" (58). Spiritual directors must remain open to whatever the Spirit may wish to do in a person's life. Again, reflection on the *Life* of St. Teresa would show that had she simply accepted the insistence of her first directors that her experiences were "from the devil," she may never have reached the intense union with God that so obviously graced her life.

Therefore, directors must be sensitive to the possibility of referring directees to someone else if necessary. St. John is clear on this point: "you should not assume that in turning from you this person turned from God" (59). And again, "directors should themselves counsel this change, and all the rest stems from foolish pride and presumption or some other ambition" (61). Failure to value this attitude as foundational in this ministry results in jealously clinging to directees rather than guiding them to the Lord with wise discernment. Directors are hardly capable of leading others to the detachment and emptiness necessary for union with the Lord when they themselves have not grown in these qualities.

The second principle for spiritual directors offered by St. John of the Cross is a reality that must pervade everything the director does. Two summary points are offered. First, only the Lord can ultimately lead a person to union with Himself. Directors are agents for the Lord, but the Lord always remains the principal agent. Second, that fact necessitates a real detachment on the part of directors: detachment from the directees[4] and detachment from the specific recommendations that are offered. Only this empowers directors to minister with the openness and flexibility necessary for willingly responding to whatever the Lord may will for a particular individual.

3. Directors must encourage the freedom necessary for the Lord to manifest His will.

This principle is truly implicit in everything that has gone before. It would not even have to be viewed as a separate point, except that St. John emphasizes freedom as an essential quality of the direction process. "Spiritual directors, then, should give freedom to souls and encourage them in their desire to seek improvement" (61). The specific "freedom" of which St. John writes must characterize the directee's response to the Lord; the response must be free to insure growth in the spiritual life. This is not meant to atrophy the ministry of directors; rather, it is to assert the primacy of responding to the Lord in freedom. There may be times when directees offer clearer insights and more effective recommendations for growth than their directors; the latter must know the significance and wisdom of those insights and recommendations. Therefore, "the director should not think that he has all requirements, or that God will not want to lead the soul further on" (57).

To ignore this incurs dissatisfaction. "The director does not know the means by which God may wish to benefit a soul, especially if it is no longer satisfied with the director's teaching" (61). Specifically, St. John cites two sources of this dissatisfaction: "either because God is making it advance by a road different from the one along which he is leading it, or because the director himself has changed his style" (61). In both cases, St. John recommends the referral that was mentioned in the reflections on the second principle. Anything else could hinder the directee's growth.

To encourage such a freedom necessitates true humility in directors. This humility is expressed in the realization "that since that soul must always advance along the spiritual road, on which God is always a help to it, it will have to change its style and mode of prayer and will need another doctrine more sublime than yours and other spirituality" (57). Obviously, the importance of both the first and second principles is evident in this statement; only a personal commitment to the spiritual life and the realization that God is truly the Guide of this life empower directors to encourage the freedom demanded by this third principle.

Besides humility, directors must have a realistic attitude toward their own knowledge and abilities. "Not everyone knows all the happenings and stages of the spiritual journey, nor is everyone spiritually so perfect as to know every state of the interior life in which a person must be conducted and guided" (57). In one sense, the cliche about not being able to give what one doesn't have is operative here, for surely the Lord can lead directees beyond the spiritual state of their directors. Admitting this, if a director continues to function as if growth has not occurred, when in fact it has, not only will the directee's further growth be hindered, but the director "would ruin" what the Lord is accomplishing.

This third principle for spiritual directors found in St. John's thought emphasizes the manner in which this ministry is to be approached. Three points are of significance. First, freedom is essential to the authenticity of the direction relationship. This insures the validity of a director's discernment as well as the directee's appropriate response to the movements of the Spirit. Second, humility demands that directors see their ministry as only one aid in revealing the Lord's will for directees; there are other channels the Lord may choose to accomplish His work. Third, an honest realism enables directors to know their competencies and the perimeters within which their ministry must take place if they are to be truly effective.

Conclusion

St. John of the Cross speaks with some specificity about different stages of the spiritual life in the section of *The Living Flame of Love* that has been under discussion here. Other principles would come to light from an examination of the entire sanjuanist corpus. So, while these principles do not pretend to be exhaustive, this is one of the only places in which St. John is concerned specifically with spiritual directors. Further, it is the only place in which he deals with that concern at such length.

The effectiveness of the direction ministry depends, not solely, but to a significant extent, on directors' personal commitment to growth in the spiritual life; within that commitment is the realization that God alone is Lord and Guide of this life: therefore, directees must be given the freedom to discover the Lord's will in their own lives. The significance of these principles in the immediate context which frames St. John's remarks is that they can enlighten directors, thus sparing them from being among the "blind men" that interfere with growth in the spiritual life.

Aware of the mystery into which their ministry brings them, spiritual directors should prayerfully reflect on the wisdom of Jesus' words to Nicodemus: "The wind blows where it wills, and you hear the sound of it, but you do not know where it comes from, or where it goes; so it is with every one who is born of the Spirit" *(John 3:8)*.

[1]In this section of his work, except for the opening paragraphs, St. John is speaking about those who have moved beyond the beginning stages of prayer.   [2]All references to *The Living Flame of Love* will be indicated by: (paragraph number). Unless otherwise noted, all references will be to stanza 3.   [3]These principles are addressed specifically to directors, even though they are foundational also to a complete sanjuanist spirituality.   [4]"Detachment from directees" in no way implies uninvolvement. Clearly, a direction relationship has some emotional ramifications. What is implied here is a loving relationship that frees directees to do whatever is necessary for a faithful response to the Lord.

Spiritual Direction According to St. Teresa of Avila

Joel Giallanza, C.S.C.

In the preceding chapter, some reflections were offered on spiritual direction as it is presented in the writings of St. John of the Cross. In those writings are found significantly important theological principles that can be of support to anyone engaged in the ministry of direction. The wisdom of St. John, as a Doctor of the Church, goes beyond both the historical period in which it was written and the emphasis of the Carmelite tradition. In truth, there is a sense of timelessness about his teachings.

Interestingly enough, within the same historical period, and the same tradition, there stands another great saint, another Doctor of the Church, whose wisdom is no less than a companion to that of St. John: St. Teresa of Avila. At first reading, the writings of Teresa may seem to emphasize only the practical ramifications of realities that St. John treats more speculatively. However, she, too, is an excellent theologian and this should not be overlooked.

It is with this in mind that these present reflections came to birth. As an outstanding figure in this history of spirituality, as well as one who struggled within spiritual direction, what St. Teresa has to say on this ministry is truly worthy of examination. By way of initial comparison, Teresa, unlike John, is not systematic in her presentation of direction; rather, her views are scattered throughout her writings. However, one part of the *Life*[1] seems to be a concentration of what she teaches con-

This article first appeared in *Contemplative Review,* 12, Summer 1979, pp. 1-9. Reprinted by permission.

cerning spiritual direction. In particular, both within and without that one part, Teresa reflects on three main areas: spiritual direction itself, the responsibility of directees, and the qualities for directors. These three will help to shape the method of investigation employed herein.

Need for Direction

It is no historical discovery to assert that Teresa had difficulties in her first experiences of spiritual direction. Indeed, for a considerable period of time, she could not even find a director who understood the path along which the Lord was leading her. Even with poor health, Teresa remained faithful to her desire for growth in prayer; but, she also reveals her frustration. "For during the twenty years after this period of which I am speaking, I did not find a master, I mean a confessor, who understood me, even though I looked for one. This hurt me so much that I often turned back and was even completely lost, for a master would have helped me flee from the occasions of offending God."[2] When speaking about the higher stages of prayer, specifically rapture, she reiterates this. "If those who guide them have not gone through this themselves, it may perhaps seem to these guides . . . that these persons are dead. . . . What these persons suffer when their confessors do not understand them is a pity" (L, 20, 21). Throughout her *Life*, Teresa alludes to her own experiences at the hands of directors who consistently misinterpreted her. But Teresa never despaired because "if after one has looked for someone, no one is found, the Lord will not fail; He hasn't failed me in spite of what I am" (L, 40, 8).

Nevertheless, Teresa insists on the necessity of spiritual direction, especially for beginners. "The beginner needs counsel so as to see what helps him most. For this reason a master is very necessary providing he has experience" (L, 13, 14). But, even as the Lord brings one to higher stages of contemplative prayer, "experience and a spiritual master are necessary because once the soul has reached these boundaries many things occur about which it is necessary to have someone to talk to" (L, 40, 8). The reason for direction is a relatively simple one: it affords some objectivity in reflecting on one's own prayer life. "There is nothing more certain in this matter than to have greater fear[3] and always to seek counsel, to have a master who is a learned man, and to hide nothing from him"

(L, 25, 14).

The alternative to this is a self-reliance which stands in opposition to growth in the spiritual life. Teresa herself had experienced this and thus points to the necessity of a director. "This self-reliance was what destroyed me. For this reason and for every reason there is need of a master and for discussions with spiritual persons" (L, 19, 15). And so it is that direction elicits humility in the directee; and this is nothing less than the realization that all growth is from the Lord. This humility is foundational to the entirety of Teresa's doctrine. "If there is no progress in humility, everything is going to be ruined" (L, 12, 4); and again, "let humility always go first so as to understand that this strength does not come from ourselves" (L, 13, 8).

Therefore, if one were to identify a primary principle of spiritual direction according to St. Teresa it would be simply that direction is necessary. It affords some objective vision of one's own spiritual state and, in that vision, calls forth humility and greater dependence on the Lord. But, one caution is worthy of mention; a distinction must be made between "necessary" and *essential*. [4] It is true that Teresa speaks of direction as a necessary means of growth in the spiritual life, especially in the early stages. However, it must not be inferred that progress in the spiritual life cannot/does not occur outside of or without spiritual direction. Such an inference would strip the Lord's grace of its power; also, it would undermine everything that Teresa is saying throughout her writings. Spiritual direction, then, is a necessary and helpful means of growth, but it is not essential; that is, it is not intrinsic to the process of growth in the Lord. The Lord *alone* is essential to growth in the spiritual life; indeed, St. Teresa's life and teaching are an incarnation of the fact that "apart from me you can do nothing" *(John 15:5)*.

Self-knowledge and Direction

Even though there are times when a particular director can limit a directee's growth — as was the case in Teresa's own life — Teresa still recommends obedience to one's director. Such obedience, however, does not remove one's personal responsibility. In other words, the spiritual director is not a spiritual magician who guarantees the attainment of perfection. Rather, spiritual direction is only one part of the exhortation given by St. Paul: "work out your own salvation with fear and trembling; for God is at work in you, both to will and to work for his good pleasure" *(Philippians 2:12-13).*

Specifically, this personal responsibility in the context of direction is to establish a discipline of self-knowledge. This discipline is important not only in the early stages of prayer, but throughout one's growth in the Lord. "This path of self-knowledge must never be abandoned, nor is there on this journey a soul so much a giant that it has no need to return often to the stage of an infant and a suckling. And this should never be forgotten. . . . Along this path of prayer, self-knowledge . . . is the bread with which all palates must be fed, no matter how delicate they may be; they cannot be sustained without this bread" (L, 13, 15). St. Teresa elaborates her understanding of self-knowledge most extensively in the *Interior Castle;* particularly, in the first, fifth, and sixth mansions. It is beyond the scope of these present reflections to explore this in depth; however, three points can serve to focus Teresa's thought on this matter.

First, as is evident in the above text from Teresa's *Life,* and as it is presented in the mansions cited from the *Interior Castle,* self-knowledge is a constitutive element of the spiritual life. St. Teresa is uncompromising on this point: "However high a state the soul may have attained, self-knowledge is incumbent upon it, and this it will never be able to neglect even should it so desire."[5] Throughout the spiritual life, the Lord can bestow great blessings on a person; even these blessings are related to self-knowledge. "I think they will never be bestowed on a person devoid of humility, because before the Lord grants a soul these favors He always gives it a high degree of self-knowledge" (IC, VI, 9). The reason for this is simply that God dwells within each person; therefore, a discipline of self-knowledge brings one closer to the Lord, and so, it holds a place of importance in the spiritual life.

Second, from this is born the realization that one is dependent on God for all things. "If we turn from self towards God, our understanding and our will become nobler and readier to embrace all that is good: if we never rise above the slough of our own miseries we do ourselves a great disservice" (IC, I, 2). At first this seems so obvious that it hardly needs to be mentioned; and yet, dependence on the Lord is a spiritual reality that can be easily overlooked on a personal level. In the busyness of everyday life, this is probably not called to mind as frequently or as intensely as it could be for sustaining one's spiritual life. This realization touches upon the importance of humility, as an expression of self-knowledge, which is foundational to all of Teresian spirituality. "But, believe me, if you find you are lacking in this virtue, you have not yet attained union . . . if you use your best endeavors and strive after this in every way that you can, He will give you more even than you can desire" (IC, V, 3).

Third, as a discipline, self-knowledge is not an activity in which one simply engages. It is a process. The text from Teresa's *Life* cited at the beginning of this section indicates that self-knowledge is not merely acquired and then passed over. "It must always be understood that she (the soul) will try to advance in the service of Our Lord and in self-knowledge" *(ibid.)*. Truly, self-knowledge must remain an active discipline throughout one's spiritual progress; indeed, it becomes a way of life — a life of prayer.

Admittedly, these three points form only a sketch of Teresa's thought on this discipline. Nevertheless, from the directee's point of view, they do shed some light on the attitude and responsibility that will foster effective direction. Even the most saintly and perceptive director will seem to be a disappointment if the directee is not committed to self-knowledge as a significant means of discovering within oneself, and growing into union with, the Lord. And so, St. Teresa asserts: "I think it is a greater favor if the Lord sends us a single day of humble self-knowledge, even at the cost of many afflictions and trials, than many days of prayer" *(Book of Foundations, 5)*.

Qualities for Directors

Thus far these reflections have considered what St. Teresa teaches concerning spiritual direction itself and the responsibility of directees in that context. It will be of value, then, to explore briefly what she says of those who are actively engaged in this ministry; namely, the directors.

In chapter 13 of her *Life,* Teresa puts forth three qualities for spiritual directors. "It is very important that the master have prudence — I mean that he have good judgment — and experience; if besides these he has learning, so much the better" (L, 13, 16). These three qualities — good judgment, experience, learning — flow from Teresa's own experience in following the advice of her varied directors. Like St. John of the Cross, St. Teresa seems to place a priority on the personal experience of the director. "A master is very necessary providing he has experience" (L, 13, 14). And again, "if one cannot find these three qualifications together, the first two are more important since men with a background in studies can be sought out and consulted when there is need" (L, 13, 16).

However, it is interesting to note that as one explores further what Teresa says regarding directors, learning is the quality that begins to take the primary position among the three.

> Let not the spiritual person be misled by saying that learned men without prayer are unsuitable for those who practice it. I have consulted many learned men because for some years now, on account of a greater necessity, I have sought them out more; and I've always been a friend of men of learning. For though some don't have experience, they don't despise the Spirit nor do they ignore it, because in Sacred Scripture, which they study, they always find the truth of the good spirit. (L, 13, 18).

Admittedly, there are times when she combines the importance of learning with experience, such as in the *Interior Castle*. "If your director, though a man of prayer, has not been led in this way by the Lord, he will at once become alarmed and condemn it; that is why I advise you to go to a man who has both spirituality and great learning if such a one can be found" (IC, VI, 8). And, in the *Book of Foundations,* Teresa combines, at least implicitly, learning and good judgment. "If a person is told to do anything, or the future is prophesied to her, in a revelation, it is essential that she should discuss the matter with a discreet and learned confessor, and neither do nor believe anything but what the confessor tells her" (8).

Nevertheless, Teresa consistently seems to place learning above the other two qualities.

> I have said this because there are opinions going around that learned men if they are not spiritual are no help to people who practice prayer. I have already said that it is necessary to have a spiritual master; but if he is not a learned man, this lack of learning will be a hindrance. It will be a great help to consult with learned men. If they are virtuous even though they may not experience spiritual things, they will benefit me; and God will enable them to explain what they must teach — He will even give them spiritual experience so that they might help us. I

208

do not say this without having experienced it, and it has happened to me with more than two. (L, 13, 19).

Indeed, almost the entirety of chapter 13 in the *Life* is an exhortation to seek out learned persons as spiritual directors.

The importance which St. Teresa attaches to learning may be unexpected at first. But this becomes less surprising when one calls to mind the difficulty she had in finding anyone who understood the spiritual experiences through which the Lord was leading her.[6] The principal frustration which Teresa seemed to experience in all of this was that, even though her directors were holy persons, they did not possess sufficient knowledge concerning the higher states of prayer. One can imagine the joy Teresa must have had upon coming into contact with one who could be considered one of her most illustrious directors: St. Peter of Alcantara. "Almost from the outset I saw that he understood me through experience, which was all that I needed" (L, 30, 4). In chapter 30 of the *Life,* Teresa writes at some length on the enlightenment that became hers because of St. Peter's explanations and encouragement. "For at that time I didn't understand myself or how to describe my experience as I do now . . . and it was necessary that the one who understood me and explained these experiences to me should himself have experienced them" *(ibid.).*

It should not be inferred that Teresa is contradicting herself by this present emphasis on experience; instead, it should be read as a clarification of her own thinking and experience. Consider: Teresa was hard-pressed to find a director who had experiences similar to her own; logically, therefore, she posits the primary importance of learning. However, once she encounters a director who understands her as well as shares similar experiences — namely, in the person of St. Peter — experience, as a quality for directors, receives prominence. It could be said, then, that experience in a spiritual director has a type of conditional primacy in Teresian thought. Put bluntly, if one can find a director with experience, that is most helpful because "if these learned men do not practice prayer their learning is of little help to beginners" (L, 13, 16). But, as if to balance that, Teresa is also prompted to say: "I do not mean that beginners shouldn't consult learned men, for I would rather a spirit without prayer than one that has not begun to walk in truth" *(Ibid.).*

Good judgment, as the third quality for directors, flows

from all that has been said concerning learning and experience. It cannot be envisioned as a quality existing in complete isolation; quite the contrary, good judgment rests upon the learning and experience of the director. Learning affords the director a clear understanding of the ways in which the Lord works at different stages of the spiritual life. Experience lends a solid confirmation of that understanding. Combined, these two constitute good judgment, or, what Teresa also calls prudence and discretion.

Teresa never loses sight of the importance of direction itself. And, it is thus that she prays for directors: "I praise You very much because You awaken so many to awaken us. Our prayer for those who give us light should be unceasing. In the midst of tempests as fierce as those the Church now endures, what would we be without them? . . . May it please the Lord to keep them in His hands and help them so that they might help us, amen" (L, 13, 21).

Conclusion

Three areas have been considered in these reflections that may help to clarify one's understanding of spiritual direction, and, in particular, the unique emphasis offered by St. Teresa of Avila. First, concerning direction itself, Teresa proclaims its necessity; however, this does not undermine the active operation of the Lord's grace outside of that context. The Lord alone is truly the source of all spiritual growth.

Second, regarding the responsibility of directees, Teresa emphasizes the foundational importance of an established discipline of self-knowledge as a constitutive element of the spiritual life. Within this discipline lies the potential to realize one's dependence on the Lord for all things; and further, the nature of the spiritual life as process becomes clearer as the depths of the self are discovered.

Third, the qualities that should characterize the ministry of directors are the areas which occupy most of Teresa's time in her reflections on direction. While experience holds a place of obvious importance, Teresa emphasizes the need for learning. This learning affords the director some understanding of the process that is integral to the spiritual life; such an understanding is valuable even though it may not have come through personal experience. These two qualities point to and lay the foundation for the third quality, good judgment. Teresa is well aware that such a director may not be found easily; therefore, she is prompted to say that directees may even have to "postpone having a master until a suitable person is found, for the Lord will provide one on the condition that all is founded upon humility and the desire to do the right thing" (L, 13, 19).

Spiritual direction, the responsibility of directees, and the qualities for directors are all significantly related to the process of moving toward union with the Lord. As a ministry within the Church, spiritual direction seems to be increasingly important. Therefore, anyone committed to spiritual growth should reflect seriously on the advice given by St. Teresa: "It should be possible to find a number of people who combine both learning and spirituality, and the more favors the Lord grants you in prayer, the more needful it is that your good works and your prayers should have a sure foundation."[7]

[1]Chapter 13, sections 13-22 in *The Collected Works of St. Teresa of Avila* (vol. 1); translated by Kieran Kavanaugh, O.C.D. and Otilio Rodriquez, O.C.D.; Institute of Carmelite Studies, 1976.   [2]*Life,* chapter 4, paragraph 7. Further references to this work will be indicated by the following: (L, chapter, paragraph).   [3]Teresa uses "fear" because this text appears in her discussion of the devil's trickery. However, the importance of direction is a fundamental principle in Teresian thought.   [4]I am indebted to John Gleason, C.S.C., for this distinction.   [5]*Interior Castle,* 1st Mansion, chapter 2; from the translation by E. Allison Peers; Doubleday Image Books, 1961. References will be indicated by: (IC, Mansion, chapter).   [6]See footnote 2.   [7]*Way of Perfection,* chapter 5. (Peers' translation.)

Thomas Merton:
Spiritual Director

Charles Healey, S.J.

Introduction

This essay will seek to investigate the thought and development of Thomas Merton concerning the subject of spiritual direction as contained in his writings. Such an investigation would seem to be both timely and worthwhile. First, there is at the present time a sustained interest and appreciation of Thomas Merton's life and writings; secondly, there is a renewed interest in the whole area of spiritual direction flowing from the renewed interest in prayer and spirituality that is occurring at the present time. We have witnessed in recent years the popularity and spread of such varied movements as the Charismatic Movement, The Directed Retreat Movement, The House of Prayer Movement and others, all differing in many respects but all reflecting the obvious concern and desire of so many for a deepening of their lives of faith, hope and love. The renewed awareness of the importance of prayer and the discernment of God's will in our lives has led naturally to a renewed interest in the subject of spiritual direction. It would seem fitting, then, to investigate the life and writings of one who is rapidly assuming the position of the most significant American spiritual writer of this century from this perspective and focus of spiritual direction.

A natural division of our subject would seem to suggest itself. First, Thomas Merton's experience of spiritual direction in his own life will be investigated. Secondly, we will consider

This article first appeared in *Cistercian Studies,* 11, 1976, pp. 228-45. Reprinted by permission.

Merton's experience of spiritual direction from the perspective of Merton as director of others. Finally, and at greater length, we will look at his ideas on the subject of spiritual direction as expressed and developed in his writings.

It might be noted here at the outset that Merton always manifested a keen interest in the archetypal figure of the "Spiritual Father" as depicted in the literature of early monasticism, that is to say, the monasticism of Egypt, Palestine, and Syria in the fourth and fifth centuries.[1] Although this will be kept in mind and developed to some extent, our main interest here will be his ideas on spiritual direction in general, particularly as they are applicable and helpful for a spirituality meeting present-day needs.

I. Merton's Experience of Spiritual Direction

a) Pre-Trappist Days

Merton's conversion experiences and his intense search for God that led him finally to the Abbey of Gethsemani in the year 1941 is carefully documented in his autobiography *The Seven Storey Mountain*. There was hardly any formal spiritual direction throughout this spiritual odyssey, and in many respects, God's grace was working in his life and influencing him more in an informal way through various persons and various books. There were, for example, the significant influences of such books as Gilson's *The Spirit of Medieval Philosophy*, and Aldous Huxley's *Ends and Means*, which led him in turn to the writings of such persons as John of the Cross, Teresa of Avila, Thérèse of Lisieux, and Ignatius of Loyola. There were also the positive influences of such friends and teachers as Mark Van Doren, Bob Lax, Dan Walsh, and Bramachari. It will be recalled that it was his Hindu friend, Bramachari, who urged him to read the classics in Christian spirituality, Augustine's *Confessions* and Kempis' *The Imitation of Christ*.

When he made his decision to become a Catholic while a student at Columbia University, he did, of course, receive some formal instruction and direction in preparation for his baptism, but this did not continue after his actual Baptism in November, 1938. Again, whatever direction occurred after this came more informally and through his friends. For example, it was Bob Lax who clarified and made explicit his deepest yearnings in a chance conversation one day with his words: "What you should say is that you want to be a saint." And to Merton's question of how he expected him to become a saint, Lax replied simply, "By wanting to."[2] There was also, as he mentions in his autobiography, the occasional advice he received in the course of going to confession regularly.[3] At other times, however, he was completely on his own. In writing about his first attempts at any kind of mental prayer, he tells us that he went through the *Spiritual Exercises* of Saint Ignatius under his own direction, even though a spiritual director is essential in this process.

When he was seriously thinking about a vocation to the priesthood, it was to his former teacher and friend, Dan Walsh, that he went for assistance in making a decision. This led to his application to the Franciscans and his acceptance, and then to his reconsideration and the disappointment and misunderstanding that followed on his part. It would seem that much of this confusion and anxiety could have been avoided if the opportunity for spiritual direction had been available to him on a regular basis. A very active and intense interior life was going on within the young Merton. God was touching him deeply with His love and His grace and Merton was struggling to respond generously. However, there was no regular direction and Merton later realized that this was a great lack. Referring to this period, we find him writing in his autobiography: "I should have sought constant and complete spiritual direction," and "Direction was the thing I most needed, and which I was least solicitous to avail myself of."[4]

This lack of formal spiritual direction need not be unduly emphasized, however, for God was leading him. The Holy Spirit was guiding him and prompting him, and Merton tried to respond as well as he could. This sense of God's providential love grew as his own life progressed and often in retrospect he recognized that God's providence was with him even though at the time he was struggling. This always left him with a sense of gratitude and awe at God's workings in his life.[5]

b) Early Experiences of Direction at Gethsemani

Gethsemani provided Thomas Merton with the direction which he needed in his own life at the time. It seems to have been a direction and guidance that was regular, consistent, sustained and capable. First of all, there was the direction that the structured monastic life gave him. Based on the Rule of Saint Benedict, it provided him with a stable way of life that allowed him to sink roots; it deepened his awareness and appreciation of God's abiding and forgiving love, and it enabled him to grow as a person, particularly in a spirit of freedom. The direction that the monastic life gave to him and the deep sense of belonging that developed in his life was extremely important.[6] There is a great deal of direction in the spiritual life built into the Rule of Saint Benedict and the ordered life of a monk.

In addition to this general direction, there was also the personal direction that was provided through such key people in the monastery as his novice master, his confessor, and his abbot. It is clear from his journal, *The Sign of Jonas,* that he availed himself of these opportunities and that he received good solid advice as he worked through his early doubts and difficulties. There were two particular areas in which this direction proved very important and valuable. First, there was Merton's attraction to the solitary monastic life of the Carthusians which flowed from an intense desire for solitude in his own life. This was a major concern during his early years as a Trappist, particularly during the years between his first vows and his ordination to the priesthood. There seemed to be no question about his vocation to the monastic life, but how it was to be lived out and in what circumstances were major questions for a time. In light of his strong attraction to the solitary life, he wondered over and over whether God was leading him to the Carthusians. With his strong desire to give himself completely to God, and the great importance he gave to seeking and finding God's will in his life, he struggled with this vocational problem. Constant, regular and capable spiritual direction was not lacking to him in the process of resolving this conflict.[7] Although his attraction for solitude was to continue and deepen, subsequent events showed that this particular tension between the Trappist and Carthusian ways of life seemed to resolve itself as he deepened and matured in his Trappist vocation and clarified his own thinking on solitude.

The second major source of conflict and anxiety in his early years at Gethsemani centered around the difficulties he experienced in reconciling his vocation as a monk and his obvious gifts and talents as a writer. Merton gives us a glimpse of this struggle to integrate the monk and the writer in the epilogue to *The Seven Storey Mountain* (where he writes of "this shadow, this double, this writer who had followed me into the cloister")[8] and in many of his entries in *The Sign of Jonas*. The constant reassurance and encouragement he received from his Trappist superiors was a source of great help to him. They obviously recognized not only his great talents as a writer and the great good he could accomplish through his writings, but also what writing meant to Merton as a person and the role it had to play in his life.[9] Merton hints at what this steady encouragement and reassurance meant to him in a passage about his first abbot, Dom Frederic Dunne: "I shall never forget the simplicity and affection with which he put the first copy of the book in my hand. . . . A few days later, he was telling me to go on writing, to love God, to be a man of prayer and humility, a monk and a contemplative, and to help other men penetrate the mystery of the love of God."[10]

In addition to the regular and ongoing direction Merton received in this area of tension between monk and writer, there were also the opportunities he availed himself of in asking visiting Trappist superiors and officials about his writing vocation.[11] It was as if he did not want to leave any stone unturned in his seeking after God's will in his life. We might also note in passing the advice he sought and received on certain occasions such as the annual retreat with its opportunity to talk with the visiting director.[12]

Thus, opportunities for receiving spiritual direction were certainly not lacking for Thomas Merton during his early years at Gethsemani. With his apparent desire to grow in God's love and to live for Him alone, he took advantage of these opportunities. A certain openness, docility, and eagerness did mark his basic attitude and outlook in this regard as he sought to grow as a person, as a Christian, and as a monk. He manifested in his own life some of that strong desire of the monks in the early desert tradition who would often travel for miles through the wilderness "just to hear a brief word of advice, a 'word of salvation' which summed up the judgment and the will of God for them in their actual concrete situation."[13]

The advice, the encouragement, the direction he did receive fell on good ground and it did bring forth fruit in his early monastic years. For example, we find him writing in his journal at a later date referring to the writing problem: "And yet it seems to me that writing, far from being an obstacle to spiritual perfection in my own life, has become one of the conditions on which my perfection will depend. If I am to be a saint — and there is nothing else that I think of desiring to be — it seems that I must get there by writing books in a Trappist monastery.''[14]

II. Merton as a Director of Others

In one of his essays in his *Contemplation in a World of Action,* Merton writes: "But in all contemplative traditions, it has been found necessary that those who have attained to some depth of religious insight should to some extent guide others who seek to attain the same experience of truth in their own lives.''[15] This was certainly true in Merton's case for shortly after his own final profession as a Trappist and his ordination to the priesthood, he was asked to assume responsibilities as a spiritual director towards those younger in the religious life. This work was to increase, particularly during his ten years as master of novices, abating only when he retired to his hermitage in the year 1965. He doesn't say a great deal about his direction of others but from some of his brief allusions, it is clear that he did it well and that he enjoyed doing it. In his early journal he writes of how the direction of the scholastics at Gethsemani and his contact with them helped him personally, particularly in his own prayer and in his desire for solitude.[16] And in a letter to a friend in 1951 he writes: "I have nothing at all against being spiritual director, in fact, I quite like it; but every moment of it makes me wish I lived alone in the woods.''[17]

It is from his fellow monks that we would expect to find the best witnesses to his capacity and ability as a spiritual director, especially those who experienced his direction personally. His abbot of many years, James Fox, who had Merton as his regular confessor for fifteen years, speaks of Merton "as a gifted director of others in the spiritual life.''[18] Flavian Burns, the abbot of Gethsemani at the time of Merton's death, delivered the homily at a Memorial Mass for Merton at Gethsemani. His words are so appropriate in this context that we might quote some of them here. Speaking of one who was "the best of spiritual fathers," Abbot Burns says:

> Still, he had a secret prayer and this is what gave the inner
> life to all he said and wrote. His secret was his secret to himself

217

to a great extent, but he was a skillful reader of the secret of the souls that sought his help. It was because of this that although we laughed at him, and with him, as we would a younger Brother, still we respected him as the spiritual father of our souls.

Those of us who had the privilege and pleasure to deal with Father Louis on intimate terms, and submit our inner lives to his direction, know that in him we had the best of Spiritual Fathers.[19]

I find it very noteworthy and significant that Abbot Burns singles out his point of Merton as spiritual director in his final tribute to him at the Memorial Mass, speaking on behalf of himself and the whole community. But when one recalls the direct contribution Merton made to the monastery of Gethsemani and his fellow monks as a spiritual director, and this over a period of fifteen years, Abbot Burns' emphasis on this point does not seem surprising.

Before leaving this section dealing with Merton as a spiritual director, we might note in passing the direction he gave to others by mail. This was incidental to his other work and he never made a set practice of it. Although it was impossible to answer all the letters he received, he seems to have made some exceptions when he felt it was called for. This often took the form of direction by way of encouragement and advice.[20]

III. Merton's Writings on Spiritual Direction

Merton's thought on spiritual direction does constitute a unified view of the subject and the process. But for our purposes here we will take certain aspects separately merely for the sake of clarity and completeness. But as we do look at the process from different perspectives, we must keep in mind the unified process that it is. This section will focus first on the nature of spiritual direction and include such aspects as the relationship between the director and the directed, the purpose and goal of direction, and the usefulness and necessity of direction in the spiritual life. Secondly, we will focus on the person who seeks and receives direction, and finally we will look at the spiritual director. Although Merton speaks of spiritual direction in various places in his writings, his most explicit treatment is found in his book *Spiritual Direction and Meditation*.

a) Nature of Spiritual Direction

As noted earlier, Merton manifested a keen interest in the original notion of spiritual direction, that is the early monastic notion which developed among the first solitaries who retired to the desert in the fourth and fifth centuries. He looks upon this original meaning of direction as "suggesting a particular need connected with a special ascetic task, a peculiar vocation for which a professional formation is required."[21] As long as the early Christians participated actively in the life of the Christian community, their spiritual needs were met by the pastoral care of the bishop assisted by the presbyters. In other words, the practice of spiritual direction was unnecessary in the early Church until men withdrew from the Christian community in order to live as solitaries in the desert. In this new context with its special ascetic task and peculiar vocation, the importance of the spiritual father emerged. But granting his interest in the early monastic origin of the term, Merton's main interest in his life and teaching was with spiritual direction as we know it today, and this is the main focus of our study of his thought here in this section of the essay.

We might begin with a definition or description of the root meaning of spiritual direction which Merton gives. He writes that spiritual direction "is a continuous process of formation and guidance, in which a Christian is led and encouraged *in his special vocation,* so that by faithful correspondence to the graces of the Holy Spirit he may attain to the particular end of his vocation and to union with God."[22] It involves, then, a continuous process of guidance and encouragement, which aims at assisting persons to deepen their union with God and to seek and fulfill God's will in their lives. This comes about by a patient and faithful correspondence to the graces of the Holy Spirit who is the true and essential director in the whole process.

Merton does emphasize that although the word "spiritual" is part of the term "spiritual direction," the process deals with the whole person in the ordinary and concrete circumstances of his or her life. He is quick to point out that you do not go to the spiritual director to have him take care of your spirit "the way you go to a dentist to have him take care of your teeth, or to a barber to get a haircut." He writes:

> The spiritual director is concerned with the *whole person,* for the spiritual life is not just the life of the mind, or of the af-

fections, or of the "summit of the soul" — it is the life of the whole person. For the spiritual man *(pneumatikos)* is the one whose whole life, in all its aspects and all its activities, has been spiritualized by the action of the Holy Spirit, whether through the sacraments or by personal and interior inspirations. Moreover, spiritual direction is concerned with the whole person not simply as an individual human being, but as a son of God, another Christ, seeking to recover the perfect likeness to God in Christ, and by the Spirit of Christ.[23]

Since spiritual direction does entail a continuous process involving the whole person, Merton attaches high importance to the relationship itself between the director and the one who seeks direction. What is called for in Merton's eyes is a normal spontaneous, human relationship. "We must not suppose," he writes, "that it is somehow 'not supernatural' to open ourselves easily to a director and converse with him in an atmosphere of pleasant and easy familiarity. This aids in the work of grace: another example of grace building on nature."[24] The relationship should develop in an atmosphere of trust, respect, acceptance, and sympathetic understanding.

Purpose

What is the purpose and goal of spiritual direction? For Merton it is "to penetrate beneath the surface of a man's life, to get behind the façade of conventional gestures and attitudes which he presents to the world, and to bring out his inner spiritual freedom, his inmost truth, which is what we call the likeness of Christ in his soul."[25] This fits in very well with the great emphasis Merton places in his writings on the theme of seeking one's true identity before God and being true to oneself. This played a very prominent part in his own personal search for God and the development of his own spiritual life, as well as in his writings.[26] The work of rescuing the inner man from automatism and leading him to a state of inner spiritual freedom and truth belongs first of all to the Holy Spirit. The spiritual director can only assist in the process, verifying and encouraging what is truly spiritual, and teaching and assisting another to discern and distinguish the inspirations of the Holy Spirit from those of the spirit of evil. Thus for Merton, "a spiritual director is one who helps another to recognize and to follow the inspirations of grace in his life, in order to arrive at the end to which God is leading him."[27]

220

Usefulness — Necessity

When is spiritual direction useful? When is it necessary? Merton addresses himself to these questions, recognizing their importance and centrality to the issue. First of all, he does not claim that spiritual direction is necessary for everyone. He holds that spiritual direction is not necessary for the ordinary Christian since it would appear that his or her needs can be met through the regular contacts with a pastor and a confessor. But Merton does stress the importance of spiritual direction whenever there is a special mission or vocation. We have noted that the practice of spiritual direction developed historically in the case of the early monks who retired to the desert, for a particular need arose for them with their specific calling and its unusual context. Merton sees the same need and necessity developing whenever there is any other special mission or vocation. He writes simply: "But wherever there is *a special mission or vocation* a certain minimum of direction is implied by the very nature of the vocation itself."[28] For Merton this would hold for lay persons whenever they have a special work to do for the Church, or are in a situation with peculiar problems. In this case they certainly ought to have a director and as some examples of this Merton writes: "For instance, workers in Catholic action, college students, professional men, or couples preparing for matrimony need some spiritual direction."[29]

Recognizing the special vocation and mission involved in the call to the religious life in its various forms, Merton stresses the necessity of spiritual direction in the case of religious. In fact it would seem that here spiritual direction is morally necessary. There is no question in his mind that spiritual direction is necessary for religious who are in the process of formation, for happiness in the religious life really depends on wise direction, especially during the early years. But even after the period of formation the professed religious needs some direction, for in some cases more serious problems are not met with until this time. Merton would see it as very important "for all newly professed religious to enjoy, if possible, a guidance that is fairly continuous, though not necessarily frequent. What is most desired is the intimate direction of someone who knows and understands them in an atmosphere of informality and trust."[30]

Merton realizes, of course, that people's needs do differ

221

and that so much depends on individual persons. Although he would hold that in general mature religious should normally be able to direct themselves, he would not want to see any religious assuming that they had absolutely no need at any time of spiritual direction. Those who have years of experience in the religious life are presumably able to direct themselves, but even they sometimes need to consult a wise spiritual guide. Merton is especially wary of persons who will listen to none but themselves.[31] Perhaps we can sum up his position here by saying that at all times, spiritual direction is of the greatest value to a religious, and that even though it may not be strictly necessary, it is always useful.

b) *The Directed*

Merton looks upon certain attitudes and basic orientations on the part of the person seeking direction as being very helpful and even necessary if the process of spiritual direction is to be fruitful. One important aspect of the attitude of the directed is a sincere and humble desire to benefit from the direction. Merton would look upon the early monks in the desert as good examples of this attitude for they would travel for miles — often through the wilderness — to consult the spiritual director, to benefit from his aid, and to hear a "word of salvation." This spirit of openness and generosity flowed from an ardent faith and a deep hunger on their part for the word of God and for salvation. This in turn had been nourished by a spirit of penance and compunction. As a result, the impact of the spiritual father's words and advice came not so much from the content itself as from the inner action of the Holy Spirit within the person seeking direction. The seed was sown on fertile soil.

Secondly, Merton does stress the necessity of a spirit of simplicity and sincerity on the part of the directed. Two extremes should be avoided. On the one hand, the person seeking direction must avoid inertia and passivity, saying nothing and waiting for the director to read his mind. On the other hand, any inclination to falsify and dramatize the situation by either exaggerating or creating any fictitious "problems" must be avoided. What Merton stresses — and this is so consistent with the emphasis in all his spiritual writings — is a spirit of simplicity and sincerity. This implies "a relaxed, humble attitude in which we *let go* of ourselves and renounce our unconscious efforts to maintain a facade."[32]

Manifestation of Conscience

Perhaps we can sum up these brief remarks on simplicity, sincerity, and a strong desire to be touched by God by recalling the great emphasis Merton places on what he refers to as the "manifestation of conscience." Since he looks upon the manifestation of conscience as absolutely necessary for spiritual direction, it would seem necessary to investigate this notion as completely as possible.

What Merton refers to as the manifestation of conscience is something apart from sacramental confession of sins and much broader in scope and in purpose. Basically what it involves is bringing the director into contact with our real selves as best we can; it involves being as honest as we can about ourselves and our motives and letting the director know "what we really feel and what we really desire, even when these things are not altogether honorable." Referring to this process, Merton writes:

> He (the director) is not interested merely in our actions. He is much more interested in the basic attitudes of our soul, our inmost aspirations, our way of meeting difficulties, our mode of responding to good and evil. In a word, the director is interested in our very self, in all its uniqueness, its pitiable misery and its breathtaking greatness.[33]

Merton realizes that this is not an easy process and he recognizes that it is difficult to be as open and free as this requires. Often we feel a certain shame and embarrassment in laying open our inmost depths, even when there is nothing to be ashamed of. In fact, it is often harder to manifest the good that is in us than the evil. But this is what is required in manifesting ourselves. Merton insists that "the director has to know what we really want, for only then will he know what we really are."[34]

But Merton also recognizes that often we ourselves do not know what we "really want," and often we have to struggle to clarify our deepest desires and aspirations. In this connection, Merton offers some reflections regarding "the will of God," for he feels that too often a legalistic concept of the will of God can lead to a falsification of the interior life. Echoing Saint Paul's reminder that we are called to collaborate with God, Merton argues that "as sons of God, we are called to use our freedom *to help God create His likeness* in our own souls."[35] As we seek to collaborate with Him in building His Kingdom in the world and His likeness within ourselves, we are not just passive and mechanical instruments.

In the case of spiritual direction, which is our main focus here, this means that it is very important for persons seeking direction to recognize their own spiritual desires and aspirations. For often the real and genuine aspirations of the heart are important indications of the will of God, and a humble and sincere desire may be a sign that God is asking this of us. Thus Merton stresses that "we must learn to speak according to our own inner truth, as far as we can perceive it. We must learn to say what we really mean in the depths of our souls, not what we think we are expected to say, not what somebody else has just said. And we must be prepared to take responsibility for our desires, and accept the consequences."[36] This is the simplicity of the child that is so important in the spiritual life.

Merton summarizes many of these points we have been discussing about the manifestation of conscience in spiritual direction in a paragraph that deserves to be quoted in full. He writes:

> This gives us a clue to what the director is really seeking to find out from us. He does not merely want to know our problems, our difficulties, our secrets. And that is why one should not think that a direction session that does not tackle a problem has not been a success. The director wants to know our inmost self, our *real* self. He wants to know us not as we are in the eyes of men, or even as we are in our own eyes, but as we are in the eyes of God. He wants to know the inmost truth of our vocation, the action of grace in our souls. His direction is, in reality, nothing more than a way of leading us to see and obey the real Director — the Holy Spirit, hidden in the depths of our soul. We must never forget that in reality we are not directed and taught by men, and that if we need human direction it is only because we cannot, without man's help, come into contact with that "unction (of the Spirit) which teaches us all things" *(1 John 2:20).*[37]

All of the simplicity, inner freedom and openness that is required for the manifestation Merton has in mind does suppose an atmosphere of love and trust. The person directed who has been open and straightforward can rightfully expect a response of acceptance and respect on the part of the director. Thus for Merton, it is up to the director to seek to produce an atmosphere of unhurried leisure in which a friendly, sincere and informal conversation can take place.

Finally, the stress that Merton does give to the manifestation of conscience in the context of spiritual direction does fit in with some of the main themes in his overall spirituality, particularly the importance he gives to such aspects as interior freedom, integrity, being true to one's self, simplicity, etc. As he writes in his *Life and Holiness:* "We can only become saints by facing ourselves, by assuming full responsibility for our lives just as they are, with all their handicaps and limitations, and submitting ourselves to the purifying and transforming action of the Saviour."[38]

c) The Director

In our treatment of the nature of spiritual direction and the person being directed, the role of the director of course has never been completely absent. But let us focus now more closely on the role of the director in Merton's thought. As we have already noted, he is anxious to rescue the role of the director from the impoverished condition where the director is looked upon only as some type of a "magic worker" who is endowed with a special, almost miraculous, authority to provide the "right formula" or the answer that will work. Merton finds this approach too mechanical and he feels that it frustrates the real purpose of spiritual direction which is to aid others to respond faithfully and spontaneously to the graces of the Holy Spirit in order to arrive at the end to which God is leading them.

Merton never wants it to be forgotten that the source of the spiritual life is the Holy Spirit and that the real director in the whole process of spiritual direction is the Holy Spirit.[39] The director must always respect a person's freedom and uniqueness before God, and he must be careful not to force upon or thrust upon a person any system or preconceived answer. An autocratic spiritual director is inverting the proper relationship and usurping what does not belong to him. Merton quotes with obvious approval the words of Dom Augustine Baker:

> The director is not to teach his own way, nor indeed any determinate way of prayer, but to instruct his disciples how they may themselves find out the way proper for them. . . . In a word he is only God's usher, and must lead souls in God's way, and not his own.[40]

Qualities of the Director

What are some of the qualities of a good director and what should be his basic attitude and approach to the whole process of spiritual direction? According to Merton, the director should be endowed with common sense, the gift of prayer, patience, experience and sympathy. The director should be one who sympathizes and makes allowances, who understands the circumstances, who doesn't hurry, who patiently and humbly waits for indications of God's actions within a person. The director should be interested in the person and all that makes up his or her uniqueness before God. It is this sense of awe and respect for the person created in the image of God that Merton feels is especially important for the director. He writes simply: "A true director can never get over the awe he feels in the presence of a person, an immortal soul, loved by Christ, washed in His most Precious Blood, and nourished by the sacrament of His love. It is, in fact, this respect for the mystery of personality that makes a real director."[41] Merton agrees that the director should have theological knowledge as St. Teresa of Avila points out, but he hastens to add that "no amount of theological study can give a man spiritual discernment if he lacks the sense of respect for souls in their uniqueness, which is a gift of humility and love."[42]

We might also recall Merton's stress that the director must indeed be "spiritual" in the full sense of the word *pneumatikos,* which implies that a person has totally surrendered himself or herself to God "and who is therefore guided by love and not by merely external or logical norms."[43] This is the person whose life is permeated by the spirit of God.

Merton also emphasizes the faculty of spiritual discernment on the part of the spiritual director in response to the manifestation of conscience on the part of the person being directed. Once we have opened ourselves to the director by means of the manifestation of conscience, the director seeks to penetrate our motives to see to what extent they correspond to the truth and grace of Christ. Merton attaches great importance to this discernment on the part of the director and writes: "The value of a director lies in the clarity and simplicity of his discernment, in sound judgment, rather than in the exhortation he gives. For if his exhortation is based on wrong judgment, then it is of little value. In fact, it may do harm."[44] Merton does look upon the faculty of spiritual discernment as a

226

grace, as a charismatic gift given by God for the sake of persons who seek to grow in God's grace and love. He does not feel that such a gift is rare; he is confident that the Holy Spirit works powerfully in His Church.

We might add one final note to the relationship between the director and the directed. Merton does not want to leave us with the impression that there is always a great deal going on in the process of spiritual direction. Once a relationship of trust and confidence is formed, the direction generally goes on peacefully and uneventfully for long periods. Great problems may seldom arise and difficulties may be few, and when they do come up they may be handled peacefully and without much fuss. One may be led to think that this is too quiet and that very little is happening. Merton cautions us, however, that "if we are wise, we will realize that this is precisely the value of direction. The life that is peaceful, almost commonplace in its simplicity, might perhaps be quite a different thing without these occasional friendly talks that bring tranquility and keep things going on their smooth course."[45] For Merton it is no small thing to navigate in such calm, safe waters as these.

Conclusion

Our study has concerned itself with the life and writings of Thomas Merton from the perspective and focus of spiritual direction. Before looking at his own thoughts on the process of spiritual direction, we considered his own personal experience of direction, both the direction he received from others and the direction he provided for others. He sought direction in his own life with a certain openness, docility and eagerness, and convinced of its importance in the spiritual development and growth of others, he gave himself generously to the work of a spiritual director.

Two general remarks might help to summarize the main points he does make in his writings on the subject of spiritual direction. These remarks center around first his own particular orientation towards direction, and secondly the close connection between his reflections on spiritual direction and the other themes he stresses in his presentation and development of the spiritual life.

First, Merton's whole approach to spiritual direction is marked by a profound appreciation and respect for the uniqueness of the individual person. He never seemed to lose his sense of awe at the mysterious ways a loving God moved in his own life and the lives of others. Along with this is an emphasis on simplicity, realism, and common sense. He situates the whole process within the human context and situation of the individual, emphasizing again and again that grace does indeed build on nature.

Secondly, what Merton writes about the process of spiritual direction fits in very closely with so many of the other themes he highlights in his spiritual writings. This is particularly true with such themes of his as seeking one's true identity (which is to be found in union with God and with one another in Christ), the centrality of seeking God and His will in our lives, and the spirit of sincerity, simplicity, and generosity that should characterize the whole search.

In his own life as a monk, Thomas Merton devoted a great deal of his time to the work of spiritual direction, seeking to lead others to a deeper penetration of the mystery of God's love in their lives. The fruit of this work was limited by its very nature to those who personally benefited from his direction. But fortunately his influence in this important area of spiritual direction can certainly continue through the written thoughts and reflections on the subject which flowed from his own prayerful experience.

[1] Cf. for example Merton's "The Spiritual Father in the Desert Tradition," *Cistercian Studies III* (1968), pp. 3-23. [2] Thomas Merton, *The Seven Storey Mountain* (New York: Signet Book, 1952), p. 233. [3] For example, upon being urged by a confessor to receive Holy Communion daily, Merton writes: "By this time, I had already become a daily communicant, but his words comforted and strengthened me, and his emphasis made me glad." cf. *The Seven Storey Mountain*, p. 260. [4] *Ibid.*, p. 224. [5] Cf. for example his reflections in *The Seven Storey Mountain*, p. 132, and his opening entry (for Dec. 10, 1946) in his journal *The Sign of Jonas* (New York: Image Books, 1956), p. 25. [6] Merton writes of his early years as a monk: "It was true. I was hidden in the secrecy of His protection. He was surrounding me constantly with the work of His love, His wisdom and His mercy. And so it would be, day after day, year after year." cf. *The Seven Storey Mountain*, p. 378. [7] Merton writes on one occasion: "I went and talked over the whole business of my vocation again with Father Abbot: and he assured me once again, patiently, that everything was quite all right and that this was where I belonged. In my bones I know that he is quite right and that I am a fool. And yet, on the surface everything seems to be all wrong. As usual, I am making too much fuss about it." cf. *The Sign of Jonas*, p. 34. [8] Cf. *The Seven Storey Mountain*, p. 400. [9] His abbot of many years, James Fox, O.C.S.O., has some interesting observations in this regard in his essay, "The Spiritual Son," in *Thomas Merton, Monk: A Monastic Tribute*. Edited by Brother Patrick Hart (New York: Sheed and Ward, 1974), pp. 59-77. [10] The

Sign of Jonas, p. 97.   [11]For example, Merton quotes in his journal what the Abbot General of the Cistercians said to him on a visit to Gethsemani: "He told me emphatically — in fact it was the most emphatic thing he said, and the only thing that seemed like an official pronouncement, an *ex cathedra* fulmination — that it was good and even necessary for me to go on writing." *The Sign of Jonas,* p. 43 (entry for April 1, 1947).   [12]Cf. for example, the entry for Dec. 6, 1948, and the advice of a retreat master in *The Sign of Jonas,* pp. 141-142.

[13]Thomas Merton, *Spiritual Direction and Meditation* (Collegeville: The Liturgical Press, 1960), p. 5.   [14]*The Sign of Jonas,* p. 228 (entry for Sept. 1, 1949).   [15]Cf. Merton's "The Contemplative and the Atheist," *Contemplation in a World of Action* (New York: Image Books, 1973), p. 180.   [16]e.g., *The Sign of Jonas,* p. 323; and p. 326.   [17]Cf. Sr. Thérèse Lentfoehr, "The Spiritual Writer," in *Thomas Merton, Monk,* p. 111.   [18]James Fox, O.C.S.O., "The Spiritual Son," in *Thomas Merton, Monk,* p. 111.   [19]Cf. "Homily" by Flavian Burns, O.C.S.O., in *Thomas Merton, Monk,* pp. 219-220. For some other observations about Merton as spiritual director by monks at Gethsemani, cf. Frederic Joseph Kelly, S.J., *Man Before God: Thomas Merton on Social Responsibility* (New York: Doubleday & Company, Inc., 1974), pp. 54-56.   [20]Some of Merton's letters are published in his *Seeds of Destruction* (New York: Farrar, Straus and Giroux, 1964). Most likely the future will see the publication of many more of his letters since he evidently carried on a vast correspondence with a variety of people.   [21]*Spiritual Direction and Meditation,* p. 3.   [22]*Ibid.,* p. 5.   [23]*Ibid.,* pp. 6-7.   [24]*Ibid.,* p. 11.   [25]*Ibid.,* p. 8.   [26]The words of Abbot Burns in his homily are very much to the point here. He writes: "But the message [Merton's] is basically the same for all. We are men of God only insofar as we are seeking God, and God will only be found by us insofar as we find Him in the truth about ourselves." cf. *Thomas Merton, Monk,* p. 220.   [27]*Spiritual Direction and Meditation,* p. 9.   [28]*Ibid.,* p. 13.   [29]*Ibid.,* p. 14.   [30]*Ibid.,* p. 16.   [31]Merton writes in one place: "The most dangerous man in the world is the contemplative who is guided by nobody. He obeys the attractions of an interior voice, but will not listen to other men. . . ." cf. *New Seeds of Contemplation* (New York: New Directions, 1972), pp. 194-5.   [32]*Spiritual Direction and Meditation,* p. 24. Merton writes in the preface of this same work: "It is also emphasized that, since grace builds on nature, we can best profit by spiritual direction if we are encouraged to develop our natural simplicity, sincerity, and forthright spiritual honesty, in a word to 'be ourselves' in the best sense of the expression."   [33]*Ibid.,* p. 25.   [34]*Ibid.,* p. 26.   [35]*Ibid.,* p. 27.   [36]*Ibid.,* p. 29.   [37]*Ibid.,* p. 30.   [38]Thomas Merton, *Life and Holiness* (New York: Image Book, 1964), p. 51.   [39]Merton writes in *Contemplation in a World of Action,* p. 284, "The only source of the spiritual life is the Holy Spirit. The spiritual life does not come from men."   [40]*Spiritual Direction and Meditation,* p. 12.   [41]*Ibid.,* pp. 25-26.   [42]*Ibid.,* p. 26.   [43]Cf. *Contemplation in a World of Action,* p. 303.   [44]*Spiritual Direction and Meditation,* p. 37.   [45]*Ibid.,* p. 42.

Further Readings

Part One:
The Nature of Spiritual Direction

Barnhouse, Ruth Tiffany. "Spiritual Direction and Psychotherapy." *The Journal of Pastoral Care* 33 (September 1979): pp. 149-63.

Carlson, Gregory. "Spiritual Direction and the Paschal Mystery." *Review for Religious* 33 (May 1974); pp. 532-41.

Coburn, John. "Contemporary Non-Catholic Spirituality and the Guidance of Souls." *Worship* 39 (December 1965): pp. 619-34.

Fleming, David. "Models of Spiritual Direction." *Review for Religious* 34 (March 1975): pp. 351-57.

Harrington, John. "The Ministry of Direction." *The Priest* 29 (March 1973): pp. 25-32.

Larkin, Ernest. "Spiritual Direction Today." *American Ecclesiastical Review* 161 (September 1969): pp. 204-10.

Lucien-Marie de St. Joseph. "Spiritual Direction — Its Nature and Dimensions." *Theology Digest* 6 (Winter 1958): pp. 39-44.

McCready, James. "Spiritual Direction as Pilgrim and Companion." *Review for Religious* 36 (May 1977): pp. 425-33.

McNamara, William. "Spiritual Direction." *Cross and Crown* 12 (March 1960): pp. 18-27.

Rossi, Robert. "The Distinction Between Psychological and Religious Counseling." *Review for Religious* 37 (July 1978): pp. 546-71.

Walsh, William. "Reality Therapy and Spiritual Direction." *Review for Religious* 35 (May 1976): pp. 372-85.

Part Two:
Preparing for Spiritual Direction

Birmingham, Madeline. "The Spiritual Direction Relationship." *Human Development* 2 (Spring 1981): pp. 28-30.

Brockman, Norbert. "Spiritual Direction: Training and Charism." *Sisters Today* 48 (October 1976): pp. 104-9.

Cantwell, Peter. "Spiritual Direction and Counseling: Some Reflections." *The Way — Supplement* 38 (Summer 1980): pp. 68-81.

Hakenewerth, Quentin. "Group Methods in Spiritual Direction." *Review for Religious* 27 (January 1968): pp. 71-9.

Pempel, Alice. "The Three Dimensions of Spiritual Direction." *Review for Religious* 40 (May 1981): pp. 391-402.

Peters, William. "Spiritual Direction and Prayer." *Communio* 3 (Winter 1976): pp. 357-72.

Rogers, Carl. "The Interpersonal Relationship: The Core of Guidance." *Harvard Educational Review* 32 (Fall 1962): pp. 416-29.

Townsend, David. "The Counselor, the Director, and the Annotations." *The Way — Supplement* 42 (Autumn 1981): pp. 40-55.

van Kaam, Adrian. "Religious Anthropology — Religious Counseling." *Insight* 4 (Winter 1966): pp. 1-7.

Part Three:
The Practice of Spiritual Direction

Armstrong, Barbara. "The Needs of Contemplatives in Direction." *Review for Religious* 41 (January 1982): pp. 28-35.

Bots, Jan, and Penning de Vries, Piet. "On Spiritual Direction." Trans. Sr. M. Theresilde. *Review for Religious* 40 (July 1981): pp. 495-502.

Connolly, William. "Spiritual Direction: It Begins with Experience — Interview." *Human Development* 1 (Spring 1980): pp. 10-18.

Corrigan, Winifred. "Initial Metanoia in Spiritual Direction." *Contemplative Review* 12 (Summer 1979): pp. 19-26.

Fleming, David. "Beginning Spiritual Direction." *Review for Religious* 33 (May 1974): pp. 546-50.

Griffin, Michael. "How to Profit from Spiritual Direction." *Spiritual Life* 13 (Summer 1967): pp. 100-109.

Keefe, Gerald. "Letter to a Person Beginning Spiritual Direction." *Review for Religious* 33 (May 1974): pp. 542-45.

Kelly, Maureen. "Reflection on the Process of Spiritual Direction." *Sisters Today* 52 (April 1981): pp. 476-9.

Kilduff, Thomas. "Spiritual Direction and Personality Types." *Spiritual Life* 26 (Fall 1980): pp. 149-58.

Shadick, Michael. "Prayer as Spiritual Direction from Within." *Spiritual Life* 24 (Winter 1978): pp. 225-28.

Squire, Aelred. "Friendship and Spiritual Direction." *Monastic Studies* 12 (Winter 1976): pp. 227-38.

Part Four: Spiritual Direction and Christian Tradition

Antonsen, Conrad. "Liturgy as a Source of Spiritual Direction." *Spirituality Today* 33 (March 1981): pp. 53-64.

Burke, Eugene. "St. Jerome as a Spiritual Director." In *A Monument to St. Jerome*. Ed. F.X. Murphy (New York: Sheed and Ward, 1952), pp. 145-69.

Corrigan, Winifred. "A Biblical Approach to Contemporary Spiritual Direction." *Spiritual Life* 25 (Fall 1979): pp. 141-50.

Culligan, Kevin. "Toward a Contemporary Model of Spiritual Direction: A Comparative Study of St. John of the Cross and Carl Rogers." *Carmelite Studies* 2 (1982): pp. 95-166.

Gratton, Carolyn. "Jesus as Spiritual Director." *Envoy* 18 (March 1981): pp. 43-7.

Merton, Thomas. "The Spiritual Father in the Desert Tradition." In *Contemplation in a World of Action* (Garden City, New York: Doubleday and Company, Inc., 1971), pp. 269-93.

Pennington, M. Basil. "The Christian Spiritual Father-Mother." *Spiritual Life* 25 (Fall 1979): pp. 151-7.

Rouse, Silvan. "St. Paul of the Cross — Spiritual Guide." *The Passionist* (no. 4, 1976): pp. 79-109.

Shine, Daniel. "Spiritual Direction and the Spiritual Exercises." *Review for Religious* 25 (1966): pp. 888-96.

Stock, Michael. "Spiritual Direction from a Dominican Perspective." *Spirituality Today* 33 (March 1981): pp. 4-33.

Sullivan, John. Ed. "Spiritual Direction in the Teresian Carmel." *Carmelite Studies* 1 (1980): pp. 3-100.

Sweeney, Richard. "Discernment in the Spiritual Direction of St. Francis de Sales." *Review for Religious* 39 (January 1980): pp. 127-41.

Recommended Books

Alekseyev, Ivan A. *Christ Is in Our Midst: Letters from a Russian Monk*. Tran. Esther Williams. St. Vladimir's Seminary, 1980.

Barry, William A., and Connolly, William J. *The Practice of Spiritual Direction*. New York: The Seabury Press, 1982.

Cameli, Louis J. *Stories of Paradise: The Study of Classical and Modern Autobiographies of Faith*. New York: Paulist Press, 1978.

Dyckman, Katherine M., and Carroll, L. Patrick. *Inviting the Mystic, Supporting the Prophet: An Introduction to Spiritual Direction*. New York: Paulist Press, 1981.

Edwards, Tilden H. *Spiritual Friend: Reclaiming the Gift of Spiritual Direction*. New York: Paulist Press, 1980.

English, John. *Choosing Life: Significance of Personal History in Decision-Making*. New York: Paulist Press, 1978.

Ginn, Roman. *Adventure in Spiritual Direction: A Prophetic Pattern*. Locust Valley, NY: Living Flame Press, 1979.

Gratton, Carolyn. *Guidelines for Spiritual Direction*. Denville, NJ: Dimension Books, 1980.

Isabell, Damien. *The Spiritual Director: A Practical Guide*. Chicago: Franciscan Herald Press, 1976.

Jones, Alan. *Exploring Spiritual Direction: An Essay on Christian Friendship*. New York: The Seabury Press, 1982.

Laplace, Jean. *Preparing for Spiritual Direction*. Tran. John C. Guinness. Chicago: Franciscan Herald Press, 1975.

Leech, Kenneth. *Soul Friend: The Practice of Christian Spirituality*. Intro. Henri Nouwen. San Francisco: Harper and Row, 1980.

May, Gerald. *Pilgrimage Home: The Conduct of Contemplative Practice in Groups*. New York: Paulist Press, 1979.

Merton, Thomas. *Spiritual Direction and Meditation*. Collegeville, MN: The Liturgical Press, 1960.

Schneiders, Sandra. *Spiritual Direction: Reflections on a Contemporary Ministry*. Chicago: National Sisters Vocation Conference, 1977.

Tyrrell, Bernard J. *Christotherapy: Healing Through Enlightenment*. New York: The Seabury Press, 1975.

van Kaam, Adrian. *The Dynamics of Spiritual Self Direction*. Denville, NJ: Dimension Books, 1976.

Tapes

Barry, William; Harvey, Anne; Lucey, Paul; and Connolly, Bill. *Initiating Spiritual Direction*. 3 Tapes. Audio Communications

Center, Inc., 2600 Lander Road, Cleveland, OH 44124.

Goergen, Donald. *The Christian Counselor: A Guide to the Art of Spiritual Direction*. 6 Tapes. NCR Cassettes, P.O. Box 281, Kansas City, MO 64141.

Contributors

Benedict Ashley, O.P., is professor of moral theology and spirituality at Aquinas Institute, St. Louis University. He has published numerous articles and books, including *Health Care Ethics,* 2nd ed. rev. 1982 (with Kevin O'Rourke, O.P.) and has recently completed *Theologies of the Body* now in the press. He is a member of the editorial board of Dominican Sources in English, a series of classics in Dominican spirituality edited by Simon Tugwell, O.P., co-published by Dominican Publications, Dublin, and Parable, Chicago.

William A. Barry, S.J., Vice-Provincial for Formation in the New England Jesuits, has written, taught and practiced extensively in the field of spiritual direction. He was a founder of the Center for Religious Development in Cambridge, Massachusetts, an urban training center for spiritual directors associated with Weston College. He is co-author with William J. Connolly, S.J., of the recent book, *The Practice of Spiritual Direction,* published by The Seabury Press.

Louis J. Cameli, S.T.D., teaches spirituality and coordinates the spiritual direction program at St. Mary of the Lake, the Archdiocese of Chicago's major seminary at Mundelein, Illinois. His most recent book is *Mary's Journey,* published in 1982 by Sadlier.

Louis Davino, O.F.M., teaches ethics and Franciscan spirituality at Quincy College, Quincy, Illinois. He is presently preparing another article for *The Cord* on storytelling and the Franciscan tradition.

James V. Gau, S.J., is a staff member at Loyola, a center for ecclesial renewal in the Ignatian tradition located in St. Paul, Minnesota. He has been directing retreats, doing spiritual direction and giving renewal workshops since 1971; during this period he also served as a religious superior and spiritual director for Jesuits in formation.

The Reverend Eugene Geromel is a parish priest with a graduate degree in psychology. He is presently Vicar of St. John the Evangelist

Church in Napoleon, Ohio. Since his article on spiritual direction, he has also written *How the Church Can Help Alcoholics, How to Care for Aging Parents* and *How to Help Your Engaged Child Prepare for a Christian Marriage,* all published by Claretian Publications.

Joel Giallanza, C.S.C., is a member of the Holy Cross Novitiate community, Waterford, New York, where he has served on the formation team for the past five years. Outside the novitiate, his ministry includes teaching spirituality, conducting retreats and workshops and giving spiritual direction. His articles on the spiritual life appear regularly in *Review for Religious, Contemplative Review, Spiritual Life, Modern Ministries* and other religious periodicals.

Charles Healey, S.J., teaches in the Department of Theology at Boston College with Christian spirituality as his main area of interest. He has been active in retreat work since 1965 and is presently an associate spiritual director at St. John's Seminary for the Archdiocese of Boston. In 1969-70, he was a Fellow in the Department of Religion and Psychiatry at the Menninger Foundation. He contributes regularly to religious journals in the United States and abroad.

Shaun McCarty, S.T., a General Councillor in the Missionary Servants of the Most Holy Trinity, teaches in the Washington Theological Union and the Shalem Program for Spiritual Directors in Washington, D.C. His ministry also includes workshops, renewal programs and writing in the area of spirituality, as well as ongoing spiritual direction for a variety of persons.

Antonio Moreno, O.P., holds advanced degrees in philosophy, physics, and architecture and teaches in the Graduate Theological Union at Berkeley, California. A native of Spain with a special interest in St. Teresa of Avila and St. John of the Cross, he offers a course on them each year in the G.T.U. His journal articles on them have appeared in both the United States and Spain. He has a special interest in the relationship of psychology and spirituality and is the author of *Jung, Gods, and Modern Man,* published in 1970 by the University of Notre Dame Press.

Matthias Neuman, O.S.B., is a monk at St. Meinrad's Archabbey in Indiana. For eleven years he taught systematic theology and served as spiritual director in St. Meinrad's seminary. For the past two years he was Resource Theologian for the Diocese of Nashville where he continued the ministry of spiritual direction at the parish level. He has recently returned to St. Meinrad's seminary where he now teaches pastoral theology.

Rose Page, O.C.D., is a member of the Discalced Carmelite monastery in Barre, Vermont, and Managing Editor of *Contemplative Review.*

Sandra M. Schneiders, I.H.M., is Assistant Professor of New Testament and Spirituality at the Jesuit School of Theology and Graduate Theological Union, Berkeley, California, where she teaches a course in spiritual direction each year. In addition to teaching and writing, she provides spiritual direction for priests, religious and laity.

Vilma Seelaus, O.C.D., is a Carmelite nun in the Carmel of Barrington, Rhode Island. She is involved in her community's formation program, gives spiritual direction, writes and speaks on spirituality and the religious life and on occasion serves as a resource person for various contemplative, interfaith, and religious groups.

Kevin A. Wall, O.P., teaches in the Dominican School of Philosophy and Theology at the Graduate Theological Union, Berkeley, California. A specialist in metaphysics and theories of knowledge, he has for years studied the nature of mystical experience in the various traditions of spirituality within Catholicism. His recent book on the Classical Philosophy of Art is to be published by the University Press of America.

The Right Reverend Kallistos Ware is Titular Bishop of Diokleia and assistant in the Orthodox Archdiocese of Thyateira and Great Britain. He took monastic vows in the monastery of St. John the Theologian at Patmos, Greece, and in 1966 was ordained priest in the Orthodox Church. Since then he has been Lecturer in Eastern Orthodox Studies at the University of Oxford and priest in charge of the Greek parish at Oxford, England. A noted author, editor, and translator of Orthodox writings, Bishop Ware is presently editing a five-volume English edition of the *Philokalia.*

John H. Wright, S.J., is Professor of Systematic Theology at the Jesuit School of Theology and the Graduate Theological Union, Berkeley, California, where he is also actively engaged in the ministry of spiritual direction. His book, *Theology of Christian Prayer,* published in 1979 by Pueblo, grew out of his course on prayer which he offers regularly at G.T.U.

PRAYER:
The Eastern Tradition   2.95

Andrew Ryder, S.C.J. In the East there is no sharp distinction
between prayer and theology. Far from being divorced they are
seen as supporting and completing each other. One is impossible without the other. Theology is not an end in itself, but
rather a means, a way to union with God.

SPIRITUAL DIRECTION
Contemporary Readings   5.95

Edited by: Kevin Culligan, O.C.D. The revitalized ministry of
spiritual direction is one of the surest signs of renewal in today's Church. In this book seventeen leading writers and
spiritual directors discuss history, meaning, demands and
practice of this ministry. Readers of the book should include
not just the spiritual elite, but the entire Church — men and
women, clergy and laity, members of religious communities.

THE RETURNING SUN
Hope for a Broken World   2.50

George A. Maloney, S.J. In this collection of meditations, the
author draws on his own experiences rooted in Eastern Christianity to aid the reader to enter into the world of the "heart." It
is hoped that through contemplation of this material he/she
will discover the return of the inextinguishable Sun of the
universe, Jesus Christ, in a new and more experiential way.

LIVING HERE AND HEREAFTER
Christian Dying, Death and Resurrection   2.95

Msgr. David E. Rosage. The author offers great comfort to us by dispelling our fears and anxieties about our life after this earthly sojourn. Based on God's Word as presented in Sacred Scripture, these brief daily meditations help us understand more clearly and deeply the meaning of suffering and death.

PRAYING WITH SCRIPTURE
IN THE HOLY LAND:
Daily Meditations With the Risen Jesus   2.95

Msgr. David E. Rosage. Herein is offered a daily meeting with the Risen Jesus in those Holy Places which He sanctified by His human presence. Three hundred and sixty-five Scripture texts are selected and blended with the pilgrimage experiences of the author, a retreat master, and well-known writer on prayer.

DISCERNMENT:
Seeking God in Every Situation   3.50

Rev. Chris Aridas. "Many Christians struggle with ways to seek, know and understand God's plan for their lives. This book is prayerful, refreshing and very practical for daily application. It is one to be read and used regularly, not just read." *Ray Roh, O.S.B.*

A DESERT PLACE   1.95

Adolfo Quezada. "The author speaks of the desert place deep within, where one can share the joy of the Lord's presence, but also the pain of the nights of our own faithlessness." *Pecos Benedictine.*

LIVING FLAME PRESS
Box 74, Locust Valley, N.Y. 11560

QUANTITY

_____ Prayer:
The Eastern Tradition — 2.95

_____ Spiritual Direction — 5.95

_____ The Returning Sun — 2.50

_____ Living Here and Hereafter — 2.95

_____ Praying With Scripture in the
Holy Land — 2.95

_____ Discernment — 3.50

_____ A Desert Place — 1.95

NAME_____

ADDRESS _____

CITY_____ STATE _____ ZIP _____

Payment enclosed. Kindly include $.70 postage and handling on orders up to $5; $1.00 on orders up to $10; more than $10 but less than $50 add 10% of total; over $50 add 8% of total. Canadian residents add 20% exchange rate, plus postage and handling.